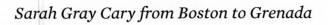

Sarah Gray Cary from Boston to Grenada

SARAH GRAY CARY
FROM BOSTON TO GRENADA

Shifting Fortunes of an American Family, 1764–1826

Susan Clair Imbarrato

Johns Hopkins University Press
Baltimore

© 2018 Johns Hopkins University Press
All rights reserved. Published 2018
Printed in the United States of America on acid-free paper

2 4 6 8 9 7 5 3 1

Johns Hopkins University Press
2715 North Charles Street
Baltimore, Maryland 21218-4363
www.press.jhu.edu

Cataloging-in-Publication Data is available from the Library of Congress.

A catalog record for this book is available from the British Library.

ISBN-13: 978-1-4214-2461-3 (hardcover : alk. paper)
ISBN-10: 1-4214-2461-4 (hardcover : alk. paper)
ISBN-13: 978-1-4214-2462-0 (electronic)
ISBN-10: 1-4214-2462-2 (electronic)

*Special discounts are available for bulk purchases of this book. For more
information, please contact Special Sales at 410-516-6936 or
specialsales@press.jhu.edu.*

Johns Hopkins University Press uses environmentally friendly book materials,
including recycled text paper that is composed of at least 30 percent post-
consumer waste, whenever possible.

CONTENTS

In researching and writing this book, I have benefited immensely from the many scholars whose writings have contributed to my understanding of the early American, West Indian, and transatlantic world in which the Cary family lived and traveled. I am grateful for the generous assistance from librarians who kindly responded to my queries and helped me locate materials. I thank Elaine Heavey, librarian and head of reader services at the Massachusetts Historical Society, for her expert assistance; Anna J. Clutterbuck-Cook and Sabina Beauchard, also at MHS, for their help with images; and Daniel Hinchen and Brendan Kieran for research assistance. I also thank James N. Green, librarian at the Library Company of Philadelphia; Timothy Salls, manager of manuscript collections at the New England Historic Genealogical Society; Carolyn Marvin, research librarian at Portsmouth Athenaeum; and George Ostler of the Chelsea Public Library for the fascinating tour of the Cary House in Chelsea, Massachusetts. Sincere thanks to Wendy Gibson, interlibrary loan librarian at Minnesota State University Moorhead, for her amazing ability to locate materials that have been essential to my research. MSUM faculty research grants have also provided valuable assistance. Thank you, as well, to the staff of the American Antiquarian Society, Beinecke Lesser Antilles Collection at Hamilton College, Boston Public Library, Congregational Library, Huntington Library, Houghton Library, John Carter Brown Library, Library of Congress, and the National Archives, Kew, United Kingdom, for assistance with materials and research.

Elizabeth Sherburn Demers, my editor at Johns Hopkins University Press, has been incredibly supportive of this project, and I am thankful for her expertise in bringing this work to print. Meagan Szekely and Lauren Straley, editorial assistants at JHUP, have kindly and thoughtfully attended to the many details of production and editing. Thank you, as well, to Juliana

McCarthy at JHUP for overseeing the editorial process, to Andre Barnett also at JHUP for her excellent assistance, and to Melanie Mallon for her expert copyediting. Thank you to the anonymous reader for the press for asking key, central questions and for offering thoughtful, erudite suggestions, which have undoubtedly improved this work.

I have also benefited from participating in various conferences where I presented papers on this project as well as from related conversations with Mary Balkun, Eve Tavor Bannet, Vincent Carretta, Richard Frohock, Lisa Gordis, Sharon M. Harris, Thomas Krise, Carla Mulford, Christopher Phillips, David Shields, Timothy Steele, Mark Valeri, and Daniel Williams. Thank you all for your kind, generous collegiality and inspiring, exuberant models of inquisitiveness and scholarship. Thank you, as always, to my family for their enduring support. Finally, I must thank Sarah Gray Cary for transporting me to Grenada in the midst of many a Minnesota winter.

Sarah Gray Cary from Boston to Grenada

Introduction

In January 1774, Sarah Gray Cary made the heart-wrenching decision to leave her three-month-old son with her mother in Chelsea, Massachusetts, in order to be reunited with her husband, who had returned to Grenada, West Indies, for business. She had hoped that the separation would be temporary, a few months at most. The decision was made with concern for the baby's health, as the islands were notorious for fevers and other maladies. With family connecting them to greater Boston, and the possibility of wealth drawing them to Grenada, Samuel and Sarah Cary were hopeful that an interval in the West Indies would bring significant financial rewards. Leaving their son, Samuel, with his grandmother, Sarah Tyler Gray, thus seemed the best choice, at least for the moment. When the Revolutionary War intervened, and months stretched into years, the separation once thought temporary lasted nearly a decade, until ten-year-old Samuel arrived in Grenada for one month on his way to England for schooling, marking his first visit to the island. Only after Samuel returned in 1789 for an apprenticeship at St. George's were mother and son able to spend their longest time together, a span of two years. This happy interlude ended when Sarah and her husband, along with seven of their children, returned to Chelsea on July 2, 1791, while Samuel remained on the island to complete his apprenticeship and to look after the family's business interests. The Carys looked forward to renovating their ancestral home, just north of Boston, across the Mystic River. The plan seemed sensible enough and promising for both parents and son.

Four years after the Carys return, however, their financial security was threatened when slave revolts broke out in Grenada in March 1795. As merchants and plantation owners, they predictably did not consider the events justifiable, nor did they imagine that the revolts would portend an end to the slave trade altogether. Not only were plans for Chelsea in jeopardy but so was the assumption that Samuel would carry on his family's work in Grenada. While Samuel sent dramatic eyewitness reports and joined the local militia, his parents responded with encouragement, even as they feared for their son's life and the destruction of their property. The fifteen-month rebellion ended in June 1796, having significantly affected the Grenadian economy. Over the next decade, the Cary family would gradually regain their financial bearings, though never at the same level as their earlier West Indian wealth, and brothers Samuel and Lucius would slowly establish their own mercantile careers. Throughout, Sarah Gray Cary provided a steadying influence that sustained and encouraged, all while successfully managing households in both Grenada and Chelsea that would eventually include thirteen children.

From their Bostonian roots to their relocation to Grenada and subsequent return to Chelsea, the Cary family story speaks to both the optimism and the uncertainty of these revolutionary times. In doing so, their experiences complicate a colonial-to-independence narrative as a linear progression; instead, they show a family in a constant state of adjustment and adaptation. We have often heard stories of valor and hardship in early America, and frequently from a man's point of view, especially from our founders, but we have less often heard from a family with ties to the West Indies, colonial America, and the newly formed United States who are confronting these difficulties while also navigating a rapidly changing transatlantic commerce. Rarer yet, we have a woman's voice at the center of this narrative, reacting to and reflecting on these dramatic events with conviction and confidence. With Sarah's quick intelligence and astute assessments, the Cary family adapted to their shifting fortunes in remarkable ways.

The Cary Family Story within an Early Boston Context

By placing the Cary family story within a larger discussion of social and economic change, I examine the intersections among religious beliefs, moral philosophies, and financial pursuits to consider how the Carys' involvement with slavery and life in the West Indies affected them, and was variously justified and a cause for concern. As Protestants and Congregationalists, they would not necessarily have turned away from wealth. Mark A. Peterson, for example, finds, "The growth of Puritanism, the continuous nurturing of its inner vitality, and the spread of orthodox churches across the New England landscape *required* the material and cultural resources produced by an expanding commercial economy." Evident in the meticulously kept shipping lists, New England provided the West Indies with ships, food, lumber, and other goods. The subsequent wealth from this trade would not have necessarily been at odds with the church. In this regard, Peterson explains, "The economic growth of early New England, based in large part on mercantile ventures centered in Boston, was the life-blood of its churches as well. Some communities were blessed with greater wealth than others, and therefore had more resources to acquire the means of grace through which salvation usually occurred." That these commercial ventures would involve slave labor was further justified on both financial and religious terms. Mark Valeri's astute examination of evangelical mercantile practices sheds light on how such justifications might have taken place: "Benevolence sanctified the practices of the successful trader. It rounded out the circle of private sentiment, commercial success, and social good." In a discussion about merchant Samuel Philips Savage and "itinerant revivalist Gilbert Tennent," Valeri elaborates on these connections: "Savage's quest for contentment along with Tennent's sermons reflected the central dynamic between religion and commerce during the mid-eighteenth century: pious merchants understood their spiritual duty to reside in the cultivation of reasonable moral sentiments in the midst of a market run by natural principles." As a result, "Savage and many of his contemporaries underwent religious and political experiences unknown to older colleagues." They "nonetheless shared a common moral vocabulary that bridged piety and trade—a vocabulary informed by pastors who elaborated the meaning of postpuritan Protestantism in Boston." Although many, especially urban, New Englanders may have shared these views, diverse opinions perpetuated these debates as New England and the West Indies grew increasingly interdependent. On these points, Wendy Warren notes, "Those tangible distinctions between the West Indies and New England do not change the reality that the English Atlantic colonies were part of one economic system, and that the people who lived there also experienced them as such. What made this Atlantic world one was slavery." S. D. Smith provides additional context: "The impact of slavery on New England has to a considerable degree been treated indirectly. Nearly all attention has been placed upon the provisioning of the plantations. . . . Notice must also be taken, however, of the dynamic role New Englanders played in creating and maintaining the plantation system in the Caribbean."[1]

This dialogue between slaveholding and benevolence continued into the eighteenth century. Wylie Sypher, for example, identifies a significant shift in attitudes toward slavery: "But until Francis Hutcheson's *System of Moral*

Philosophy (1734–1741), no writer formulated ethical principles inimical to slavery as an institution. The import of Hutcheson's argument against slavery is great, because his benevolistic objections signify a collapse of the entire 'classical' rationalization of the oppression of man by his fellow-man; his ethics of pity overcomes an ethics of reason." Regarding connections between Protestantism and philanthropy, Amanda B. Moniz finds, "By the mid-eighteenth century, then, there was widespread agreement that human beings were sociable and sensitive to their fellow creatures' feelings. Yet the possibility of *universal* benevolence remained in dispute." And as David Brion Davis points out, "There were many planters in Virginia, Jamaica, and St. Domingue who were open to the spirit of the Enlightenment. They did not, however, decide to give up their slave property after reading Montesquieu, *The Virginia Gazette*, or *The Weekly Magazine or Edinburgh Amusement*. The question of abolishing slavery was ultimately a question of power."[2] From these various perspectives—economic, religious, and ethical—the Samuel and Sarah Cary family attempted to reconcile their own source of wealth with their religious beliefs as they confronted changing attitudes toward a pursuit of fortune linked to the slave trade and to the transatlantic sugar trade that had initially enabled it.

The next generation who inherited these issues also confronted contradictions in need of reconciliation. Samuel and Lucius, for example, who were educated within an Enlightenment ideology that promoted individual rights, were also living in an era of social revolution, in which upholding a hierarchy that justified the inequities of slavery was becoming increasingly difficult. Christopher Leslie Brown elaborates on these competing issues: "North American colonists found that their campaign for independence, in ways increasingly impossible to ignore, made the institution of chattel slavery a moral issue and, as a consequence, a political liability." Sharon M. Harris also notes this pervasive contradiction: "Systems of oppression were ironically entrenched in the rhetoric of liberty during the Revolution and in the early Federal period." Simon Gikandi comments on a similar contrast: "In its simplest form, the project of Enlightenment, considered to be the high point of modernity, was conceived as the production and valorization of the subject as autonomous, self-reflective, and unencumbered by immediate experience."[3] In this regard, as Samuel and Lucius enjoyed the benefits of a self-reflective education, they were not necessarily encouraged to address the actual experiences of slavery. Instead, they maintained, along with their parents, an attitude of benevolent paternalism toward their slaves, attitudes that were neither exceptional nor unusual. From their perspectives, we learn how two young men born into privilege inherited the right to happiness, yet struggled to see it manifest not only for themselves but for all of humanity. This study tracks the Cary family's search for financial success and their subsequent reversal of fortune, as it provides a unique perspective on a seminal period of early American history, one that begins with the first colonial enterprises of New England and reaches into the narrative of a newly formed democracy striving to fulfill the promises of its revolutionary intent.

Samuel Cary and Sarah Gray Cary: Brief Family Histories

These discussions between ministers and merchants are particularly relevant to the Cary and Gray families in that Samuel's father, Captain Samuel Cary, was a successful merchant throughout the West Indies and in London, and his mother, Margaret Graves Cary, was a devout Calvinist. Sarah's father, Ellis Gray, was a Congregationalist minister who would have been privy to such debates, and her mother, Sarah Tyler Gray, was a pious New Englander. Sarah and Samuel are each descendant from prominent New England families. James Cary of Bristol, England, migrated to colonial Massachusetts in 1639, and Edward Gray arrived in Boston from Lancashire, England, in 1686. Samuel Cary graduated Harvard College in 1731, and on December 24, 1741, he married Margaret Graves, the twenty-two-year-old daughter of Thomas Graves and Sybil Foster Avery from Charlestown, a village that Margaret's grandfather, Thomas Graves, had settled in 1629.[4] Ellis Gray graduated Harvard College in 1734, received his MA in 1737, and served as the second minister of the New Brick Church from 1738 to 1753. On September 20, 1739, Ellis Gray and Sarah Braem Tyler were married. In *Sibley's Harvard Graduates*, Clifford K. Shipton notes about Sarah, "This lass of seventeen had sharply practical qualities which her husband lacked and recognized, so he relinquished the family and financial cares to her efficient management."[5]

As children, both Samuel and Sarah were separated from their fathers. Captain Cary was often away at sea, for intervals up to six years, whereby Margaret Cary assumed charge of the household. She recounted these separations in her diary, as on May 15, 1742, five months after their marriage: "This day I received the agreeable news of the safe arrival of my dear consort in St. Kitts. Lord, be pleased to grant that we may make a right improvement of so great a mercy." Upon the birth of their first child, Samuel, on September 20, 1742, Margaret records, "This day God was pleased to appear for me in a wonderful manner, in a time of great difficulty and distress, and made me the living mother of a living and perfect child. Lord, what shall I render to thee for all thy goodness and mercy vouchsafed unto me?" On November 19, 1748, she writes, "This day God was pleased to return my dear consort after an absence of almost four years. Lord, grant that I may be thankful for this thy great mercy to me, and that we may both bless and praise thy name together."[6] Recollections about Samuel Cary's childhood portray him as "lively." Margaret Graves Cary, the eldest daughter of Samuel and Sarah, for example, provides this description of her father's childhood in an 1843 letter to her nephew George Blankern Cary: "He was allowed great freedom, as he was the eldest son and his father generally absent. He gave frequent entertainments to his friends at his mother's house, and heeded her direction, and she did everything to make his home happy." Having shown an early interest in business, Samuel was apprenticed to Gilbert DeBlois, a wealthy Bostonian merchant who dealt in a diverse inventory, as indicated in the *Boston Evening Post*, March 21, 1757: "A very neat and large Assortment of Hard Ware Goods," along with "Rasins, Currants, Spices of all Sorts, Bohea Tea."[7] Margaret also described Samuel's assignments: "Mr. Deblois employed him in frequent journeys to traders with whom he had dealings, particularly at Middletown, in Connecticut, and he loved to allude in later life to the pretty girls he had seen weeding onions in that neighborhood, not very refined, one would suppose." Overall, the apprenticeship "passed over so well, and with so many proofs of Mr. D.'s confidence in his integrity and ability that his father could find no fault there." Still, Captain Cary expressed concern that his son's "affections might be too early engaged, and he might form an imprudent connection."[8]

In Lucy Allen Paton's 1919 biography of Samuel and Sarah's granddaughter Elizabeth Cary Agassiz, founding president of Radcliffe College (1894–1900), Paton offers this description of Samuel: "Handsome, gay, and fond of society, he was no favorite with his serious-minded father." This conflict apparently prompted Margaret Graves Cary on her deathbed to insist that Captain Cary treat Samuel fairly regarding inheritance, as Samuel's daughter Margaret Cary reports: "She therefore made him promise to give him a thousand pounds sterling." Clifford K. Shipton notes, "Probably this came from her property, for the Captain was a man of no such wealth."[9] When Margaret Graves Cary died on October 8, 1762, Captain Cary honored his wife's request and gave Samuel "a letter of introduction to his friend Mr. Manning, of St. Kitts," and said, "'There, sir, that is all you will ever have from me. Do what you please with it,—throw it into the sea if you like,—but don't apply to me for more.'" William Manning was also asked to assist Samuel, as Margaret notes, "in such a manner as to secure his residence in the island for some years."[10] Despite any apparent misgivings, Captain Cary provided support for his son, who would then head off to the West Indies in search of his fortune.

For Sarah Gray, absence from her father was even more dramatic in that the Reverend Ellis Gray died unexpectedly, at the age of thirty-seven, on January 7, 1753, from an "apoplexy," a stroke or cerebral hemorrhage. Two months later, Sarah Gray was born and then baptized on March 11, 1753, by the Reverend William Welsteed.[11] Sarah was the youngest of four children. She and her brothers, Ellis, William, and Edward, lived with their mother on Hanover Street, in North Boston. Sarah Tyler Gray's brother-in-law, Thomas Gray, assisted the family financially and paid for the children's education after their father died. The Reverend Ellis Gray was remembered as a distinguished minister, as noted in the *Boston Gazette* on January 16, 1753, which describes his character as "a manly Seriousness, and deep Sense of Religion; a singular Modesty and Innocence of Manners; a Taste for the most solid and useful Branches of Literature"; his temperament as "a natural Sweetness of Temper and Openness of Heart, improv'd and exalted into Christian Benevolence, and *godly Sincerity*"; and his preaching style as "a clear, and pathetick Elocution; a Manner of Preaching, that discovered at once the Solidity of his Judgment, and the Warmth of his heart." In Samuel Mather's funeral sermon, delivered on May 6, "The Walk of the Upright, with Its Comforts," he recalled Ellis Gray: "Thro' the happy Influence, no doubt, of parental Instruction, He appeared from *his Childhood* to be very grave, serious and well disposed: And, as he discovered an early Inclination to the *Ministry*; so, with a View to preparing Himself for it, He *gave Himself to Reading, Mediation and Prayer, that his Profiting might be made manifest* in due Season *to all Men*."[12] Sarah was thus raised in a prominent household in colonial Boston at mid-eighteenth century, a busy port city with a diverse, animated population, and one that would eventually take up arms against its British forebears.

Samuel's mother, Margaret Graves Cary, died on October 8, 1762, an event recorded in the diary of her son the Reverend Thomas Cary: "October 2d 1762. My hond Mother was taken sick of the fever and Flux and the 8th She died at a Quarter after 4 of the Clock in the Afternoon and on the 13th was buried—Being 43 ye[a]rs old the July preceding her Death."[13] A year later, Captain Samuel Cary recorded his last will and testament on the "fourteenth day of November," which states, "I give my House and Land in Boston in the County of Suffolk in the Province aforesaid [Massachusetts] . . . to my Son

Samuel Cary and his heirs for ever." After allotting monies to his brothers, Richard and Nathaniel, for various reasons, Samuel Cary willed the rest of his estate to his three sons, Samuel, Thomas, and Jonathan.[14] Captain Cary then left Boston for a year, as Thomas notes: "Novbr 30th my Father Sailed for England in Capt. Hunter." Then eleven months later, on October 10, 1764, Thomas records in his diary, "My father returned from England."[15] In spring 1764, Thomas's brother Samuel sailed to the island of St. Christopher (St. Kitts) in the Leeward Islands of the Lesser Antilles.

Courtship and Marriage

In summer 1770, Samuel returned to Boston, as Thomas notes in his diary for July: "The Beginning of this Month my Bro. Sam'l arrived after an Absence of five Years and Six Months." Though Samuel had received a wound to his hand prior to his departure from St. Kitts and came home with his "arm in a sling," his daughter Margaret depicts his return rather triumphantly: he "had a black man with him, who frequently drove a chaise in which he took his rides; dressed elegantly; was perfectly easy in his circumstances; and had that perfect ease and knowledge of the world which, with good manners, betokens a gentleman." During his visit, Samuel's cousin Samuel Otis invited him to a ball "held at a public house over the Neck." Margaret's father "declined at first, on the plea of his lame hand and inability to dance, and besides, he did not want to have anything to do with the ladies; but finally Mr. Otis prevailed and he went." It was here that Samuel Cary and Sarah Gray first met. He was twenty-seven, and she was seventeen. Margaret also notes that although her father "had no thought of giving up his liberty," two weeks later, he contrived a meeting whereby his landlady, who kept a shop in the front part of her boarding house, arranged for Sarah "to stop on her way to Thursday lecture and give her opinion" of recently purchased silks. While Samuel was having his hand dressed in a nearby room, a signal was sent so that he appeared "to the door of the shop just as Miss Gray was preparing to quit it," and after exchanging pleasantries, "he invited himself to pass the evening." Margaret adds that her father "loved to describe her dress and manners. . . . She had found out, he said, his taste for simplicity and neatness, and dressed herself in a striped linen gingham gown, buff and white. . . . 'She did not lay out much upon the supper . . . a little celery, a little bread, a slice of butter. Ah! She was cunning enough; she knew how to win me.' And from his account, they were almost immediately engaged." In Margaret's recollections of these events more than seventy years later, there is a strong sense that these stories have been woven into the family history, and in highly romantic terms. After a five-month stay, Samuel left Boston on December 5, 1770, as Thomas notes: "Bro Sam'l Sailed for Grenada." The *Boston Post-Boy* also marked his departure in its Shipping News on December 10: "Capt. Smithwick sailed Wednesday for Granada, in whom went Passenger Mr. Samuel Cary of Charlestown." Notably, Samuel is identified here, a contrast to his initial, anonymous departure five and a half years earlier.[16]

As a counterpoint to this nostalgic narrative, just three months before Samuel arrived, the Boston Massacre occurred, on March 5, 1770, so that by July, the British officers had been arrested, and preparations for the trials had begun. The trials would take place in October and November, just prior to Samuel's departure in December. Boston newspapers included frequent reports that would then have become the subject of tavern talk and conversation throughout the city. Still, there is no mention of these events in either Margaret's account or Samuel's correspondence. The omissions are significant because of the direct connections to Sarah Gray's family. Her great-uncle John Gray had inherited from his father, Edward Gray, the ropewalks in Boston that had been the scene of an altercation between British soldiers and the ropemakers just prior to March 5, and Samuel Gray, Sarah's cousin, was one of the first casualties of the Boston Massacre. Frederic Kidder thus reports, "There were then killed and wounded, by a discharge of musketry, eleven of his Majesty's subjects, viz: Mr. Samuel Gray, killed on the spot by a ball entering his head."[17] As a British subject and as a merchant, Samuel may not have wanted to alienate his British business associates, and Margaret, in her role as family historian, may have preferred to preserve a romantic story of her parents' meeting and engagement. These omissions are thus interesting as they show how narratives are cast and edited to emphasize certain events and to minimize or conceal others.

To return to Samuel and Sarah's engagement, after eighteen months of separation, during which "love-gifts were frequent — a harpsichord from England . . . a gold watch; a mahogany waiter, with a beautiful set of tea gear, etc. etc.," there were concerns that Samuel's intentions may not have been serious.[18] Margaret then explains to George Blankern Cary, on March 9, 1843, that despite letters and "love-tokens . . . all was not peaceful and serene," adding, "Your grandfather had appeared as a rich West Indian, which in those days included everything that the imagination could paint. The engagement made something of an éclat, and feelings of envy, mixed with wonder, brought out a variety of remarks. . . . 'Mr. Cary had only amused himself,

—he would never return.'" Samuel Otis allegedly sent a letter to Samuel at St. Kitts with a report of other men showing interest in Sarah at a recent ball, and in an apparent response, Samuel Cary returned. "It was one afternoon, at the close of September, 1772, that my mother had been taking a ride with Captain Jonathan Cary, and in driving up to the door he exclaimed, 'My brother!'" Within a month, Samuel and Sarah were married. Thomas Cary, who attended the wedding, thus wrote in his diary on November 5, "Bro Saml married by Dr. Pemberton to Miss Sally Gray." Margaret also called attention to the notoriety of their wedding date: "That day was always one of confusion in Boston while under the British government. It was the celebration of the anniversary of 'Gunpowder Treason and Plot.' The South Enders and North Enders, each carrying about a representation of Guy Fawkes with a lantern in a cart, were in the habit of meeting at the mill bridge, and what began in ridicule ended in fight." Apparently, Jonathan Cary "joined in the frolic, directly after the wedding" and was later "brought in senseless," but without "fatal consequence and no lasting inconvenience."[19] Meanwhile, on November 10, the *Essex Gazette* announced their marriage: "Mr. Samuel Cary, Merchant, to Miss Sally Gray of the late Rev. Mr. Ellis Gray." Samuel and Sarah then moved into the Chelsea house, which had originally been built as a hunting lodge in 1659 for Richard Bellingham; the house had passed into the family through Margaret Graves Cary's inheritance.

In summer 1773, Samuel returned to Grenada, and prior to his departure, John Singleton Copley was commissioned to paint Samuel and Sarah's miniatures to commemorate their marriage. According to Erica E. Hirshler of the Museum of Fine Arts in Boston, these portraits "are the only documented pair of ivory miniatures by Copley to survive and are among the most intimate, refined, and precious objects the artist ever produced"; the "settings Copley provided for Samuel and Sarah Cary indicate the personal nature of these tiny paintings. *Samuel Cary* (cat. no. 77), mounted in a bracelet, was clearly intended to be worn by a woman, while *Sarah Gray Cary* (cat. no. 78) is encased in a locket that could be worn on a ribbon or chain or kept in a gentleman's pocket."[20] Meanwhile, Sarah and her mother, Sarah Tyler Gray, remained at Chelsea and, on August 1, 1773, became members of the church, thus marking their residency.[21] Sarah gave birth to the couple's first child, Samuel, on October 7, 1773. Three months later, in January 1774, Sarah reluctantly left her newborn with her mother to reunite with her husband in Grenada. The daughter of a respected Bostonian reverend and the son of a successful merchant and sea captain thus began a new life together far from their New England home. Together, the Cary and Gray families would serve as merchants, captains, ministers, and householders and become notable figures in early Boston history.

Overview of Chapters

At the center of this study is Sarah Gray Cary, who maintained an extensive correspondence with her sons through extended periods of separation between Chelsea and the West Indies. After working on Sarah Cary's correspondence for an edited collection of letters, I became increasingly interested in knowing more about both sides of her correspondence.[22] I then began gathering manuscript letters from Samuel and Lucius, as well as Samuel Cary Sr., with the generous assistance of Elaine Heavey, librarian and head of reader services and staff at the Massachusetts Historical Society. As a result, what had initially appeared to be a collection of fascinating letters written by a thoughtful, articulate, intelligent woman to her family and friends evolved into multivocal conversations of a family at the center of a dramatic period of American history.

This book is organized chronologically and thematically, set against the backdrop of the transatlantic sugar and slave trade, slave revolts, and the early abolitionist movement. By placing the study within a larger discussion of social and economic change, and by considering the language of sentiment and reason in the family's correspondence, I examine how attitudes toward slavery inform the family's discourse and how these attitudes were ultimately challenged as slavery was no longer justified, let alone tolerated. In addition, I discuss the merchants with whom Samuel Cary Sr., Samuel Cary Jr., and Lucius Cary worked and corresponded in order to understand how their transatlantic networks operated. Chapter 1 thus provides an overview of the transatlantic sugar trade, which drew Samuel Cary to St. Kitts in 1764 and later to Grenada. Chapter 2 focuses on Sarah Cary's arrival to Grenada in 1774 and her adjustment to her new home. Chapter 3 begins with the family's return to Chelsea, on July 2, 1791, while their eldest son, Samuel, remained in Grenada to finish his apprenticeship and oversee the family's plantation and business interests. Chapter 4 marks the dramatic changes on the island when slave revolts broke out in 1795 and subsequently affected the family's financial security. In chapter 5, I examine the family's attempts to recover economically, while Samuel and Lucius sought new trade opportunities. The final chapter begins in 1810 as once again Sarah was guiding her family through crisis and toward renewal.

A Note on the Texts and Primary Sources

The primary source for this book is the Cary Family Papers housed at the Massachusetts Historical Society (MHS), Boston. When manuscript letters are not available, I cite quotations from the Cary family letters in *The Cary Letters: Edited at the Request of the Family* (1891), compiled by Caroline Gardiner Gray Curtis. Another key primary source is Samuel Cary's Letterbook for the Simon Plantation, St. Kitts (1765–1772), Special and Area Studies Collections, George A. Smathers Libraries, University of Florida, Gainesville. Primary sources for family history are largely from the New England Historic Genealogical Society, including the Diaries of the Rev. Thomas Cary of Newburyport, Massachusetts, 1762–1806. I have slightly modernized my transcriptions of the Cary family's writings with an eye for readability regarding spelling, abbreviations, and punctuation. Several images of the manuscript letters are also included in this book to show the dimensions of the letters and to illustrate the handwriting and expressiveness in each. Where there are gaps in information regarding the identity of some of the people cited in the letters, I have tried to compensate with information from contemporary eighteenth- and nineteenth-century sources. Fortunately, when correspondence spans years, as with Sarah Cary's forty-five-year correspondence, a biographical portrait emerges from the letters themselves, even though the archival historical record may have left a fainter trace.

CHAPTER ONE

Seeking Fortune

Samuel Cary in St. Kitts and Grenada, 1764–1773

When Samuel Cary left Boston for St. Kitts in pursuit of a fortune, the lure of the West Indies promised riches and stature for merchants and planters engaged in the lucrative and expansive sugar trade. With great potential for wealth, the islands attracted ambitious young men such as Cary, who was eager to continue in his family's proud mercantile traditions and become part of the growing transatlantic economy. Before departing, he placed two advertisements in the *Boston Post-Boy*: "Charlestown, March 26, 1764. To Be Sold, By Samuel Cary, jun, About one hundred Quintals of Jamaica Fish." The second ad, on April 16, did not cite a specific location. With one ship departing from Boston on March 17, 1764, and three additional ones from the Port of Piscataqua, in New Hampshire, Samuel likely arrived at St. Kitts sometime in April–June 1764.[1] Once landed, Samuel Cary presented William Manning with his father's letter of introduction, and, as Margaret Cary reports, Manning then encouraged Samuel "to hire a large building to use for himself as a store, and to let the adjoining rooms. . . . Here he was for several years engaged in successful merchandise, buying cargoes and disposing of them."[2] Within a year, Samuel was hired as a manager for the sugar estates of Charles Spooner and John Bourryau, as indicated by his earliest ledger entry: "St. Christopher's March 9th 1765." Spooner was Bourryau's uncle, and each of them owned several plantations on the island. According to Spooner's will, he owned estates in "St. Mary Cayon and Christ Church, Nichola Town, St. Christopher, called the Level or Prospect, with 287 slaves of various ages."[3]

Although the estates for which Samuel worked were profitable, he initially experienced periods of financial instability. On February 10, 1766, he wrote to Manning, who had since returned to England, "I find it so difficult to live that I certainly will not refuse anything that I may do without being censured by the people among whom I live, times are so hard that I should have been happy had my hond. Father thought some years ago of a Trade."[4] Samuel's criticism of his father is interesting considering the alleged falling-out regarding the son's inheritance before he left for St. Kitts. On October 5, the younger Samuel responds defensively to Manning's criticism about a recent purchase of slaves: "You thought I had taken the advantage of buying them myself for less money [than] they would fetch from any other person, as to the expression I made use of it was only to endeavor to prevent your thinking me capable of doing a thing that was mean." And even though Cary had consulted with "the most able People here and no one disapprove[d] of what I did," Samuel conjectured that a "Mr. Stephens is displeased at my tak-ing a Commission," and thus asked Manning to pay Stephens a commission to avoid any ill will. Although this reference to Samuel's direct involvement in the slave trade is unique in his ongoing correspondence, he would con-tinue to participate. Two months later, on December 6, 1766, Samuel wrote to Joseph Sill, the London banker for the St. Kitts estates, beginning with an acknowledgment of "the great friendship that has long subsided between you and my Hond. Father," and then explaining that "Mr. Bouryeau and Mr. Spooner have been so kind as to appoint me their agent here," which leads to a disclosure—"am young and thoughtless but flatter myself fond of reproof: being almost a stranger to the customs of this part of the world"—and a request: "As their business rests in your hands it would be doing a great piece of service to your old Friend as well as to his Son if you will be so kind as to inform me of the errors committed . . . should be happy if you would point out what steps I can take to benefit their Interest."[5] Thus, even as Samuel defended his business practices, he was willing to seek advice in matters of trade. He learned quickly, for as his three-hundred-page letterbook attests, Samuel corresponded and negotiated business with an extensive network of merchants and planters both on the island and throughout the West Indies and Great Britain. This proliferation of planters is clearly indicated in Sam-uel Baker's *A New and Exact Map of the Island of St. Christopher in Amer-ica, According to an Actual and Accurate Survey Made in the Year 1753*, which shows estates owned by British, Scottish, Irish, and French merchants.[6]

Significantly, Samuel Cary's arrival also coincided with the conclusion of the Seven Years' War and the signing of the Treaty of Paris in February 1763, by which the British had acquired territories from the French, referred to as the Ceded Islands, including Dominica, Grenada, St. Vincent, the Grenadines,

Samuel Baker, *A New and Exact Map of the Island of St. Christopher in America, According to an Actual and Accurate Survey Made in the Year 1753.* C-651l-000. Courtesy of the John Carter Brown Library at Brown University.

Tobago, and St. Lucia. Andrew Jackson O'Shaughnessy describes the subsequent economic growth: "Over the years 1763–73 the values of the islands' exports to Britain increased from £62,915 to £859,981 sterling. Their exports rose as a percentage of the total trade of the British Caribbean from 3.1 percent in 1763 to 32.3 percent in 1773." Regarding Grenada, Beverley A. Steele notes that "when the British took over the island of Grenada, they found a country . . . full of potential, in which there were over 300 estates and farms varying in size from 1363 acres to 20 acres." Trevor Burnard offers a larger view yet: "In retrospect, the Seven Years' War marked the high-point of West Indian planter power." Hilary McDonald Beckles provides additional information about this planter's earlier status: "The West Indian sugar planter of the mid-17th century was celebrated as the most successful agricultural entrepreneur of the time." In this regard, Beckles also notes, "Facilitated by a transcontinental complex of brokers, agents, and financiers, the West Indian sugar planter held the known world with his gaze and made 'good' with the extensive array of goods produced. Using their economic success to maximum effect, they lobbied and bought their way into metropolitan Parliaments and Imperial Courts in an effort to protect and promote the world they had made." With disruptions that included the American Revolutionary War among other conflicts, markets vacillated and were often volatile. Burnard marks these trends: "Indeed, in economic terms Britain's West Indian colonies were economically viable until at least the middle years of the second decade of the nineteenth century. They entered into real economic decline only in the late 1820s, as the reality of the abolition of slavery became clear to a panicked planter class."[7] In Samuel Cary's three decades in the West Indies, he thus experienced both the prosperity and the decline, including his own panic about keeping his family solvent.

Samuel Cary and Plantation Management at St. Kitts

Two years into his appointment as a manager, Samuel wrote a twenty-three-page manual entitled "Some Directions for the management of a Sugar Plantation," dated March 18, 1767, which describes the methodology necessary for maintaining a productive, efficient estate. Cary thus begins, "Although there is no general rule to be given for the management of a Sugar Plantation, yet there may be some very good ones laid down founded on Experience, that may serve as a guide to the owner, and more so to the raw and unexperienced young manager." Citing experience as his guide and addressing the manual to both owners and potential managers, Cary includes this job description: "And first, as to your manager, let him be a man bred up to the planting business, of an unstained Character, good tempered, and one that loves home; let him hold no other employment but the management of your Estate. As he must give all orders and directions himself, so he should see the most of them put in execution, the more the better, the less so much the worse."[8] In addition to emphasizing a manager's familiarity with "the planting business," Cary stipulates that a manager be "of an unstained Character" with a singular focus on the estate. Regarding the very construction of such a persona, Philip D. Morgan notes, "The dominant social ethos and cultural metaphor of seventeenth- and early-eighteenth-century Anglo-America, patriarchalism, embodied the ideal of an organic social hierarchy." To this point, he also observes, "Suffusing the thought of the age, the patriarchal outlook was an austere code, emphasizing control, obedience, discipline, and severity. Yet patriarchalism also involved protection, guardianship, and reciprocal obligations. It defined the gentleman planter's self-image and constituted the ideals and standards by which slaveholding behavior was judged."[9] Cary's description of a confident, "good tempered" manager reflects similar characteristics.

This insistence that the manager be solely committed to the estate and "give all orders and directions himself" would have been particularly important in a system that was largely directed by absentee owners. J. R. Ward elaborates: "By the 1760s perhaps a third of the British West Indies' sugar plantations belonged to absentees, a proportion that was to grow steadily until the early nineteenth century." Eric E. Williams finds that absenteeism "had serious consequences in the islands. Plantations were left to be mismanaged by overseers and attorneys." There were other disadvantages that Cary may not have fully anticipated. David Watts, for example, finds, "Absenteeism, both of a temporary and permanent nature, additionally provided a type of instability all of its own."[10] To offset such possibilities, Cary notes that a manager "should never sleep out of the Estate, for fear of Accidents of fire," and includes these additional duties and tasks: "He should understand something of Architecture, as he will have under his Care, Masons, Coopers, Carpenters, &c.; that he may not only be able to find fault, but at the same time point out a remedy to prevent it for the time to come." Regarding the marital status of a manager, he notes, "If the Estate is small, get a single man; if large, let him be a married man, as his wife will be very useful to your sick & breeding women." This last directive, while primarily a financial concern, would have potentially reduced a need for continual importation of slaves. This is not to suggest that Cary would have disregarded humanitarian con-

Samuel Cary, "Some Directions for the management of a Sugar Plantation," March 18, 1767. Samuel Cary Papers, Collection of the Massachusetts Historical Society.

Some Directions for the management of a Sugar Plantation.

Although there is no general rule to be given for the management of a Sugar Plantation, yet there may be some very good ones laid down founded on Experience, that may serve as a guide to the owner, & more so to the raw & unexperienced young manager. — And first, as to your manager, let him be a man bred up to the planting business, of an unstained Character, good tempered, & one that loves home; let him hold no other employment but the management of your Estate. As he must give all orders & directions himself, so he should see the most of them put in execution, the more the better, the less so much the worse. He should never sleep out of the Estate, for fear of Accidents of fire; he should understand something of Architecture, as he will have under his Care, Masons, Coopers, Carpenters &c.; that he may not only be able to find fault, but at the same time point out a remedy to prevent it for the time to come. If the Estate is small, get a single man; if large, let him be a married man, as his wife will be very useful to your sick & breeding women.

cerns, nor that there was no debate about the treatment of slaves. For instance, the Anglican minister, naval chaplain, and antislavery advocate James Ramsay was preaching in the parishes of Christchurch, Nicola Town, and St. John's in 1762–1777 and in 1779–1781, which correspond with the times when Samuel Cary was also living there. Caroline Quarrier Spence underscores Ramsay's significance, in that he was "one of Britain's leading authorities on the French slave laws. . . . Priests, he noted, were charged with visiting slave plantations to make inquiries into the behavior and religious improvement of the slaves; they were also tasked with interceding in disputes on slaves' behalf from time to time." Ramsay was thus attentive to a more humane approach to slavery. Lowell Joseph Ragatz, moreover, notes in his 1928 study, *The Fall of the Planter Class in the British Caribbean, 1763–1833*, that Ramsay "had become embroiled with the colonists in consequence of his having given plantation hands religious instruction, opened an attack on the trade and slavery as he knew them from first-hand information and personal experiences." Ramsay's *An Essay on the Treatment and Conversion of African Slaves in the British Sugar Colonies* (1784), for example, would later become a key document for the antislave debates and initiate a pamphlet war with merchant and proslavery advocate James Tobin.[11] Although these publications fall outside Samuel Cary's time at St. Kitts, the discourses that inspired them may help explain how Cary could call for a principled manager while not directly criticizing the institution of slavery.

Unlike colonial America, where plantation owners most often resided on their estates, the absenteeism of the West Indies placed even more emphasis on the manager to keep order. Justin Roberts elaborates on this complex structure in his analysis of a "successfully run" eighteenth-century Barbadian "absentee-owned" sugar plantation and describes a "multi-tiered hierarchy of experienced and knowledgeable local managers," in which "the plantation was controlled by an attorney and an overseer. Attorneys were knowledgeable locals who acted as legally empowered representatives for the absentee owners. Overseers — sometimes called 'managers' in Barbados — were more directly responsible for day-to-day operations. On smaller estates, they often took on the dual role of attorney and overseer." With up to six-month gaps between correspondence, these responsibilities became all the more pressing. B. W. Higman, for example, notes that "many decisions had to be delegated to overseers, agents, attorneys, and local merchants" and finds, "The overseer was typically a free white unmarried man, with a practical knowledge of agriculture, eager to become an owner himself."[12] Charged with both transatlantic and inter-island communications, the manager was thus expected to maintain order.

Absenteeism not only reflected the business model of slavery, but also attempted to shield the owner. As Nicholas Draper elaborates, "By removing the slave-owner from personal contact with the enslaved, absenteeism lifted the slave-owner out of the 'philosophy of fear' that informed the world-view of the resident white owner, attorney or overseer." This physical distancing thus deemphasized the effect that slavery had on the individual. Christopher Leslie Brown provides additional insights on these issues: "Slavery often was out of mind because it was very much out of sight. The British enjoyed the fruits of slavery while incurring few of its social or cultural costs. Not faced daily with the dangers of living in a slave society, the residents of the British Isles had no immediate reason to dwell on the customs taking shape several thousands of miles away. The anxieties that gave urgency to colonial debates about controlling the growth of slavery meant little to those safe from the prospect of insurrection or revolution." Yet, even as owners acquired great wealth, their acceptance in British society was not guaranteed, as Draper explains: "Absentee slave-owners experienced a position of ambiguity: tied to the colonies but not of them, in British society but seen (certainly until the early nineteenth century) as 'West Indian', insulated from the accusation of personal cruelty but nevertheless living from the fruits of slavery, often making claims to gentility but at times the object of an overwhelming national movement of profound hostility towards the 'sin' of slavery." Such contradictions also identify the attraction. Andrew O'Shaughnessy encapsulates this mindset: "West Indian whites were not committed to permanent settlement, and their ideal of returning home to the mother country gave white society a transient quality. They treated the islands as little more than temporary abodes to facilitate their spectacular reentry into British society." Still, absenteeism was lucrative, as O'Shaughnessy points out: "Absentee estates in Grenada were worth upward of a million pounds of sterling in 1778." Moreover, in Natalie A. Zacek's discussion of the French colonization of St. Kitts, 1713–1763, she observes, "As far as the great majority of the men of influence in both metropole and colony could see, the proper business of a settlement such as St. Kitts was the enrichment of the mother country, and it would achieve this goal almost exclusively through the cultivation, refining, and sale of sugar, that rich man's crop."[13] The economic draw brought even more pressure to bear on the plantation manager to secure profits. Physical distance may have diminished the realities of slavery, but it did not erase the truth of enslavement.

Along these lines of efficiency and productivity, "Some Directions for the management of a Sugar Plantation" is organized into eighteen sections: "Servants on your Estate"; "Negroes & Cattle"; "Opening land to plant Canes"; "Planting Canes"; "Supplying Canes"; "Hoeploughing your Cane banks"; "Stripping the trash off Canes"; "Making Dung"; "Additional Care of the Negroes"; "December"; "February 1ˢᵗ"; "February 12ᵗʰ"; "March"; "April"; "May"; "June"; "July"; "August." In the section "Servants on your Estate," Cary begins by explaining that servants "should be regularly fed from the manager's own table, and their time of dinner not exceed two o'clock, that they may go to their business immediately after. To have clothes when they ask for them, in moderation, and it is the manager's business to see that their Clothes are wash'd clean and carefully mended, so that they may shift from head to foot twice every week." Order is thus maintained with a regular schedule. There are also occasional modifications, as he explains: "There are many Estates who give their Servants a weekly allowance of Rum and Sugar; this I look upon to be one of the worst plans that can be followed." Instead, Cary recommends, "Let a forty Gallon Cask of Rum and a Keg of Sugar, be opened, and set it down in the day-book, and as they all eat and drink together, let them make use of it whenever they have occasion; — by this method they will never have it in their power to dispose of either rum or sugar among the negroes, who are very artful and cunning among young folks." He also advises, "When they ask to go abroad on Sundays," servants should be granted permission but under certain conditions: "one at a time, and a careful negro sent with them to take care of them, and also the beast they ride. This will produce good Servants. When they are free, they should, if they have behaved well, be entitled to the first Vacancies." Such incentives again underscore a plantation as a business. Cary's distinction between "servants" and "negroes," in turn, indicates that indentured servants were still part of the plantation system in 1767, while the overall omission of the word "slave" appears to mask the realities of slavery itself. These references to "servant" rather than "slave" appear to be in keeping with practices in Boston; Vincent Carretta notes: "As in New England, the term *servant* was used in England to describe both free and unfree workers, but the latter would have been extremely rare in England in 1773."[14] Samuel Cary apparently also saw some distinction.

This emphasis in Cary's "Directions" on a sugar estate's efficiency and order, moreover, was one that had been developing for more than a century as planter-merchants cleared land and planted cane, using native and then slave labor. Susan Dwyer Amussen provides additional details about the scope of the slave trade: "Between 1651 and 1700, English ships carried over 350,000 Africans into slavery in the Americas." She also reports, "Between 1661 and 1700, more than 245,000 slaves arrived in the English sugar islands, the vast majority in Barbados and Jamaica." Trevor Burnard reports, "The trade increased in volume during the seventeenth and eighteenth centuries, reaching its peak in the latter half of the eighteenth century, when 3,440,981 Africans were transported out of Africa." With specific regard to the West Indies, he notes, "The height of importations into the Caribbean came in the eighteenth century. Over 2 million Africans were landed in the British Caribbean in that century." Concerning both the "intercolonial" and the "transatlantic" slave trade, Gregory E. O'Malley finds, "In the first few years that these islands were in British hands, intercolonial slave traders sent numerous shipments from the older colonies, especially Barbados, carrying several thousand slaves. . . . After the first several years of British occupation, however, transatlantic deliveries to the Ceded Islands accelerated, and this intercolonial trade quickly declined. Intercolonial merchants engaged heavily at the moment when British settlers flocked to the new territories but before transatlantic traders flooded them with enslaved Africans."[15] This dramatic escalation speaks to a frenetic desire for wealth—one at the grave cost of human life.

Staggering numbers of African men, women, and children were not only captured and torn from their homelands, but also suffered the "horrors of the Middle Passage," as Frederick C. Knight discusses: "Africans experienced the Atlantic slave trade as a waking nightmare."[16] After disembarking, Africans then confronted an extremely debilitating climate. Richard S. Dunn, for example, identifies several "deadly diseases" they encountered: "malaria, yellow fever, dysentery, dropsy, leprosy, yaws, hookworm and elephantiasis, to name the chief seventeenth-century killers and cripplers." Climate along with inhumane treatment contributed to an alarming mortality. According to Marshall Smelser, "The life expectancy of a West Indian slave was but seven years [after start of bondage]." Slaves were also denied equality before the law, as Dunn explains: "The Negro was defined as a chattel and treated as a piece of conveyable property, without rights and without redress."[17] The overwhelming drive for profit thus drove the slave trade as the sugar trade expanded.

As sugar production encouraged and justified the system of slavery, the once neutral term "plantation" became associated with the institution of slavery itself. To these points and with specific regard to the Caribbean, B. W. Higman notes, "Growing sugar did not, in itself, entail the plantation or slavery.

It was the emergence of the plantation as the dominant mode of enterprise that determined the structure and contents of the landscape and the character of daily life. The sugar plantation not only covered a relatively large area of agricultural land, it also required a large work force committed to labour exclusively for the plantation, a substantial factory complex, and a hierarchical system of management." Despite attempts to minimize the harsh realities of slavery, they persisted, and this system's turn toward cruelty and violence was variously justified. In Lorena S. Walsh's magisterial study *Motives of Honor, Pleasure, and Profit: Plantation Management in the Colonial Chesapeake, 1607–1763*, she identifies a critical turning point: "Few slaveowners had moral qualms about the institution of human bondage until after the end of the Seven Years' War. Until then, most planters accepted slavery as at worst a distasteful necessity, and some rationalized, even romanticized, their role as slaveowners as a positive good." Philip D. Morgan's expert discussion of eighteenth-century Chesapeake describes additional factors that contributed to the portrayal of the planter: "A shift toward romantic sentimentalism, which was closely linked to a more affectionate family life, helped created a climate in which slaves could be viewed more sympathetically." The view of slaveowners would only become less sympathetic, as Walsh notes: "Although it is possible to view some of the elite planters' struggles as heroic, and some of their managerial and entrepreneurial successes as admirable, from a present-day perspective their activities as slaveowners cannot be judged other than morally reprehensible."[18] Samuel Cary is thus entering plantation management as these questions and issues are being raised and debated.

On another front, contemporary moral arguments against slavery expressed by Anthony Benezet, Quobna Ottobah Cugoano, Olaudah Equiano, and Ignatius Sancho, among others, advocated convincingly and powerfully for the end of the slave trade and for the abolition of the institution of slavery. Despite their efforts, the will to abolish slavery required more resolve, as justifications persisted. Christopher Leslie Brown elaborates on a prevailing attitude: "Most in Britain had tended to think of colonial slavery and the Atlantic slave trade as unfortunate and distasteful but beyond the power of anyone to address effectively." Brown also marks a shift in perspectives from resignation to rejection: "If particular individuals and groups could be held responsible for slavery, then they also could be held responsible for correcting the wrongs they created. By describing complicity in slavery as proof of collective vice, disputants in the Revolutionary era helped define opposition to slavery as proof of collective virtue."[19] Brycchan Carey marks several factors that contributed to changing attitudes, including an emphasis on sensibility and emotion, so that consequently, "As British involvement in slavery grew, greater numbers of British people came into contact with both slaves and the products of slave labour, and the number of those expressing disquiet grew in proportion."[20] Along these lines, Philip Gould cites legislative actions, such as the Rhode Island 1787 antislavery statute An Act to Prevent the Slave Trade and to Encourage the Abolition of Slavery, which calls the slave trade " 'inconsistent with justice and the principles of humanity, as well as the laws of nature, and that more enlightened and civilized sense of freedom which has of late prevailed.' " Gould provides additional commentary about the language, as it "registers several important features of early antislavery writing," including "its appeal to natural law and natural principles of justice" and "the assumption of a moral and cultural position . . . that participating in the African slave trade severely jeopardizes." Such opposition to slavery thus signaled larger changes: "This language also begins to suggest that the slave trade threatened cultural assumptions connecting commerce to the refinement of manners."[21] Antislavery discourse would persist in calling out the incongruity of claiming genteel and pious ways while operating in the world of slaveholding, and these efforts would eventually lead to abolition: on March 2, 1807, the United States passed the Act Prohibiting Importation of Slaves; and on March 25, 1807, Great Britain passed the Abolition of the Slave Trade Act of 1807, which brought an end to the slave trade in the Caribbean by 1811. The Slave Emancipation Act of 1833 freed all slaves in the British Empire, ending slavery in the British Caribbean on July 31, 1838. With consideration of this timeline, Hilary McDonald Beckles observes, "The abolition of the British slave trade has traditionally been presented as a benevolent act by the British state that acquiesced under the mounting pressure of opposing intellectual voices and the mass advocacy of religious and humanitarian activists. There is a substantial literature that details this rich history, but it does not, however, give adequate attention to the political role of enslaved communities in the Caribbean, who in the context of the wider Atlantic dimensions of the transatlantic slave trade, were its fiercest foes."[22] These assumptions were thus contrary to the reality of the enslaved. Notably, the United States would take another twenty-seven years and undergo a civil war before enacting the Thirteenth Amendment to abolish slavery in December 1865.

Along this broad arc from slavery to abolition, the once admired profession of planter-merchant, which had inspired several generations of Cary men to pursue careers in the West Indies, became increasingly tainted. Lowell J. Ragatz notes that "the British West Indies were developed as exploita-tion colonies. Tropical heat, the flocking out of adventurers, and easy credit in Great Britain combined to that end." He also observes that their "decline" was not solely due to efforts to end the slave trade; several factors played a role, including "a wasteful agricultural system, the rivalry of newly-exploited tropical territories, adherence to a policy of restricted trade . . . vicious fiscal legislation in the mother country, and forty years of intermittent warfare." Although the decline theory in general has been challenged as additional economic data have become available, the planters' reputation continues to be evaluated, as Trevor Burnard describes: "The prevalent metropolitan conception of planters shifted during the eighteenth century as abolitionist denunciations of planters became central to discursive treatments of West Indian character. But even people who praised West Indians as men of good character and ready hospitality deplored their immorality, their venality, their tendency to excess in all things, and most of all their violence to their slaves, as well as their greed for food, money, and pleasure of all kinds." Ini-tial approval of the West Indian planter thus declined as antislavery senti-ment grew, and as a result, Burnard explains, "Planters were wealthy, but depictions of their wealth were undercut by representations of decadence and corruption coded as luxury, effeminacy, gluttony, racial degeneracy, or sexual hybridity."[23]

The next section of Samuel Cary's plantation manual, "Negroes & Cattle," is another example of how language is used to objectify the slave as a com-modity. It begins: "As Negroes and Cattle are the two great engines of a Sugar Plantation, they must of course be first attended to, the land being good for little without them; therefore, let me advise that the negroes be well fed, and be sure never to work them beyond their strength, always remembering that fair and easy goes far in a day." Although he does advise a "fair and easy" ap-proach, abolitionists would condemn the comparisons between humans and animals as profoundly inhumane. In plantation ledger books, in general, this objectification is made even more obvious, as cattle and slaves are both listed as property of the plantation. Considering the devastating mortality rate of enslaved Africans, Cary might have been responding to a need to retain the workforce rather than depend on constant importation. He then provides details about the slave's diet: "What twou'd be understood by good feeding is the following: Four quarts of Corn or Beans, and four Herrings per Week for each full grown Negro." A "good feeding" may be synonymous with a "good serving," but the language again implies comparisons to cattle, as the two subjects are paired in one section. Cary also recommends that slaves "be allowed one afternoon every week to work their own Ground," where they would presumably grow food to supplement their meager weekly portions. This practice also benefits the slaveholder by potentially reducing the importation of food. Simon P. Newman explains the effects of such plots in Barbados in the early eighteenth century: "However essential garden plots were to the health of the enslaved, they were nonetheless dependent upon the whims of planters and managers. Moreover, the enslaved were required to work on them to produce their own food, making them part of regulated labor rather than an independent enterprise."[24] Not only was sugar cane cultivation labor intensive, but, as frequently noted, the tropical conditions were extremely harsh, which often led to illness. Samuel Cary thus includes these instructions: "Whenever they are at hard labour, such as holeing, hoe ploughing, digging up the bottom of Cane-holes, give them toddy twice every day vizt. at about ten o'clock in the morning, and four in the afternoon, and if at any other time they get wet in the field, order each negro a glass of rum immediately; this method prevents colds and fevers." In *Candid and Impartial Considerations on the Nature of the Sugar Trade* (1763), John Campbell downplays "*Granada* fever," observing that it "is at present far from being so terrible as it formerly was; proves very rarely mortal, and as it chiefly proceeds from the humidity of the air, occasioned by the thickness of the woods, it will very probably be entirely removed, whenever the country is brought into a thorough state of cultivation."[25] Sugar production thus potentially reduces the potential for fevers, or so it seems.

As Cary's section on "Negroes & Cattle" continues, he appears to recommend some moderation for slave labor, while still focusing on efficiency and profits. For example, he suggests, "The days for allowance should be Tuesdays and Thursdays, and give the afternoon on Friday — this divides the week and gives them a bellyful, with ease in their labour, and I know good and humane treatment will do much better than punishment." Again, Cary seems to hold mixed directives: to maintain a slave population subject to excessive labor while attempting to mediate their suffering. J. R. Ward provides additional background, noting that in the 1770s and 1780s, "amelioration served as a response both to the immediate problem of the slaves' reproduction and to the challenge against the legitimacy of slavery itself. In general, West Indian prosperity fostered greed and cruelty, while misfortune brought moderation and restraint."[26] Cary's recommendation of "good and humane treatment" suggests some attention to moderation. Still, such gestures signal an inherent contradiction in slavery. To enslave is never humane, and attempts to mollify the harm and justify the profits only appear self-interested. As "Directions" indicates, however, to participate in trade as a West Indian merchant in 1767 required an acceptance of these practices, and the manual thus projects an image of a competent manager whose methods will maintain a productive workforce.

Cary next provides instructions on how to plant and harvest the cane, followed by a section on the "Additional Care of the Negroes," with information about clothing allotments, work schedules, and medical treatment related directly to the constant effects of hard labor and the harsh climate. This section begins, "Supposing this to be the month of November, give the Negroes their Clothing and don't let them work after Sunset, neither turn them out too early in the morning." He then addresses the role of a physician on the plantation: "Let your sick house be well attended to, and oblige the nurses to do their duty, and see that the doctor's orders are punctually observed, and good Kitchen physic called for; this depends on the Manager more than any one else, therefore when the Doctor visits the sick house, he should do his endeavour to be present and consult with him, and see which is most requisite for your sick folks, the Physick from the shop, or that from the kitchen." The manager's attention to the sick house and consultation with the doctor indicate a business-minded approach and emphasize the importance of an attentive overseer. This section then ends with a note of caution: "The northerly winds set in at this time of the Year, and epidemics and other kinds of fevers may ensue, but from experience I know that good nourishment and care perform two thirds of the Cure, particularly to negroes, who, at this time of the Year, are many of them very low in flesh." The phrasing "good nourishment and care perform two thirds of the Cure" again appears to counter harsher treatment, even though the overall focus is on maximizing production.

The concluding sections of the manual are divided into months from February to August and describe the various stages of processing the sugar cane, culminating with the distilling of the sugar itself. These descriptions, in turn, suggest an "integrated plantation," as Trevor Burnard and John D. Garrigus explain: "An 'integrated' sugar plantation is one that not only grows sugarcanes but also transforms them into sugar crystals."[27] In "Directions," for example, a chart labeled "To make Rum" precedes a section titled "To clay Sugar," followed by "Distillery from Tyrrell Hebert"; and the section "For Sugar Boiling" provides these notes: "If the Juice be rich, temper low, Strike High, but not so as to bind the Molasses, — If Juice poor, temper high, Strike low." For "August," Cary writes, "I shall now conclude, observing that

there are ten thousand other little manoeuvers to be done on a Sugar Plantation, which comprehends the whole, all which the Manager should be entire
master of." These sections show that cultivating, curing, and producing sugar
was both labor intensive and dangerous, with the sugar works reaching extremely high temperatures, and the round-the-clock refining process contributing to fatigue and serious accidents.

Although the practice of slavery is of course abhorrent to modern sen-
sibilities, the language and attitude about slavery expressed in this manual
are not unusual. This discussion is thus not intended to single out or dispar-
age Samuel Cary, for reading this manual with a focus on how slavery was
viewed and justified, not just by any one person but for all involved in this
larger historical moment, shows how the dramatic expansion of the sugar
trade and the subsequent accumulation of wealth dominated the discussion
and determined the focus. As S. D. Smith notes in his discussion of Edwin
Lascelles and coauthors' *Instructions for the Management of a Plantation in
Barbadoes. And for the Treatment of Negroes, etc.* (1786), "It is tempting to
condemn the *Instructions* for sacrificing humanitarian principles for profit
and to ridicule many of its practical proposals. Neither response, however,
is historically justified. While shocking to a modern audience, the proposals
for plantation management articulated concepts similar in nature to poor
law reform within Europe."[28] In Samuel Cary's later correspondence are in-
dications that he disapproved of the West Indian culture in general, but any
objections he may have had in March 1767 appear to have been overruled by
a general acceptance of an enslaved labor force. To his immediate purpose,
"Some Directions for the management of a Sugar Plantation" emphasized
the importance of a skilled manager who would maintain order and keep the
plantation profitable.

Cary's role as manager appears to have improved his financial situation
significantly over the two years since he commented to William Manning,
in 1766, "I find it so difficult to live." On July 26, 1768, in a letter to Manning,
he includes a note about his income: "The Salarys I receive amount to upwards of four hundred pounds per year so that with the few cargoes I buy
maintains me and adds a trifle every year to my stock."[29] To put this salary in
perspective, consider the average income of the era, as Alan Taylor describes:
"In 1774 on the North American mainland, the free colonists probably aver-
aged £13 annually per capita, compared with £11 in Great Britain and £6 in
France."[30] Samuel Cary's salary of £400 in 1768 was thus already much higher
than the average colonial American salary.

Samuel Cary's portrait of a manager with "an unstained Character" who is "good tempered, and one that loves home" gestures toward an idealized persona of high principles, who somehow transcends both the West Indian climate and the corruptions of the slave trade. In creating this ideal, Cary situated the plantation manager as much in the world of sentiment as in economics. An efficiently run sugar plantation was thus the result of attention to details and an emphasis on order. The manager would then project an admirable identity rather than be subsumed by corruption. Yet even though wealthy West Indian planters were admired, they were also chastised for their opulence. To counter these depictions, Samuel Cary presented a plantation manager who aspired to retain his good character while operating a successful estate. These intentions are also evident in several contemporary sources.

The West Indian Sugar Plantation and Planter:
Literary Portraits and Considerations

James Grainger's *The Sugar-Cane: A Poem, In Four Books* (1764), for example, provides an idealized portrait of both manager and plantation. The 2,560-line poem, dated "Basseterre, Jan. 1763," is based on Grainger's observations while living on St. Kitts as a physician and a planter. Although Samuel Cary mentions Grainger in his business correspondence, he does not appear to have commented on Grainger's poem in his letters. Still, they likely interacted while both lived on St. Kitts, especially considering Grainger's close relationship with John Bourryau, whose estates Cary was managing. Grainger was a native of Duns, Berwickshire, Scotland, as David S. Shields describes: "Born sometime between 1721 and 1724 . . . Grainger studied medicine at the University of Edinburgh, worked as a physician's apprentice and army surgeon, traveled in Europe, and in 1753 received his M.D. and secured an appointment in the Royal College of Physicians." Moreover, John Gilmore notes, in "October 1753," Grainger's regiment "left Scotland for the south of England." Grainger then "as he himself put it 'sold out of the army' " and moved to London where he "practised medicine." In 1754, Grainger "had become acquainted with a young man of about 16 called John Bourryau," a student at Trinity College, Cambridge. Gilmore elaborates on their relationship: "John Bourryau was described as Grainger's 'pupill', and Grainger referred to him as 'my patron' and said that he 'had in great measure, the superintendence of his Studies'—presumably some payment was involved." In 1752, John Bourryau's father, Zachariah, had passed away, leaving John a fortune that included an estate on St. Kitts. Six years later, in 1758, John turned twenty-one, and "thus had control of his fortune. He now proposed to Grainger that 'as a strict Intimacy had long subsisted between us', he should accompany Bourryau on his travels for a period of four years, promising to settle on him in return an income of £200 a year for life." In 1759, they left England for the West Indies.[31] Two years after the publication of *The Sugar-Cane*, James Grainger died of West Indian fever, on December 16, 1766. In a letter to London merchant Charles Bowken on February 11, 1767, Samuel Cary notes, "Dctr. Grainger lately dead his Executors cannot at present say whether he was paid or not, if not that is good."[32] Though this comment is clearly from a financial perspective, it does indicate that Cary knew Grainger and conducted business with him or his estate. A month after this letter, Samuel would write his plantation manual.

Regarding the significance of *The Sugar-Cane*, Thomas W. Krise describes the poem as "perhaps the best major work to come out of the West Indies in the period. . . . This long georgic poem details the entire process of running an eighteenth-century sugar plantation, from choosing the proper fields to the selection and 'seasoning' of newly arrived African slaves." In the preface, Grainger describes his poem as a "West-India georgic," a reference to Virgil's *Georgics* with its attention to agriculture and husbandry. Jim Egan finds Grainger's description noteworthy in that "the label implies that these seemingly irreconcilable differences can be overcome. The label implies, in other words, that colonial vision can be effectively expressed in the forms given to British poetry by the classical period."[33] The style thus lends dignity to the planter's role. On this point, Richard Frohock observes, "Grainger evokes discourses of conquest, cultivation, and science in weaving his image of the planter-protagonist and elevating him as an embodiment of British imperialist virtue." David S. Shields elaborates on these connections: "Agriculture for Virgil was the quintessential imperial act, for the imposition of control upon nature, upon the newly conquered or colonized lands, was the justification of Roman power." Markman Ellis addresses similar themes: "As Grainger develops his case, he argues that the georgic vision of the virtue of labour is one of the new techniques of cultivation and commerce associated with the improvement of the estate in Britain and its colonies. This is appropriate to the form." From yet another angle, Steven W. Thomas observes, "The poem's Georgic form presented the reader with the ideological contradictions of commerce and the slave trade, as the Georgic paradoxically both celebrated the national character of the virtuous farmer and his plantation and implied a critique of slavery, or at least, a utopian desire to reform the plantation complex." Cristobal Silva offers additional insight: "Indeed, part of what makes *The Sugar-Cane* so compelling is that it stands as a record of Grainger's own evidently quixotic struggle to assimilate plantation slavery into a humanitarian vision of eighteenth-century commerce. With one foot firmly in the British tradition and the other on a West Indian plantation, Grainger's reliance on a mode like the georgic places great pressure on the poem to mediate between two irreconcilable positions."[34] As these various approaches and reflections suggest, Grainger's *The Sugar-Cane* attempts to elevate the role of the planter, even as it expresses anxiety, if not mixed messages, about the institution of slavery itself.

These attempts to portray the sugar plantation as industrious and the planter as hard working and sympathetic are also reflected in Samuel Cary's description of the plantation manager as both efficient and benevolent. The degree to which this persona was constructed through an act of self-examination and questioning of slavery may not have been a subject for manuals or letters, and yet, the need to construct the persona in the first place suggests some degree of justification, if not self-consciousness or even defensiveness. Similar to Cary's portrait of a manager, the planter in Grainger's poem is both in control and apparently sympathetic. Books 1–3 of *The Sugar-Cane* include details about planting the cane and managing the plantation. Book 4 then shifts the focus from sugar production to slavery. Concerning book 4 as a whole, Shields observes, "Here conflicts between man of science and man of feeling became acute in the narrator's persona. The welter of cross-purposes dramatized the predicament of a progressive man, ambitious to serve as spokesman for the material improvement of mankind brought about by imperial expansion, yet compelled by economic circumstance to employ and justify slavery." The poem is thus not a call to abolish slavery, but instead it offers an idealized scenario of an industrious, sympathetic planter. Regarding the poem's stance toward slavery, Frohock contends that "Grainger's primary purpose is to address the pragmatics of slave management, and discussions of practicalities, such as how to cure slaves of various maladies, far outweigh his intermittent treatments of slavery at the level of abstract principle." To these points, Ellis finds, "Adopting the form of the georgic allows Grainger to describe the wealth and prosperity that flows from industrious application to sugar husbandry. But his treatment of slavery exposes the limits of both his chosen form of the georgic, and the ideology of the plantation system it describes." Thomas draws additional comparisons: "Like Virgil's *Georgics*, a poem about farming during the Roman Empire, *The*

Sugar-Cane is neither simply a poem about farming, nor a moral allegory for the nation, but an embodiment of the author's emotional and ethical stance toward the empire." Carla Mulford observes how Grainger's planter-persona adapts a rational, scientific approach: "Throughout the poem, the man of science employs a comparative method as he sifts through his book-learning, demonstrating his presumed control over his environment in comments that again and again evidence his knowledge gained from experiences with Native American and African peoples."[35]

These various and at times conflicting roles are evident in book 4 that begins with an invocation "Genius of Africk!" and then describes the African slave's sacrifices: "Yet, planter, let humanity prevail.—/Perhaps thy Negroe, in his native land,/Possest large fertile plains, and slaves, and herds." The speaker thus acknowledges the African as a dignified landholder, dressed in "the richest silks, from where the Indus rolls,/His limbs invested in their gorgeous pleats." Now, displaced, he grieves for his family left behind: "Perhaps he wails his wife, his children, left/To struggle with adversity."[36] In doing so, the speaker appeals to the planter's humanity in an attempt to reconcile the role of a respectable planter in charge of enslaved labor. Frohock expands on these intentions: "Grainger's ideal planter channels sympathy for enslaved Africans, generated from recognition of their humanity, into amelioratory rather than emancipatory effort. The planter's benevolence thus makes him a more efficient manager of his commodities."[37] In Grainger's poem and to an extent in Cary's manual, the planter aspires to bring order while also maintaining a humane persona. The need to do so suggests but does not confirm that this construction was inspired by an awareness of or concern for the harshness of slavery.

James Grainger's interest in plantation management is also evident in *An Essay on the More Common West-India Diseases: And the Remedies Which That Country Itself Produces: to Which Are Added, Some Hints on the Management, &c. of Negroes*. Printed anonymously in London in 1764, three years before Samuel Cary would begin his plantation manual, Grainger's work recommends adopting a humane approach to slavery, an approach that he argues would also result in financial benefit. "An Essay on the Management and Diseases of Negroes, Part the Fourth," for example, begins, "But it is not enough to take care of Negroes when they are sick, they should also be well cloathed and regularly fed. The neglecting either of these important precepts is not only highly inhuman, but is the worst species of prodigality. One Negroe, saved in this manner, more than pays the additional expences which owners of slaves by this means incur." As Samuel Cary would do in his manual, Grainger presents the plantation manager as efficient and attentive. Tending to the health of enslaved Africans is thus presented as a matter of humanity and within an economic context. To do otherwise invites criticism: "But supposing it did not, it ought seriously to be considered by all masters, that they must answer before the Almighty for their conduct toward their Negroes. Where neither humanity nor self-interest, are able to make masters treat their slaves as men, the Legislature should oblige them. This the French have done much to their honour."[38] Grainger thus references earlier, French efforts toward amelioration, and by evoking a higher divine law, he more emphatically addresses the planter's "conduct," as it, too, is subject to judgment.

Representations of the Planter's Persona

Along similar lines of investigation, Rhys Isaac examines Virginian Landon Carter's plantation journal, which he began in 1756 and continued for twenty-two years. Carter also casts the planter's life in a classical literary context, as Isaac explains: "Landon, of course, knew the Roman Virgil's pastoral *Eclogues* and his poetic celebration of country works and days in the four books of the *Georgics*, so the great poet's influence is pervasive." The planter not only brings order to the landscape, but does so within the context of paternalism. Isaac thus finds that "Landon, according to his worldview, knew that he had a patriarchal duty to all on his estate. *Care & protection* was what the feudal lord owed his dependent inferiors. In return, of course, they owed him service, deference, and obedience. This was very much how Landon saw his relationship to his enslaved workers. It was congruent with his own sacred obligation to his own sometimes harsh, sometimes-benign master, God."[39] In this sense, both Grainger's poem and Cary's manual present similarly contrasting portraits: a benevolent, efficient planter engaged in the violent world of enslaved labor.

Samuel Cary may have also been familiar with Samuel Martin's *An Essay upon Plantership* (1755), a defense of slavery that appears to advocate for humane treatment of slaves. If not directly familiar, Cary may have read James Grainger's preface to *The Sugar-Cane*, which references Martin—"I have often been astonished, that so little has been published on the cultivation of the Sugar-Cane"—and finds that "an Essay, by Colonel Martyn of Antigua, is the only piece on plantership I have seen deserving a perusal. That gentleman's pamphlet is, indeed, an excellent performance; and to it I own myself indebted."[40] As Natalie A. Zacek and other scholars speculate, Grainger may have modeled his planter, Montano, on Samuel Martin. Zacek, for example, notes, "Martin imagined his relationship to his slaves in paternalist terms. ... The planter, then, is charged with the responsibility to behave as a father to this family, his slaves, and his community."[41] By contrast, Gordon Turnbull's *Letters to a Young Planter; Or, Observations on the Management of a Sugar-Plantation* (1785), which also adopts the tone of a concerned planter, claims that the Africans are "much happier than the peasantry in most parts of the globe, when they have not the misfortune to be subjected to the caprice, or the tyranny of a bad master. Under men of sense, or of feeling, I will take upon me to aver, the negroes are better clothed and fed, and better lodged, than the poor labouring people of many countries in Europe."[42] Turnbull, who owned a large plantation at Grenada, near St. George's, thus downplays the adverse conditions of slavery by adapting a paternalism that conflates race and class.

As previously noted, Samuel Cary's own managerial duties involved keeping accounts balanced, collecting bills, paying accounts, and informing investors of the current growing conditions. These tasks were complex and difficult, as his business correspondence illustrates. For example, in a letter to Peter Symons on March 10, 1769, Samuel notes, "The prospect of a crop is so terrible that I fear Kiddall's Lime will not pay a freight this year. The Planters can poorly afford to build the coming fall this being an old settled country they have it in their power to chuse the year to build or repair and this does not bid fair to be a profitable one either to the Planter or Tradesman."[43] Despite a poor crop and the reluctance "to build or repair," Samuel tries to reassure Symons and maintain trust, even though the uncertainty remained. Sheryllynne Haggerty addresses similar factors and finds that "merchants clearly perceived and managed different types of risks appropriately. They were painfully aware of the need for personal trust, especially because they had to work in a system where institutional and general levels of trust were constantly in flux."[44] Financial connections were also becoming increasingly interdependent. John J. McCusker and Russell R. Menard elaborate on these "intertwined" economies: "The West Indies interacted with the mainland colonies in several ways: they served as a major market for colonial exports, particularly foodstuffs and wood products; they supplied a variety of goods that the continental colonists imported, processed, consumed, and reexported; and they provided an important source of foreign exchange that helped balance colonial accounts and pay for British manufactures."[45] Cary illustrates the complications of transatlantic and intercolonial transactions in his letter to William Hammond on September 25, 1769: "The last month I got an order from Carew's Executors on Henderson and Murray for One hundred and fifty Pounds Sterling being rent due 31 July last, now send you Wm. Woodley's first Bill on Mills's and Warrington for £135.19 / Sterling which is all I have received of the order to get the balance in a few days. Mr. Hart promised to give me £50 Sterling to remit you by this opportunity but has not yet done it."[46] In these attempts to address the concerns of planters, merchants, and owners, Samuel Cary notes the significant amounts of monies being exchanged, illustrating the interconnected, corporate nature of managing a sugar plantation.

Samuel Cary's correspondence with William Manning also reveals the strains of record keeping. For example, on July 26, 1768, Samuel's decision to underwrite a Mr. Hutchinson without Manning's consent led to mistrust on both sides, contributing to a falling-out six months later. In his letter to Manning on January 9, 1769, Cary thus begins: "I received your unkind and unfriendly Letters." After recounting financial matters dealing with Manning's brother as well as other transactions, Cary concludes with an overview of their relationship and then signals a significant change: "I have received a great many favours from you for which you have my sincere thanks, wish to be in friendship with all men but believe me Sir I'll not brook Ill treatment from any and be assured there's not a more independant one living . . . it's high time we had come to a settlement which desire you would order."[47] In addition to other contributing factors, this letter indicates another reason for Samuel's discontent with St. Kitts.

Samuel Cary and the Simon Estate in Grenada

In spring 1769, Samuel Cary's attentions turned more definitively toward Grenada when John Bourryau offered him a position as manager of the Simon sugar plantation, a 466-acre estate in the Parish of St. Andrew, on the eastern side of the island, "at equal Distance from the Sea and the Mountains, about Three Miles in a direct Line from the Town and Harbour of Grenville Bay."[48] These prospects appeared even more promising when Bourryau assisted Cary in purchasing a 140-acre estate in the Parish of St. Mark, on the western side of the island. Samuel hinted at these developments to his uncle Richard Cary on March 30, 1769: "Pray — excuse my not saying more as I am this moment going to embark for the windward Islands." On June 16, 1769, Samuel elaborated for his other uncle Nathaniel Cary, a shipmaster in Boston: "Since I had the pleasure of writing to you last I have been at Grenada, where I have bought a Coffee Estate which will I hope make me one day or other very easy, tho at present, things are so bad here that it seems almost impossible for even time to get the better, beg leave to refer you to my Father for the particulars." Samuel also notes economic growth: "When I was at Grenada some Gentlemen begged me to help them to a Ship loaded with Lumber one that would carry 300 or 350 Hhds Sugar not to exceed that number and to be loaded with such lumber as they shall direct." In addition to "Boards," "Staves and Hoops" are also in need of shipping, as Samuel then asks: "If you can prevail on any one to ship the whole Quantity they write for at £4 they'l be the more oblig'd to you."[49] This request again illustrates the strong connections between New England merchants and the West Indies, specifically Grenada.

On June 17, 1769, Samuel Cary made an entry in his account book with the header "Plantation, Mount Pleasant," writing beneath it, "Cash paid the Marshall Rochards Execution as 'Cousin . . . £159.15.9," then adding on the next line "paid the Marshall his Costs . . . £53.4.0." The next twelve entries, dated July 27 through December 5, all begin with "Ditto," that is, payments to the Rochards estate.[50] Thus, as Samuel Cary traveled between Grenada and St. Kitts that year, he was actively engaged in establishing his Mount Pleasant estate. On July 25, 1769, Samuel informed Joseph Sill of these new developments: "My good friend Mr. Bourryau was so kind as to take me with him to Grenada and has there done more for me than I ever should have been able to have done for myself, by buying a Coffee Estate upon such easy terms that it's impossible I think but it must turn out well am preparing to go and live there." On September 15, he wrote to Peter Symons with a similar report: "Our friend Mr. Bourryau and Self have been among the Windward Islands and with his assistance I have bought a small Estate at Grenada which will cause my leaving this Island, and settling there tho' not as a Planter, mean to carry on business at Grenville Bay." In addition to noting this purchase, Cary also explains to Symons why this move to Grenada from St. Kitts might be more favorable for business: "Money is so hard to be called in here that it's impossible to fix a time, but anyone may chuse to deal with both Islands," a comment that echoes his remark to Nathaniel Cary that "things are so bad here."[51]

Samuel's plans, however, were unexpectedly interrupted when John Bourryau died suddenly on October 5, 1769. According to Bourryau's last will and testament, signed December 24, 1766, and proved on March 1, 1770, he willed the Simon estate to his sisters, with his uncle Charles Spooner serving as their guardian and subsequently as a trustee of the estate, for which Joseph Sill would be agent and banker.[52] On October 26, Samuel wrote from St. Kitts to Joseph Sill, "Before this can reach you, you have without doubt heard the melancholy news of the death of our good good Friend Mr. Bourryau. He died at Grenada the 5th Inst. greatly lamented by all his Friends, but as there's none whose loss is so great as mine can't think any ones sorrow equal to what I feel." In light of these events, Cary assumed that his manager position would not go forward: "The loss of my dear Friend has caused me to drop all thoughts of going into business at Grenville Bay, shall as soon as possible settle my affairs here and turn Planter have already added 33 Negroes to the 34 I had with the Estate and hope next year to make a pretty good Crope." On the same day, Samuel wrote to Charles Spooner with a similar summary of events: "I should have taken an earlier opportunity of informing you of the death of my good Friend Mr. Bourryau had I not been in bed with a fever." Cary then relays details about the recent plans he and Bourryau had made: "He was so kind as to take me with him to Grenada the beginning of this year and there assisted me in buying a small Coffee Estate at St. Marks about 3 miles from yours." As Cary continues, he reiterates his assumptions about his potential role as manager of the Simon estate: "The scheme he had formed was that I should have lived at his house and carried on business at Grenville Bay but that is now at an end and I am settling my affairs here as fast as possible to commence planter and settle at St. Marks but as I have a great deal of Lumber on hand and monies out here, fear it will be the last of next year before I shall be able to leave this." He then references his "late illness," which leads him to explain, "I fear must be obliged to go for a month or two to N America before I fix to windward."[53] Thus, within seven months, Samuel's plans had been significantly altered.

In the beginning of 1770, Samuel Cary, now twenty-seven years old, continued to sort out the legal rights to the coffee estate. After discovering from Samuel Sandbach, planter, merchant, and future agent, that the plantation was still in Bourryau's name, Samuel contacted various parties to clarify the legal ownership. On January 5, he sent an update to Charles Spooner and Joseph Sill that Sandbach "says they are agreeable to this agreement which was in Mr. Bourryau's name tho he knows the Estate was bought for me." Bourryau had, in fact, written several letters about this transaction, including those sent to Samuel and "several others relative to the Estate." Although the situation appeared to be heading toward resolution, Samuel remained worried and cautious: "Must own at first Mr. Sandbach's Letter made me very unhappy as I had a few days before contracted with a Merchant here for all the Goods I had on hand at a low price, laid out my money for Negroes and etc. and thrown my self wholey out of business." He did, however, receive some guidance regarding the need to "file a Bill in Chancery" to begin the process. Meanwhile, he reports, "I have made the first payment and shall be ready to make the next and the whole as they become due." In a letter to Joseph Sill on the same day, Samuel explains that a lawyer named McFarran, who "in hopes of being twice paid drew the deeds in Mr. Bourryau's name and never mentioned me." Cary adds, "When I left Mr. Bourryau I asked if it was not proper to leave a power, he said there was no need of it for that he could sign as my attorney and no one (he supposed) would dispute it." Not only was the legal issue at stake, but Samuel had "borrowed two thousand Pounds Sterling here for three years," noting that "the Bill I sent you was part with which made the first payment £3150 my own money which is about £4100 Currency have laid out in Negroes and etc. for the Estate reserving as much as will make the next payment due in July." Samuel then explains how he will repay these loans: "I have the present Crop . . . which is now finish'd and turn out 15000 Coffee so that if it does not increase the next year I shall be straightened to make the payment and add a few Negroes — suppose by sending my Crop home I might venture to ask for some credit, pray how much may I expect for the Crop mentioned." He describes these details to Joseph Sill not only to present his dilemma, but also to elicit Sill's support: "As there's few I choose to advise with and I have lost my friend know you'l be so good as to excuse my troubling you with a State of my affairs and give me your advice freely."[54] Cary was thus hopeful that the future crops would enable him to repay his debts.

Meanwhile, the legal difficulties prevailed. On January 12, 1770, Cary writes from St. Kitts to Sandbach that he had "followed [his] advice and given the Trustees a full account of the conveyance of the Estate and sent them copy's of Mr. Bourryeau's Letters under the Seal of a Notary," adding that "money received for this year's Coffee and what raised from next crop will go to make the payment in 1771." He also apologizes for not coming in person to settle these affairs because of his ill health and sends directions to be relayed to the plantation manager, Alex Gray, to "plant as much as he can and I'll find Negroes to keep it clean tho I think he has enough with what I now send him." Samuel includes instructions for his manager and attorney to increase the size of the coffee house and to attend to the health of his slaves; in addition, he sends a specific directive to Sandbach: "I must beg you'l give orders to inoculate my Negroes if the small pox should be in any of the Neighbouring Estates or there's the least prospect of its spreading." Adding to Cary's troubles, he had learned by the first week in January of his father's passing on December 4, 1769, which he tells Sandbach about in the closing sections of his letter: "I have just rec'd the melancholy acct. of the death of my Father which will carry me to Boston as soon as my affairs here can be settled."[55] Samuel's brother Thomas recorded further details of their father's death in his diary: "Novbr 28 1769 My hond Father taken ill with the bilious Cholic, died between 12 and 1 Morning Dec 4 and on the 7th buried from Uncle Richd Carys having completed his 56th year in Novbr."[56] Within three months, Samuel Cary had lost two important people in his life, his father and his business mentor.

With his personal and professional life in turmoil, Samuel wrote several letters to Mr. Gray about managing Cary's coffee estate. On January 12, 1770, he explained that he was sending eight Negroes to work on the estate: "Quashy and Joe will be of great service they have lived five years with me and never needed correction, dare say they will not deserve it, pray get them a good House the others must be fed by hand as they are new except Titus." He then added, "Mr. Smith has promised to lend you Herrings till I can get up 10 or 15 barrels which will not be long." Unlike the plantation manual, with its generalized passages about slavery, here Cary writes about specific slaves with whom he has lived and worked for five years. In doing so, he provides directions: "First if you find it necessary give the Negroes 7 instead of 6 per week, and Joe, Quashy and Titus till they have some Land planted give them 8 or 9 but if this will cause any disturbance give to them as you do others." He not only encourages Gray to "get them a good House" and recommends their "great service," but also acknowledges the potential for "disturbance," should they be considered somehow favored.[57] Moreover, in his 1767 plantation manual, Samuel wrote, "What twould be understood by good feeding is the following: four quarts of Corn or Beans, and Four Herrings per Week for each full grown Negro." Here, then, he appears to be requesting that Mr. Gray provide extra servings of fish as a possible reward. Although actively involved in the buying of slaves himself, Samuel seems to suggest more humane treatment of his slaves.

On another topic related to his slaves, Cary asks Gray about a purchase of oznabrig, a coarse linen cloth made in Osnabrück, Germany, and used for slave clothing, and requests a clearer accounting of funds: "It appears to me that you have used a great deal of Oznabrig as I have no Journal can't tell what use you have made of it the Negroes was fully cloathed that went from this." He then provides instructions: "Beg you'l embrace the first opportunity of inoculating my Negroes if the small pox breaks out in any of the Estates near you, don't wait till it gets into mine but immediately begin and Innoculate." As this caution against smallpox was crucial to the health of the Africans and the community as a whole, these comments seem to suggest a concern that was not solely financial. In addition to instructing Gray to attend to the health of his slaves, Cary tells him, "Quashy has prevailed on me to buy his Wife and Child Emma and Frances which I also send you by this opportunity if you have occasion to keep a wench about the House pray she may be the Person as she washes and Irons exceeding well and understands cooking." In this letter, Samuel also includes a list of "Negroes sent up": "Joe, Quashy, Titus, Nero, Scipio, Emma and Frances, Charlotte and Liberty, Clarrisian, Violet."[58] As this list indicates, Africans were assigned names by the slaveholders, reflecting certain naming practices. Richard S. Dunn, for example, observes that "classical tags were also thought amusing: Dido and Venus for the women, Pompey, Nero, and Scipio for the men. All of this suggests the ambiguous status assigned the black man in the English sugar islands. Torn from Africa, excluded from European culture, he was placed in limbo somewhere between the dumb beasts and rational men." Trevor Burnard discusses these practices in specific regard to the plantation system: "Africans were renamed on arrival on the plantations, and although planters were very often careful not to give names intended to humiliate, they were fond of giving slaves names derived from classical mythology or names of grand imperial places." In doing so, Burnard finds, "Masters did not need to act with such cruelty and meanness in areas where there were no obvious correlation with work performance. It betokens an underlying contempt for Africans and an indifference to their concerns and feelings." John Wood Sweet provides additional connections: "Like the biblical Adam naming the creatures of the earth, or parents naming children, masters assigning new names to captive Africans symbolized their dominance, the totality of their possession, and their determination that a servant's identity could be reshaped at will." Colleen A. Vasconcellos observes naming practices of children in Jamaica and finds, "While some names assisted children in developing an identity apart from their English owners or fellow slaves, other names served as constant reminders that they were slaves first and children second." Burnard explains that because slaves most often did not choose their names, "slave names are more a guide to what whites thought of blacks than an entrée into slave consciousness. . . . Slaves recognized the humiliation implicit in the names that they were given. When freedom afforded them the opportunity to name themselves, slave names became almost entirely extinct."[59] Naming practices were thus an attempt to assert control and deny slaves their identity.

Samuel Cary's account book, 1770–1776, includes a ledger titled "Plantation, Mount Pleasant," which documents his relationship to his slaves; for example, an entry for December 5, 1769, lists the amount of "£1.16." as "paid the Midwife for Charlotte." At the end of this book is a three-page ledger titled "Memorandums &c for Mr. Billington," which includes sixteen items by way of directions "for the Manager of Mt Pleasant Estate." It is signed "SC" and dated "Simon July 1st." As Samuel was either in Boston or Chelsea in July 1770 and July 1773, he probably did not sign the ledger in those years. Several of the memorandum items refer specifically to the management of the slaves: "4th To allow the Negroes every Indulgence consistent with carrying on the Business of the Estate"; "8th Pray pay great Attention to your Negro Houses, let them be placed as far apart as possible and put in Order in Crop Time when thatch is plenty"; "9th To mark every Negro as soon as bought and enter his or her Name and Description into your Book, such as height, Age, Country &c inoculate them if the Small Pox should be in the Island as soon as the Season will permit." In this last item, the phrase "To mark every Negro," which does not seem to appear in his letters, may refer to recording, as in a ledger, rather than to branding, for example. That the phrase "to mark" is followed by the details of identification, however, still indicates objectification in itself. Following the memorandum on separate pages is "Instructions for Distilling," with similar details to those in Cary's "Some Directions for the management of a Sugar Plantation," of March 18, 1767. Together, these documents appear to recommend a plantation manager who is both efficient and attentive.

Contemporary Accounts of Slavery: Quobna Ottobah Cugoano, Olaudah Equiano, and Alexander Falconbridge

Contemporary accounts also describe the treatment of slaves, such as that of Quobna Ottobah Cugoano, who arrived on Grenada as a slave at the same time that Samuel Cary was setting up residence there. In an "N.B." to Cugoano's *Thoughts and Sentiments on the Evil and Wicked Traffic of the Slavery and Commerce of the Human Species . . .* (1787), he writes: "I was requested by some friends to add this information concern[ing] myself:—When I was kidnapped and brought away from Africa, I was then about 13 years of age, in the year of the Christian aera 1770; and being about nine or ten months in the slave-gang at Grenada and about one year at different places in the West-Indies, with Alexander Campbell, Esq."[60] Vincent Carretta, editor of *Thoughts and Sentiments,* notes that in 1763, Alexander Campbell purchased "two sugar estates on Grenada with more than three hundred slaves for more than £40,000."[61] Campbell's Tivoli estate was approximately twelve miles north of the Simon estate. Mark Quintanilla elaborates, noting that the estate "was ideally situated in the heart of the richest Grenadian plantation lands of St. Andrew and St. Patrick parishes. . . . Tivoli's strategic location on the River Antoine provided it with a water supply that would generate power for a mill. In addition, the estate was next to the Great Road, which was important because it provided direct access to Greenville, the major regional marketing center on the island." According to the Legacies of British Slave-ownership database, in 1772 Campbell purchased "Mount Liban, Rose Hill, Saint Cyr and Achalles [sic] estates, also in Grenada. In 1777 he added (with Ninian Home) the St John estate and half of Paraclete."[62]

Cugoano not only provides an important perspective on one of the most prominent merchants and plantations on Grenada, but also testifies to the pains of slavery: "Being in this dreadful captivity and horrible slavery, without any hope of deliverance, for about eight or nine months, beholding the most dreadful scenes of misery and cruelty, and seeing my miserable companions often cruelly lashed, and as it were cut to pieces, for the most trifling faults; this made me often tremble and weep, but I escaped better than many of them." From the slave's point of view, Grenada was a place of terrifying brutality. Cugoano, for example, describes several incidents of harsh punishment: "For eating a piece of sugarcane, some were cruelly lashed, or struck over the face to knock their teeth out. . . . Thus seeing my miserable companions and countrymen in this pitiful, distressed and horrible situation, with all the brutish baseness and barbarity attending it, could not but fill my little mind with horror and indignation."[63] Regarding *Thoughts and Sentiments* in general, Roxann Wheeler identifies a central challenge: "Cugoano faces a difficulty many writers did: claiming that color variations are a natural phenomenon (rather than God's curse or an unnatural degeneracy from white skin) and that a variety of skin colors should not signify anything other than the wonder of the Creation."[64] In his narrative, Cugoano thus testifies to the cruelty of the slave trade and addresses criticism about the moral character of life in the West Indies.

Olaudah Equiano's *The Interesting Narrative of the Life of Olaudah Equi-*

ano, or Gustavus Vassa, the African (1789) provides another contemporary account of the West Indies. As a twelve-year-old on a slave ship that arrived in Barbados in 1757, Equiano and his fellow Africans "were sold after their usual manner, which is this:— On a signal given, (as the beat of a drum), the buyers rush at once into the yard where the slaves are confined, and make choice of that parcel they like best." Equiano then describes the horrors and brutality that followed: "The noise and clamour with which this is attended, and the eagerness visible in the countenances of the buyers, serve not a little to increase the apprehensions of the terrified Africans, who may well be supposed to consider them as the ministers of that destruction to which they think themselves devoted. In this manner, without scruple, are relations and friends separated, most of them never to see each another again." As Vincent Carretta, editor of *The Interesting Narrative*, explains, "Equiano refers to what was known as the *scramble*." Alexander Falconbridge's *An Account of the Slave Trade on the Coast of Africa* (1788), as Carretta notes, describes a similar event. In the section "Sale of the Slaves," for example, Falconbridge recalls, "Being some years ago, at one of the islands in the West-Indies, I was witness to a sale by scramble, where about 250 negroes were sold." He then describes them being "placed altogether in a large yard, belonging to the merchants to whom the ship was consigned. As soon as the hour agreed upon arrived, the doors of the yard were suddenly thrown open, and in rushed a considerable number of purchasers, with all the ferocity of brutes."[65] The horrors of this scene become evident as he describes how the slaves were "seized" and how, in the process, "the poor astonished negroes were so much terrified by these proceedings, that several of them through fear, climbed over the walls of the court yard, and ran wild about the town; but were soon hunted down and retaken." As Ellen Hartigan-O'Connor observes, "Slave auctions treated human beings as one more type of commodity." Both Equiano and Falconbridge attested to the objectification. Stephanie E. Smallwood explains, "At the carefully staged performance surrounding the sale of captive Africans, the agents responsible for overseeing the process were keen to cater to their audience's comfort and pleasure." Remarking specifically on the seventeenth century, Smallwood notes, "When slave sales in the English Caribbean generally took place on shipboard, prospective buyers were ferried out to the slave ships in boats provided by the company. The norms of hospitality required agents to serve wine and 'refreshments' to prospective buyers, to keep the mood jovial and the atmosphere pleasant."[66] Cugoano, Equiano, and Falconbridge thus testify in their contemporary accounts to the inhumanity of slavery and, in doing so, provide important perspective about the world that Samuel Cary had entered.

Samuel Cary was still facing ongoing legal matters related to his coffee plantation and serving in his now tenuous role as a manager at Simon when he became seriously ill in January 1770 and retreated to Nicola Town, in the hills of St. Kitts, for a "change of air." Although his physicians thought he was dying, Samuel recovered and returned to Grenada in February, where he wrote letters to several business associates. On February 18, he wrote to London lawyer Peter Robert Luard, John Bourryau's nephew, acknowledging the mutual loss of "our dear Friend Mr. Bourryau," an event Cary describes as "the greatest misfortune . . . the loss that this Island and Grenada has met can never be made good." Addressing legal issues, he notes, "the deeds for the little Estate he was so kind as to buy on my account were drawn in his name so that I am oblig'd to file a Bill in chancery to get a Title which will be attended with expense as well as giving my friends much trouble." Samuel then reflects that the "loss of him and my honoured Father who dyed the 3rd December in a fit of the Cholic had deprived me of strength and spirits, what's left is intirely at your service if you can think of any thing I can do for you it will make me happy." On the same day, Cary writes to Joseph Sill about the cause of Captain Cary's fatal illness —"a fit of the Cholic which lasted only 4 days"—and then makes this request regarding his brother Jonathan, who was in London attending a mariner's academy: "Pray do me the favour if Cox should not have sailed for this Place to inform my Brother of my Father's death if I write to him he will be more shock'd than the kind manner which you'l please to make it known to him." Despite the difficulties, it appeared that he would retain the estate. Joseph Sill wrote on March 26, verifying that it was clear from Bourryau's letter that "this Estate was bought for you and by you, tho' the Conveyance is to him, we do not hesitate a moment to admit your Right to it." Two days later, on March 28, Sill wrote Cary again, extending his condolences and noting that Captain Cary's "memory I shall always revere."[67]

After a two-month visit to St. Kitts, Samuel returned to Grenada, where he would write to Charles Spooner on May 17, 1770, including a note about his father's passing: "Tho Heaven seems determined to rob me of every thing that's dear, I need not tell you the loss I have met with in the death of my Hond. Father its now left me nothing to fear." He then relays a report of Spooner's estate: "Both Negroes and Trees look clean and healthy and your loss of Negroes trifling to what it had been which drawback in my opinion is not enough attended to by the planters in the wind Islands." He concludes by telling Spooner, "I shall sail in a few days for Boston hope to be at Grenada again by the first Janry next." Two days later, on May 19, he received the wound to his hand, as previously mentioned, which is referenced in a letter from William Arrendell, at St. Kitts to Captain John Kiddall: "Mr. Cary intended to write to you himself but has hurted his hand and can't." In noticeably altered handwriting, Samuel writes on May 27 to Joseph Sill, explaining his delayed response in answering letters: "Some days ago I hurt my hand and am not able to hold a pen." He then adds, "Shall sail for Boston the day after tomorrow from whence shall do myself the pleasure of writing to you and the other Gentlemen."[68]

Samuel Cary in Boston, 1770–1771: Family, Business, and Health

Samuel Cary arrived from St. Kitts to Philadelphia in June 1770, as noted in a letter to William Smith on September 3: "After a very agreeable passage of 12 days spent 9 there, then set out for NYork where I was oblig'd to wait 12 days for an opportunity to go to R. Island." And in July, Thomas Cary includes a notation in his diary for the 27th: "Returned to Newburyport with Bro Sam'l."[69] After a week's stay with Thomas, Samuel "went home" on August 7 to Chelsea, where he reconnected with family and friends—and was first introduced to Sarah Gray. He also maintained contacts with business associates. In his September letter to Smith, Cary includes details about his inheritance: "My part of my Father's Estate will be £2200 Stl £1000 in money the other in House and Land which is not in my power to dispose of at present without a great loss. . . . I hope in the year 1774 or 5 I shall be free of debt." Samuel's plan to pay off his debts would prove more difficult than he imagined. He also tells William, "The Journey has been of great service to my Health — am now as well my dear Friend as ever you knew me" and "impatiently waiting an opportunity for Grenada w[h]ere you may depend on my being in November."[70] On September 3, 1770, Cary also wrote to Richard and Thomas Oliver to gauge their interest in investing in his plantation: "There's 139 Acres Land and 60 Negroes, the Cost of it made between 12 and 13000 this Season I hope it will make a little more." After summarizing the potential for profit, Samuel notes that he will "sail for Grenada in a month" and makes these final requests: "Please to inform me of the price of Coffee and the charge attending it, pray order a hogshead of the best Wine by the first ship from Madera to Grenada."

Although Samuel Cary proved to be efficient and hardworking, his position as manager, while respected, was also a subordinate one in the eyes of Charles Spooner and Joseph Sill. Writing from London, November 19, 1770, for example, they enclose a copy of Spooner's September 10 letter, which had been "directed to Boston," and state, "We . . . flatter ourselves strongly that you will accept of the proposal therein made you, or at least that if your Own Views at Grenada will not permit you to undertake the management of the Estate, you will accept of being our acting and confidential attorney and give all the assistance in your power to state the affairs of Mr. Borryeau [*sic*] at Grenada and collect in all the outstanding debt." The phrase "if your Own Views at Grenada" could have referred to Cary's legal difficulties or to other concerns instead. They then add, "Relying firmly that your friendship to the Family & us—will induce you to accept our proposals, we shall proceed to give you our further sentiments about our Grenada Concerns, and that you may be perfect master of what we have hitherto done about them." Thus, they are entrusting Samuel Cary to manage their business "concerns." On November 28, moreover, Joseph Sill reveals to Samuel, "When we made you the offer . . . we at the same time had the View of connecting to ourselves a person on whose fidelity, attachment and Industry we could place the fullest confidence and we rely that we shall not be mistaken in that respect."[71] As they affirmed the hierarchy of owners, lawyers, agents, and managers, they also signaled the scrutiny and pressures that Cary would face as manager. Upon returning from Boston, in late January 1771, after "a passage of fifty days," Cary received a letter from Joseph Sill on March 5: "We hope your scruples would vanish after your arrival at Grenada." Samuel appears to have dispelled such doubts, for on April 2 and 17, he wrote several letters confirming that he had taken possession of his role as manager. To Sill, on the 2nd, he provided a financial overview, and on the 17th, he sent specific notes about the inventory. To Spooner, on the 17th, he sent a summary of legal transactions and financial matters related to his coffee plantation.[72] On the same date, Cary also wrote to Peter Robert Luard that the person who had lent him £2,000 now wanted a mortgage on his property. In the letter, Cary expresses hope that Luard might provide credit and mentions another possible source of income: "If my friends can Sell a House I have in Boston they will remit you the money; part of my Crop my Attorneys disposed of to pay debts the Plantation owed and the remainder I sold on my Arrival." Having made his case, Samuel then asks Luard, "you'l please to debit me with your Commissions." These attempts to find financial backing for his coffee plantation reveal his vulnerability as the owner of a small estate. As a measure of the overall finances at Simon, Samuel Cary's entry in an account book for "Yearly Expencies of the Simon Estate/Sent home 20 July 1771" lists the salary for "Manager 500."[73] So, even though the owners disputed his commitment, if this note refers to Cary's salary, then his financial position appears to have been secure.

Samuel Cary continued to struggle with financing his own estate, Mount Pleasant, and with securing a profit from his coffee crop. James W. Roberts elaborates on these circumstances: "After world coffee prices plummeted in 1772, Cary spent nearly three years converting Mount Pleasant to sugar and incurred debts for labor and capital equipment that effectively chained his finances to Spooner and Luard."[74] Even though Cary eventually found other investors, the estate continued to struggle. Moreover, on February 26, 1772, Joseph Sill wrote that the trustees had advertised the Simon estate "for public sale" and that they worried about his health for fear that bad management might jeopardize the estate.[75] The *London Gazette* had already run the first of four notices on February 15, 1772: "TO be sold by Publick Sale; at Garraway's Coffee-House in Exchange-Alley, London, on the 18th Day of February, 1773, by Order of the Trustees, pursuant to the Will of John Bourryau, Esq; deceased." The estate is then described as "a Plantation called Simon, situated on the River Simon in the Quarter of Marquis in the Island of Grenada, containing 466 Acres of cleared Land, whereof about 360 are in Canes, the Remainder in Pasture and Provisions, together with 350 seasoned Negroes; among which are many Creoles and several Tradesmen." The livestock and sugar works include "60 Mules and above 40 Head of Horses, Cattle, &c. and a compleat Set of Works, consisting of a Water-Mill, Boiling-House, Curing-House, Still-House, and all other Buildings necessary for carrying on a Sugar Plantation, together with an excellent Dwelling-House. The Buildings are partly new within these few Years; the whole in compleat Repair." The advertisement then provides contacts: "For further Particulars enquire of Mr. Sill, at Mr. Luard's, Copthall-Cnoit, Throgmorton-Street, or at Mr. Palmer's. Philpot-Lane." These notices reinforced the hierarchy of owners and managers, showing how economic factors dictated decisions. Although the sale suggested that Samuel's position as manager might be in jeopardy, on November 5, 1773, Joseph Sill writes that it is good to hear that Samuel's "health is perfectly restored, the disagreeable altercation that passed between us is eternally buried in oblivion on this side of the Water."[76]

This precarious situation, however, prevailed throughout Samuel Cary's tenure as manager. According to the Legacies entry for John Bourryau, "Although the estate was advertised for sale in 1773, it appears to have then become bound in Chancery p[r]oceedings, and readvertised for sale 20 years later."[77] By 1792, the original administrators of the Simon estate had all died: John Bourryau in 1769, Charles Spooner in 1790, and Joseph Sill in 1792. The pending sale might have also contributed to the Carys' decision to depart Grenada in June 1791. The first notice of this second attempt to sell the estate then appeared in the *London Gazette*, March 3, 1792.[78] Thus, as the Legacies entry for Bourryau explains, there was a protracted legal battle for the Simon estate, preventing it from going back on the market for decades.

Subsequent notices provide additional details about the estate and inventory. For example, the November 29, 1793, notice mentions shipping options, as the estate is "about Three Miles in a direct Line from the Town and Harbour of Grenville Bay, (where the Government have established a Port and Custom-House for entering and clearing out Vessels, on which there is a Storehouse belonging to the Plantation) so that while it is free, on the one Hand, from the Expence and Inconveniency of a long laborious Cartage, it is, on the other, secure of seasonable Weather, from it's Vicinity to the Mountains." The notices also document changes in the slave population: in 1773, there were "350 seasoned Negroes, among which are many Creoles and several Tradesmen," and in 1794, there were "264 Negro and other Slaves." The posting on March 1, 1794, reveals an additional six acres of cane cultivated, and a list of the "Particulars of the Buildings" that now include a mill house, a boiling house, a curing house, a still house, a cooper's shop, a cattle and mule pen, and two begass houses. In 1786, 387 hogsheads of sugar were produced yielding "nett Sales, including usual Commission £7798.17.3." In 1793, the crop was 330 hogsheads, "The Whole not yet sold, but supposed will net upwards of £9000." In addition to describing the sugar works, the notice provides detailed descriptions of the housing: "A Dwelling-House, built of hard Wood"; "Kitchen and Pantry"; "Two Store-Rooms . . . An Hospital, with Three Rooms, shingled Roof"; "Two Overseers Dwelling Houses"; and "Seventy-six Negroe Houses." Other details noted are a consistent water supply from the "Rivers Simon and Cacoieie"; good soil, "among the best in the Island"; and "the Situation very healthy." The Legacies database provides a summary of the valuation of the estate: "In 1789 the Simon estate had been valued at £72,194 sterling, and in 1794 it was offered for sale at £72,000 (with the next or ensuing crop) or £65,000 (without the next or ensuing crop)."[79]

As these ads indicate, the Simon estate included substantial acreage, numerous dwellings, and elaborate sugar works.

⌒

Samuel Cary's first decade in the West Indies had thus proved to be both challenging and profitable. And though the ending of one conflict, the Seven Years' War, facilitated Cary's entrance into the sugar trade with the opening of the Ceded Islands to British control, the American Revolutionary War would present a new set of issues affecting both trade and family security over the next decade. As a third-generation merchant in the West Indies, Samuel Cary must have had some sense of the harsh climate, but he probably could not have anticipated how the increasing transatlantic slave trade would bear on the moral aspects of managing a sugar plantation. His portrait of a "good tempered" manager might have been one way to offset the realities of slaveholding, if not an attempt to justify his role in this system. Cary had not only associated his position with success and fortune, but also identified his own role as manager more within the realm of a benevolent figure than a tyrannical or greedy one. As such, he shows how a well-intentioned person could be swayed to participate in the slave trade. How consciously Samuel Cary debated this decision is unclear from his correspondence, but that he lived near James Ramsay and James Grainger while working for Charles Spooner and John Bourryau suggests that such debates existed. After Sarah Gray Cary arrived at Grenada in spring 1774, and they set up their household, both Samuel and Sarah would be tested even further regarding their genteel New England assumptions about society. As the next chapters show, these transitions are by equal parts rewarding and difficult.

CHAPTER TWO

Building Prosperity

Sarah Cary and Family in Grenada, 1774–1791

Sarah Cary's departure from Chelsea was both hectic and dramatic. Not only was she distraught about having to leave three-month-old Samuel behind, but with the Boston Harbor impassable, Sarah had to depart north of the city, as she would explain to her son Henry years later: "I believe you have heard me regret my want of opportunity after marriage to improve in music. It was all in vain. A voyage to the West Indies in winter, and sailing from Portsmouth — Boston harbor being blocked with ice — obliged me to leave my harpsichord behind." Margaret Cary relays a similar account: "Oh, how often she regretted not having yielded to the dictates of her feelings and taken her infant with her! But both parents had consulted the interest of the child, and they hoped the separation would not be long."[1] Thomas Cary notes his sister-in-law's departure in his diary by first marking his brother Jonathan's arrival "at Portsmouth" on January 5, which was then verified a week later in the *New Hampshire Gazette*: "Custom House, Piscataqua, January 13, Inward-Entries, Ship Sally, Jonathan Cary." On February 8 Thomas notes that "Sister Cary & Ned came" to Newburyport, and on February 15 that he "went to Portsmouth with Sister Sally." Thus, his diary explains how Sarah traveled from Newburyport to Portsmouth. British shipping records show that Jonathan Cary, ship master, was cleared for departure from Portsmouth to Grenada on February 15, 1774, on the ship *Sally*.[2] With an approximate sailing time of five to six weeks, Sarah would have arrived at Grenada in late March or early April 1774. In Sarah's letter to Henry, she adds, "The following month, the revolution broke out, and then all intercourse was stopped between us." As Sarah mentioned, the Boston Port Act closed Boston Harbor on June 1, a prelude to the Coercive Acts, referred to as the Intolerable Acts by the colonists. In May, Jonathan Cary confirms Sarah's arrival in a letter to Joshua Wentworth, who co-owned the *Sally* with John Davenport, noting as well that this is his "third letter" since landing: "Brother Sam and Sally are both well but are [on] the other side the Island so that I don't see them no more than if they where [*sic*] in Boston as he is busy taking of his Crop and I have employment enough here, that I can't go to see him."[3] From these accounts, Sarah had not only departed Boston under tense conditions on the eve of the American Revolution, but as the following chapters address, she now faced a very different life on the Simon estate, just north of Grenville Bay on the island of Grenada.

This move would require radical readjustment not only climatically but socially as well. Having grown up in the bustling colonial city of Boston during the 1750s, Sarah would have been afforded educational opportunities and social interactions as part of her family's strong church community. Grenada was, by contrast, a colonial outpost in the British Empire's thriving West Indian sugar trade. According to Bryan Edwards, in *The History, Civil and Commercial, of the British West Indies* ([1793] 1819), "Grenada is computed to be about twenty-four miles in length, and twelve miles in its greatest breadth, and contains about 80,000 acres of land, of which although no less than 72,141 acres paid taxes in 1776, and may therefore be supposed fit for cultivation, yet the quantity actually cultivated has never exceeded 60,000 acres. The face of the country is mountainous, but not inaccessible in any part, and it abounds with springs and rivulets." Edwards also calculates that "the number of white inhabitants, in the year 1771, was known to be somewhat more than sixteen hundred; in 1777 they had decreased to thirteen hundred." In regard to "the negro slaves," Edwards reports, "By the last returns preceding the capture of the island in 1779, they were stated at 35,000, of which 5,000 were in Carriacou, and the smaller islands."[4] When Sarah left Boston in 1774, the city's population as recorded in the 1770 census was 15,520, and its size was around 750 acres, according to William A. Newman and Wilfred E. Holton, who also note that "Boston was about two miles long north to south and had a maximum width of about a mile and a half."[5] Sarah would have had the opportunity to travel outside Boston, which would have expanded her world as well. She had been accustomed to living in a densely populated city, and she now found herself living in comparative isolation. When Samuel Cary had arrived, five years earlier, the area around Simon had been populated largely by single men serving as agents, but by 1774, several families had since moved in, as Margaret describes: "Mrs. Williams and her daughter, Mrs. Van Dussen, arrived from England, their husbands being already there;

also Mrs. Proudfoot came out with her husband, and Mrs. Horsford, from Antigua"; together, they "formed a very pleasant association. My mother was intimate with them all, but particularly with the last-named."[6] For Sarah, this community would provide a sense of familiarity and valuable connections. In her subsequent letters to family and friends in Boston, she would also present an important counterpoint to the emphasis on commerce and trade that dominated, for example, her husband's correspondence. Instead, Sarah would express mixed emotions as she acknowledged the potential for fortunes and questioned the sacrifices required to achieve them.

As noted in the *London Gazette,* January 30, 1773, the Simon estate included an "excellent Dwelling-House" with "partly new" buildings. Margaret Cary provides an extended description in a letter to her nephew George on March 9, 1843, noting that the house sat "on a high flat hill" with "a beautiful lawn." She includes a sketch of the floor plan, which shows "a dining-room to the south with a pantry beyond, and a drawing-room to the north, with a housekeeper's room at the west side, opening to the west gallery; above were three chambers, besides a dressing-room over the northeast end of the gallery, and a similar square room over the north end of the west gallery for a study." There was also "a play-room for the children," as well as her "father's writing-room, where he received persons on business, and a large storeroom with provisions. Beyond the kitchen, a little farther to the north, was the hospital." She describes her mother's activities as "taken up in the care of her children, in regulating her household, in reading to my father, writing to her mother, and entertaining company," adding as well that one of the family cooks "had been sent to Paris for his education." Margaret also recalls, "My father was on horseback every morning, riding round the plantation and giving directions, or rather seeing that the directions given every night were going on properly; then to La Baye, returning home to dinner; at leisure in the afternoon to visit, or receive company, or read." She describes the grounds of the estate in a similarly genteel tone, with a "beautiful stream of water . . . meandering between the verdant grassy banks," a vegetable garden, and "a cashew walk," which she compares in length to "one side of the Boston Common."[7] In her next letter, Margaret adds, "The plantations all around were beautiful and in complete cultivation. . . . The verdure of the green can hardly be imagined. It was what the poets would call a laughing green . . . and in the least cultivated parts of the country Nature seemed to frolic without any restraint."[8] Margaret thus conveys a bucolic scene of a gardenlike, industrious plantation, with the river's "meandering between the verdant grassy banks," her mother's household routines, and her father's leisurely afternoons.

Margaret also presents slave life as part of a well-ordered estate, with housing for "between two or three hundred negroes." She then directs her reader to "look beyond the river, on another hill, and you see the negro-houses, shaded with palm-trees, cedar-trees, and roseaux." The "sugar-house," located down the hill, included "a distillery over it, the begass-house, and the mill." Here, she refers to the sugar-making process that included the extraction of juice from the sugar cane, where the pressed cane, or begass, was stored in a house for fuel. The canes were then transported by "mules laden with canes, each with a boy conducting; men receiving the canes and feeding the fires." Margaret also includes a description of the daily roll call: "Every evening after tea, the negroes assembled in the open space before the west gallery, each bringing a bundle of sticks for fuel for the kitchen, the men on one side, the women on the other, and an elderly man as a leader in prayer between them. They all cast their fagots before them, and answered to their names as the list was called. Then they knelt reverently and joined in prayer, kissed the ground, and rising, sung a hymn and departed."[9] Bernard Moitt corroborates such scenes in eighteenth-century Caribbean practices: "After prayers, which were obligatory but not always observed, roll call was taken —a measure which permitted the slave driver to report sick and absent slaves to the *économe* (overseer), who was in charge of the day-to-day operations of the plantation. It was left to the économe and the *gérant* (*géreur* in creole)—a manager who ran the plantation in the absence of the *colon* (owner)—to verify the number of absentees and to ensure the care of the sick, a daily rate as high as 22 percent on the Lugé Plantation in Saint-Domingue in the period of 1778–91."[10]

As a child, Margaret may not have understood these actions as driven by management and control, instead recalling the scene in which the slaves "knelt reverently and joined in prayer, kissed the ground, and rising, sung a hymn and departed." By contrast, Moitt describes a slave's extended workday: "Before leaving, each slave gathered animal feed or firewood. . . . After the evening meal, prayers, and the taking of a head count, slaves were free to return to their huts. The only exception to this routine was at harvest time, when slaves were required to work at night. During this period, the workday lasted for about eighteen hours, and the other six were often dedicated to searching for food."[11] Endless work and meager sustenance thus counter

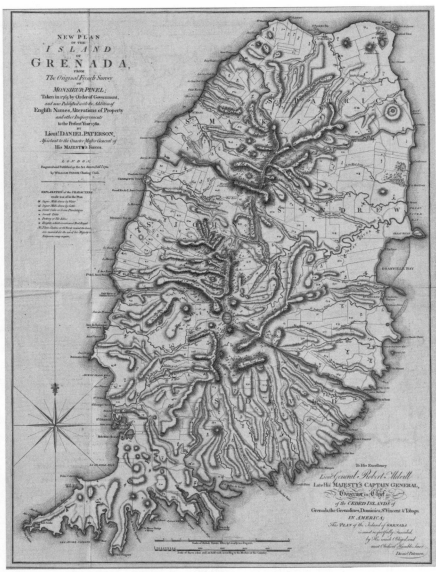

Daniel Paterson and Pinel, *A New Plan of the Island of Grenada, from the Original French Survey of Monsieur Pinel; Taken in 1763 by Order of Government, and now Published with the Addition of English names, Alterations of Property, and other Improvements to the Present Year 1780 by Lieutt. Daniel Paterson.* C-6105-000. Courtesy of the John Carter Brown Library at Brown University.

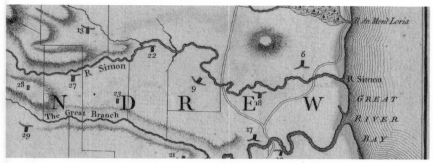

Detail of Paterson and Pinel, *A New Plan of the Island of Grenada*, showing the Simon estate, Parish of St. Andrew, Lot 27. The Cary family lived on the Simon plantation, where Samuel Cary served as manager.

Detail of Paterson and Pinel, *A New Plan of the Island of Grenada*, showing the Mount Pleasant plantation, Parish of St. Mark, Lot 25. Samuel Cary's coffee estate, Mount Pleasant, was on the Little River Crawfish, just south of Point Duquesne and approximately twenty miles northeast of St. George's. Samuel Cary eventually converted the coffee estate to a sugar plantation. The Cary family lived here during the rainy season.

idealized portraits. Margaret does offer a more critical view of Grenada: "O beautiful country! Dear native land! Had thy moral excellence been equal to thy natural advantages, how gladly would I have clung to the soil which yielded daily fresh flowers to the feet!" She then draws another contrast: "But the fragrance of the air, the beauty of the clouds, the rich luxuriance of vegetation, the bright radiance of the moon, the all-prolific sun, tempered only by the east wind which rose daily from the ocean, — all, and much more, could not satisfy the rational mind."[12] She follows with notes about her father, who "had that vigorous cast of mind that was always looking for improvement," in both conversation and books. So, her comments might have referred to a lack of intellectual stimulation on the island, but they might have also reflected antislavery sentiment.

Despite any hopes that Sarah's separation from young Samuel would be temporary, the onset of the American Revolutionary War not only prolonged their time apart but also made regular communications with Boston and Chelsea nearly impossible. Although Sarah must have anticipated some level of disruption following the closing of Boston Harbor, it may have been diffi-cult to foresee the escalation of conflicts leading to the Battles of Lexington and Concord on April 19, 1775, and the subsequent ten-month Siege of Bos-ton, which lasted until March 17, 1776. Even more directly related to the Cary family was the Battle of Chelsea Creek, May 27–28, 1775, the second military engagement of the Revolutionary War, as Mellen Chamberlain elaborates: "In the winter of 1775–6, during the siege of Boston, some of Washington's troops occupied the Cary mansion as barracks."[13] Moreover, in an observation about wartime disruptions, Andrew O'Shaughnessy notes, "Soldiers went to great lengths to avoid the notorious postings in the Caribbean. . . . Absenteeism among officers—like that among sugar planters—was a chronic problem." More specifically, he points out, "In Grenada in July 1775, more officers were absent than present. . . . Officers frequently complained that the high cost of living made it impossible to live like gentlemen—even in Jamaica, which paid lieutenants and their superiors an additional subsistence allowance."[14] The war not only halted communications but also prevented the Cary family's return before the war ended. As such, remaining at Grenada became less of a choice and more of a compromise. Meanwhile, their decision to send four-year-old Margaret to London in 1779 for her education further committed them to remain.

The war also affected the sugar trade, decreasing production and profit margins. David Watts, for example, elaborates: "The result was that between March 1774 and March 1778, the amount of sugar reaching London annually from the British West Indies fell from 131,000 to 76,000 casks." Shortages led to escalating costs, and even though "sugar prices soared over the war period . . . rates of profit on estates remained low, ranging from means of 7% in the Ceded Islands to 2% to 3% elsewhere."[15] Sugar production on Gre-nada was slow to recover, as Samuel Cary explained on August 25, 1778, to William Smith, after surveying both of Smith's estates, which were located near Mount Pleasant. Regarding Smiths' Revolution Hall, Cary reports, "I am happy to find your own Estate has produced more than was promised; if the Sugar gets to a good market Your revenue must be great, which I hope and pray may continue." As to the Diamond estate, which Smith co-owned, Samuel reports, "The plants and those Rattoons from the Land that's been dungd look exceedingly well." Samuel then addresses the effects of the war on shipping and commerce: "The troubles have made us all economist[s] and our wants can never be so great as they have been. Tho the Repairs of our old Buildings will call for great Supplys soon." Having heard that the British were planning to send troops to reclaim islands from the French, he writes, "There seems a Storm gathering, it will burst on or near us, the troops having left Philadelphia, and a large Quantity of Salt provisions being arrived at Barbadoes, stored for Government, we begin to think that as soon as the hurricane months are over, We may expect the Troops in this part of the world. They think so at Martinico by the preparations making there, their want of Salt provisions will insure Success — we feel secure here, I wish we may be so." Samuel Cary's economic concerns were justified, for as Mark Quintanilla notes, "between 1776 and 1792 the Grenada sugar exports actually declined seven percent."[16] In other words, for nearly the entire time that Sarah and Samuel were on Grenada, the economy was less dependable than Samuel had anticipated on his arrival in 1769. Moreover, while Samuel's main concerns were about commerce, on August 25, 1778, he speculates to William Smith about a possible resolution: "I would hope as the troops are about to leave N. A. that a Settlement will take place, it appears to me that none ever will shout of independance, both Countrys may by that be saved from Ruin." With similar hope for resolution, he writes to Joseph Sill on October 20, 1778: "We are informed that the Army is about to leave N. America, if that is the case hope we shall have peace."[17]

In Sarah's first extant letter from Grenada, on October 29, 1779, to Mary (Polly) Smith Gray, she begins, "It is with the utmost satisfaction my dear sister I sit down to assure you how much pleasure I feel at the agreable connexion you have form'd with my Brother." As Sarah notes, Mary Smith and Edward Gray had married on December 11, 1777, an event that Abigail Adams anticipates in a letter to John on October 20, 1777, regarding her cousin Mary Smith: "She marries in about 2 months to a Mr. Gray, a Brother of Mr. Eliss Grays of B—n [Boston]."[18] Sarah then describes her new home: "I wish I had anything entertaining or new to communicate, but you must expect nothing from this, when I tell you that I am situated in a fine Island, every corner of which abounds with the most beautiful prospects, I have said every thing, for we have little society here." By contrast to Margaret's nostalgic view of her childhood home, Sarah conveys a sense of isolation. And where Margaret recollects a "pleasant association" between families, Sarah, who is writing this letter when Margaret is about four years old, describes her disappointment with having "little society." She also notes the difficulty of finding safe transport for her letters: "I hope you will do me the justice to believe that nothing should have prevented me from writing you long before, but the uncertain Channels through which our Letters have been hitherto conveyed." These "uncertain Channels" had made letters vulnerable to loss and even confiscation, which Sarah found increasingly frustrating: "It is distressing to be obliged to live in a state of separation from our Friends at any rate, but it becomes intolerable when we are deprived of corresponding with them. — I have received but 2 letters in 3 years from any of my Family, I am convinced, however, that they do write, but some particular Friends we have here, pick up all the Letters; imagining, I suppose, that we hold a treasonable correspondence."[19] The separation was hard enough, but the potential accusation of carrying on "a treasonable correspondence" only intensified the stress. As Sarah's remarks about interrupted communications indicate, letters were often subject to delay for various reasons. Barbara Maria Zaczek notes, for example, "In passing between the sender and the recipient, the letter is prone to all sorts of mishap: it can be intercepted, misdirected, or misplaced, and thus fall into the hands of a third party who may take advantage of its existence." This last possibility supports Sarah's speculations about her own correspondence. All letters were thus vulnerable to some degree. While Sarah Cary may have been less concerned about her letters being treated maliciously, she was frustrated by the interruptions. Samuel Cary's business transactions were also frequently disrupted, causing even more frustrations. Konstantin Dierks elaborates on such circumstances: "Wartime complicated what was daunting enough in peacetime: the conduct of transatlantic trade entirely by letter with clients one would never meet, to a place one would never see. The ground, as it were, beneath that trade was constantly shifting, subject to incessant glitches, problems, and disputes."[20]

As the war continued, the Carys were subjected to scrutiny, not only for their Bostonian roots but perhaps as well because brothers Jonathan and Thomas were sympathetic to the Patriot cause. In Ednah C. Silver's *Sketches of the New Church in America on a Background of Civic and Social Life* (1920), she offers additional background: "Although Mr. Cary was a British subject, he sympathized with the colonists, and at one time harbored some American sea-captains, 'so that the governor threatened to send him to London and have him put in the Tower and punished as a rebel.' " Here, Silver is citing Margaret Cary's letter to her nephew George, which then continues: "But he minded no risks; and when General Cornwallis's army was taken, and the news reached Grenada, Colonel Williams rode over to Simon, and, giving the intelligence, charged my father not to stir from his own house, for he knew that he could not conceal his pleasure, and it would be dangerous for him to express it."[21] Nevertheless, Samuel Cary did serve in the British militia as captain of the First Company of the St. Andrews Regiment on Grenada, as noted in the Revolutionary War orderly books at the Massachusetts Historical Society. Various notations describe his duties and activities. For example, on December 23, 1778, "Capt. Cary" is listed to serve "For Guard tomorrow" and "For Fatigue at day break tomorrow," and on December 30, Cary is noted as one of the captains to preside "For a General Court Martial tomorrow."[22] Thus, Samuel Cary did comply with British rule. In other developments, the French captured Grenada on July 4, 1779, and held control until September 3, 1783, when the Treaty of Paris returned the island to the British.

Moreover, before the end of the war, Sarah would suffer the loss of all three of her brothers. William, a doctor, died on May 17, 1772, and Edward died at age twenty-nine, on December 21, 1779. In Elizabeth Storer Smith's letter to her son Isaac on April 12, 1780, she provides details about Edward, her son-in-law, noting his "bad state of Health, which kept increasing on him till the 21 Decr when it pleas'd a wife and holy Providence to remove him from us, your Sister is come back to live [with] us again."[23] On May 25, 1780, Sarah Cary writes to Mary Smith Gray, "I am unable to determine which predominates most in my mind at present, real grief for the loss of your dear departed Husband, or the tender participation I take in your distresses, both afflict me, I wish I cou'd Say any thing that wou'd afford you comfort, but alas I stand too much in need of it myself." Sarah then expresses her own grief: "I loved my Brother, and feel most sensibly his Death. Many happy hours had I promised myself I shou'd, in some future Day pass in conversation with Him and you. The connexion indeed gave me pleasure; but we must submit to the dispositions of Heaven which however distressing, are always Wise, and intended for our advantage." While Sarah recommends that they each "submit to the dispositions of Heaven," she also seeks solace: "I don't know anything so likely to console a serious mind for the loss of a beloved object, as the agreeable prospect of an hereafter; Where Friendship will be truly permanent, and uninterrupted by those Things which so often occur in this

Life, to disturb our domestic comforts, and make them less compleat. My Tears flow too fast to dwell longer on this melancholy subject." Sarah then responds to Mary's questions about visiting Chelsea: "Be assured nothing wou'd afford me so much pleasure; but it is at present our Lot to live in a State of Separation from every thing that cou'd give Life a relish; we must submit for a time, though I wou'd fain flatter myself that will soon expire. Heaven grant it may." Even though Sarah acknowledges that the situation requires submission, she still does not find that the prospects for success justify the separation. In her grief, Sarah was acutely aware of the sacrifices that had kept her from "everything that cou'd give Life a relish." The goal of financial gain appeared far less important than the desire to be home.[24]

One year after Edward Gray's death, Sarah's only surviving brother, Ellis Gray, encountered a series of misfortunes when his ship, the *Sally*, whose captain was Samuel Andrews, was captured by the French at Martinique. Ellis Gray wrote to John Adams on July 25, 1780, for help, and John Thaxter, John Adams's private secretary, then reported to Adams on September 19: "The Judge, he says, declares in his decree of condemnation Vessel and Cargo to be Dutch Property, but that the Vessel was navigated by Englishmen," and consequently, "Mr. Gray requests your Assistance."[25] Adams then wrote from Amsterdam to Benjamin Franklin on September 29, explaining that "Mr. Samuel Andrews, formerly of Boston lately of Demarara, is going to Paris upon Business, respecting a Vessell taken by the French and carried into Martinico." Franklin responded to Adams from Passy, France, on October 8, 1780: "I received the letter you did me the Honour of writing to me by Mr. Andrews, and shall render him every Service I can in his Application." On March 12, 1782, Samuel Andrews wrote to Adams from Paris, where he had been detained for sixteen months, to thank him for interceding and to request that he write to Franklin "upon this head and that my friend Mr Gray had wrote you, or if agreable send him the origanel."[26] These exchanges not only acknowledge Ellis Gray's stature as a merchant and his connections by marriage to John Adams, but also mark the ongoing problem of privateering. Stephen Conway, for example, explains how the conflicts during the American Revolutionary War between England and the colonies, as well as "the entry of France and Spain into the war," collectively affected trade on the sugar islands: "The threat from enemy privateers and naval vessels increased greatly, some of the islands themselves were taken by the French—Dominica in 1778, St Vincent and Grenada in 1779, Tobago in 1781, and St Kitts and Nevis in 1782—and Jamaica, the most important of the British islands, was

frequently seen as under threat." As Conway notes, trade in the West Indies was not only interrupted but potentially dangerous. A year after his ship
was captured, Ellis Gray died at the age of forty-one, on July 11, 1781.[27] With
Sarah's siblings all passed away, she suffered these losses at a distance, and
as the wartime interruption to her correspondence continued, she felt her
isolation more acutely.

Contributing to this isolation, Sarah's correspondence remained subject
to interruptions. For example, Mary Smith Gray Otis, now remarried to Samuel Allyne Otis, wrote in November 1783 that she had not received a letter
from Sarah since March 1782. When Sarah responded on March 10, 1784,
she offered this explanation: "How my Dear is it that my Letters Miscarry?
if I had not wrote you repeatedly in that time, I shou'd be perfectly at ease,
because you must have become indifferent to me, and in that case I wou'd not
regret the complaint in your Letter." Noting that if a correspondence should
drop off, it indicates indifference, Sarah confirms that this is not the case, but
rather "the reverse," and that she had written "very frequently." And in regard to young Samuel, Sarah adds, "I am glad to find you and Mr. Otis approve
of Master Sam's coming out here," noting as well, "at the same time I smile
when reading that part of your Letter where you say 'a Boy in his Station
of Life ought &c:' ah, My Dear, you little know what you say, at least, if you
allude to any future prospect of Fortune." Having tempered these assumptions, Sarah does appreciate "the Friendship which has subsisted between
our two Gentlemen My Dear and which absence, nor time can lessen, is one
very great reason why I impatiently wait the time of our return to America."
She then acknowledges, "I Shall ever feel indebted to you and Mr. Otis, for
the Tender attention you bestowed on My Dear Boy when in America," and
to Samuel Otis in particular, "who has so faithfully acted the part of a Friend,
in being a Father to my Son." Sarah is exasperated by the prolonged absence
from Chelsea as it prevents her from visiting her son and her mother, as she
notes earlier in the letter: "Upon the subject of my dear Mama, I scarcely
know what to say, my feelings for her are not to be expressed, but how shall
I inform her that it is impossible for us to see her next Summer, it is a difficult and even dangerous task." The dangers of traveling are not specified,
but Sarah may be alluding to the prevalence of privateering. Regarding her
mother's perceptions of their life in Grenada, Sarah notes, "She thinks we are
building up a Fortune for ourselves, without bestowing a thought on her." In
doing so, she again weighs the sacrifices of separation against the potential
for fortune. It had been ten years since she had arrived in Grenada, and any

Sarah Cary to Mrs. Otis, Simon, March 10, 1784. Cary Family Papers III, Collection of the Massachusetts Historical Society.

Simon 10th March 1784

My Dear Mrs. Otis

I cannot to the full extent of my wish, express to you my extreme chagrin, at the complaint which accompanied your agreable favor of the 18th Novembr delivered by my dear Boy, you say you have not had a Line from me since March 82, how my Dear is it that my Letters Miscarry? if I had not wrote you repeatedly in that time, I shou'd be perfectly at ease, because you must have become indifferent to me, & in that case I wou'd not regret the complaint in your Letter, but my Friend you must do me the Justice to believe the reverse, I have frequently wrote you, very frequently, I cannot indeed say how often, nor can I remember their several dates, because I never copy my Letters, but indeed you are very dear to me, and my Heart tells me that I have never been remiss in my attention to you; I feel the same attachment as when we were [. . .]

initial hopes that this move would be both relatively short and significantly profitable were now in doubt.

Samuel and Sarah did return to Chelsea for six months beginning in summer 1784, when they visited family and friends, including her mother, Sarah Tyler Gray, as well as her former sister-in-law Mary Smith Otis and her husband, Samuel. Thomas Cary notes their arrival in his diary on July 22: "Bro & Sister's Cary got to Boston." On this visit, the Cary family was accompanied by Fanny Fairweather, who was referred to as the family's "black servant." "Good old Fanny," Margaret recalls, "was of the party, and the old lady undertook to teach her to read, and she did make some progress. My grandmother would have kept her with her. But no; if mistress stayed, she was willing to stay, too; but if she went, Fanny would not be left behind."[28] Although Fanny's unwillingness to "be left behind" was expressed as obedience, Margaret's details about her grandmother teaching Fanny to read and offering her the choice to stay may indicate abolitionist sympathies. The Carys departed on January 26, 1785, as Thomas notes: "My Bro'r Sam & Ux sailed from Beverly," a town just north of Salem, Massachusetts.[29]

Once home, Sarah writes to Mary on March 29, 1785, and imagines her life in Boston: "Considering the Month of March, I suppose then every thing that is agreable, a lovely Infant, a doating Mother, a fond Husband, Relations of all sorts, Numerous Friends, Cakes, Cordials, and etc. and etc. and etc. and to crown the whole, your happy Self." Having presented this scene of domestic harmony, Sarah asks whether Mary "intend[s], like other Town Ladies, to sacrifice the pleasure of nursing the dear one to fashion?" adding, "If you do, I pitty you, for you are possessed of too much sensibility to do it without giving yourself great pain." Sarah then acknowledges that her letter may appear disjointed: "I have much on my mind to say to you, but the truth is, I have already wrote you a strange sort of unconnected Letter, this you will probably observe before you get thus far, I have for this, only one apology to make, and that is, the extreme anxiety I feel, occasioned by the Inoculation for the Small Pox, of My dear little Boy and Girl." Writing only three hours since the "operation," Sarah tries to downplay the dangers: "I cannot help strange foreboding of mind, on the introduction of so fatal, and Shocking a distemper, into My Family; Softened indeed by the art of the Physician, but even then, sometimes dreadful in its consequences."[30] These fears were, of course, real, as inoculations involved introducing live smallpox pustules into the bloodstream and then waiting for the body to fight off the infection. Letters enabled Sarah to maintain connections with Mary Polly Otis, and they provide insights into domestic routines and motherhood. On May 20, 1786, she again writes to Mary and expresses her frustration over the "state of separation from those we love and value," including her mother, from whom she had not received a letter "since last December." Twelve years after her arrival at Grenada, Sarah, who was now thirty-three and the mother of six children, ages one to twelve, remained deeply connected to her Massachusetts home: "I assure you I am more than ever desirous of returning to Chelsea, whether it is, that as I find the more I see of life, the less worthy it is of pursuit; or that growing old, I am anxious to get to a resting-place or that the pleasing picture Mama draws of the improvements upon the Farm, operate Stronger than usual upon my mind, I know not; but I feel an impatience to quit this Country, that I have not felt before." Sarah's desire to return home thus intensified. She also adds a note about Mary's sister-in-law Mercy Otis Warren: "When you see Mrs. Warren, tell her I very often think of her, and always with pleasure, at the same time present for me, my affectionate regards."[31] On May 24, 1787, Sarah again envisions Mary "engrossed by domestic care," and draws this contrast: "It is not here, as in Boston, that children are sent to school to be out of mamma's way, or confined to a nursery in the upper part of the house. Here they play, sing, dance, bathe, all under my own eye. We are always together. I am nurse, school-mistress, and mother, alternately." She then places this scene in a larger context: "And I am of opinion that Providence designed me for the situation, for I feel no regret at refusing to join in a ball or other amusements at our capital. To a woman of fashion, what an insipid animal I must be!"[32] Sarah again references the dictates of "fashion" in contrast to her simplified life, even as she considers her situation providentially designed.

Concurrent with these other events, Samuel Cary, in addition to participating in the transatlantic slave trade, "was also active in inter-island slave sales, investigating Antiguan estate auctions and arranging transshipments between Grenada, St. Vincent, and St. Kitts," James W. Roberts finds in his detailed discussion of Cary's business transactions. Furthermore, Margaret Cary notes that her father served as a member of the General Assembly at Grenada, which sent him "occasionally" to St. George's, where "he was always very independent in his principles, and sometimes gave his vote against the governor."[33] At the same time as this appointment, Roberts notes, "Cary served on a committee to answer queries regarding the nature of slavery and the slave trade at Grenada to provide Spooner, as agent, the means to represent the islands before a Select Committee investigating the slave trade in London."[34] Thus, while Samuel Cary may have written infrequently in his letters about purchasing slaves, his position as plantation manager on St. Kitts and Grenada and his role as a plantation owner at Mount Pleasant required his direct involvement.

Margaret and Samuel's Education in England

During this same period, Sarah and Samuel were also making arrangements for their children's education in England, as few options were available in the West Indies. In a discussion about Scottish merchants in the Caribbean, Douglas J. Hamilton observes, "For those wealthy whites who remained in the islands long enough to raise families, the problem of education was solved either by bringing out a tutor from Britain or by dispatching their children back there to school."[35] Moreover, as the British were on the verge of retaking Grenada from the French, Margaret would later explain that she was sent away "just before this war," noting as well, "It was always an important object with my father to have his children well educated, and he always did in this respect to the very utmost of his ability."[36] In 1779, at the age of four, Margaret left Grenada, and for the next ten years, she received an education that would have been equal to if not better than that of her Bostonian counterparts.

On the voyage, young Margaret was placed in the care of Captain Cox, and upon her arrival, Charles Spooner and his wife welcomed her into their household. In Samuel Cary's letter to Charles Spooner on May 1, 1780, after acknowledging Joseph Sill's death and mentioning an apparent falling-out between Spooner and Sill, Cary explains that an illness in 1776 had prompted him to make a will: "[I] took the Liberty to mention you as Executor and Guardian to my Children, for as times were they had nobody else to look up to." He then provides additional details about the decision to send Margaret to England: "The communication between this and Boston being shut by the unhappy War, and my little Girl beginning to take notice of things in this most unchristian Country, made up with people of all countries and rudest in their manners of any place, so unlike the Leeward Islands," and as a result, Samuel notes, "my Wife and Self thought it our Duty to send her away tho' our stay here might be prolong'd by it, and as we had heard a good Character of Mr. Cox and he had received from me every assistance in my Power, thought it best to send her by him never having an Idea of her being noticed by You." Samuel thus explains their decision while also making an interesting comparison between Grenada, in the Windward Islands, and St. Kitts, in the Leeward Islands. He then expresses his appreciation to the Spooner family: "These are Ties, My dear Sir that's almost too much for one who is so fond of his Family as I am of mine — and in doing every thing I can shall not be able to make amends."[37] This letter not only explains Samuel and Sarah's concerns about Grenada but also acknowledges that their decision would prolong their stay. Samuel Cary's reference to "the unhappy War," moreover, can be read in terms of economic concerns as well as his own allegiances. Their sons Samuel and Charles would also be sent to London for their education, further extending the Carys' stay on the island.

Five months later, Charles Spooner sent the first of several updates about Margaret, as recorded in Samuel's letterbook. On October 2, 1780, from Mottisfont, Hampshire, Spooner writes, "I am going to Town in a few days when I shall see Capt. Cox . . . I shall then see your Daughter and if I find she is at a proper School, and under such Management as appears to be right, I shall not remove her, if otherwise I shall, in any event she shall always pass her Holidays with me, and you may depend upon our affectionate regard to her, and paying every attention to her in our power." Spooner's attentiveness must have been reassuring to Samuel and Sarah, for he also notes, "I never was a Father but I think I can form a Judgement of a parent's Feelings at such a distance from his Child, but beg you and Mrs. Cary will make yourselves perfectly easy as to her." On December 4, from London, Spooner remarks on young Margaret's "very Amiable disposition," and on February 4, 1781, he sends praise: "I congratulate you, upon having a child of the most pleasing disposition, I ever was acquainted with. Full of spirits and good humour, yet of a sedate solid understanding, included by no perverseness of Temper." Additionally, he offers, "If you have any thing in particular to recommend as to her Education, it shall be duly attended to." Samuel appreciated these reports, as indicated in his responses from Simon on February 15: "Now beg leave to tell you how perfectly happy your Letter made us on Acct. of our little Girl"; and on April 13, "Your Account of our Little Girl is very flattering, hope that she will appear in as favourable a light to Mrs. Spooner, to whom my Wife begs leave to join me in most respectful compliments." With a tenderness not often displayed in his letters, and especially not to his business associates, Samuel Cary expresses his appreciation, adding as well his endearments for "our Little Girl."[38]

Caroline Curtis notes that in Margaret Cary's "magazine articles, written for young people," she describes her education as directed by "two French and two English" teachers, and her studies as including "drawing, music, writing and ciphering, geography and astronomy, composition and dancing," along with "history and poetry . . . embroidery, flowers, and filigree." Mar-

Samuel Cary to Charles Spooner, Simon, May 1, 1780, with partial transcription. Samuel Cary Papers, Collection of the Massachusetts Historical Society.

The communication between this & Boston being shut by the unhappy War, & my little Girl beginning to take Notice of things in this most unchristian Country, made up with people of all countries & rudest in their manners of any place, so unlike the Leeward Islands, — that my Wife & Self thought it our Duty to send her away tho' our stay here might be prolong'd by it, & as we had heard a good Character of Mr. Cox and he had reced from me every assistance in my Power, thought it best to send her by him. [. . .]

garet also describes a sampler she produced when she was ten years old, with "about ten lines from a piece of poetry of Rowe's, called the 'True End of Education.' It was worked with fine black silk, in small letters, on very fine canvas, on one thread. It cost me many tears, but was completed at last, and was framed and sent to Grenada."[39] Nicholas Rowe's eleven-line poem begins with an extended question: "And therefore wer't thou bred to virtuous knowledge, / And wisdom early planted in thy soul, / That thou might'st know to rule thy fiery passions." The final couplet answers the question: "A long and shining train; till thou, well pleas'd, / Shalt bow, and bless thy fate, and say the Gods are just." Regarding poetry and pedagogy, Kevin J. Hayes observes, "Children's authors found religious poetry especially appropriate for young readers," as in, for example, Isaac Watts's verse for children. Hayes further explains, "Reading and memorizing religious verse facilitated meditation." In *Learning to Stand and Speak: Women, Education, and Public Life in America's Republic*, Mary Kelley discusses a similar curriculum for female education in the 1760s and 1770s for Martha Laurens Ramsay of Charleston, South Carolina, one that "leaves no doubt that she enrolled in the informal curriculum imported from Great Britain. Ramsay read widely in natural history, biography, astronomy, philosophy, and history. She took pleasure in polite letters, especially English and French prose and poetry. Equally well versed in godly books, Ramsay immersed herself in Bibles, psalm books, and devotional works." Overall, this course of study considered a woman's education seriously and prepared young girls to participate actively in polite civil society. The cost of Margaret's education, however, was notable, for as Charles Spooner explains, writing from "Mottisfont March 6, 1782," "I sent you near twelve months ago your Daughters School Bill and desired your opinion upon it. . . . Never having received and answer to this, I have still continued her there, and I shall continue to do so, till I hear from you to the contrary. I believe it is a good school, but can not think it a cheap one." In Cary's ledger titled "Cash paid on Account of Miss M. Cary, 1779–1780" is this entry: "To Miss Blackburns for 12 Months of School, 26.5," that is, £26, an expense that would have contributed to the Carys' decision to stay at Grenada.[40]

Sometime in 1783, ten-year-old Samuel, "who had been sent for to Grenada, and stayed at home just one month," Margaret recalls, and five-year-old Charles joined their sister in England. The boys were accompanied by "one of Mr. Horsford's sons, a fine boy," the teenage George Horsford.[41] Samuel's academic subjects were those considered appropriate for a young man's education and, especially, to prepare for a career as a merchant. In his August

23, 1789, letter from London to his grandmother, Samuel describes his recent academic standing: "It is now about a year since all our class was examined, when, to set my vanity in a blaze, I was declared to be the best, after an examination which set us all tilting. When I left school I was reckoned the first Latin scholar; the second in French; in arithmetic there were several before me; in writing I was excelled by many; in geography I was the first, rather I believe because there was no one who knew much of it on account of my own excellence."[42] And to further illustrate his linguistic accomplishments, on October 7, Samuel wrote a letter to his father in Spanish, accompanied by a translation by Thomas Lynch, of Boston. Such fluency would befit a young man preparing for a clerkship and later to become a merchant operating in the transatlantic world.

Margaret and Samuel Cary Return to Grenada

In late November 1789, brother and sister returned to Grenada. When Sarah and Samuel, who were at Mount Pleasant, spied the *Grenville Bay* passing by the western coast of the island, Samuel left immediately for Gouyave, later named Charlotte Town by the British, where he took a sloop to St. George's and arrived at Belmont, north of the Simon estate, the next day at "ten o'clock" to greet his children and bring them back to Mount Pleasant. Margaret describes their return in a letter to her nephew George on April 14, 1843: "My brother, who was sixteen, was in all respects a gentleman in his appearance and manners; he had left school almost a twelvemonth before, and had been placed in Mr. Manning's counting-house, attending to business and studying the Spanish and Italian languages. He had a great deal of conversation with my father. I answered his questions, but had little to communicate."[43] She also includes a portrait of her brother Samuel in one of her magazine articles: "He had his gold watch; hair dressed, frizzed and curled at the sides with powder; small-clothes, with knee-buckles (pantaloons had not made their appearance); silk stockings, and shoes with buckles, — a tall and handsome person. He was perfect in my eyes; sometimes finding fault with me, but I never saw anything amiss in him." Margaret also remarks, "He had brought the last new book, — a present to my mother. It was a poem, called 'The Shipwreck,' by Falconer. And then he talked so well!" Samuel thus appeared to have entered genteel society with his powdered hair and buckled shoes, bearing the gift of William Falconer's *The Shipwreck: A Poem, in Three Cantos* (1762). The poem was reprinted in Philadelphia in 1788 and titled *The Shipwreck: A Sentimental and Descriptive Poem, in Three Cantos*, which may be why Margaret calls it "the last new book." She then adds this note about her brother's future: "A few days only were allowed the mother and son to enjoy this happy meeting. He then went with my father to St. George's, to be placed in a mercantile establishment, where he made himself very useful, and so gained the confidence of his employers that before he was twenty-one he was left executor by one of them."[44] Samuel thus joined the offices of Thomas Morris and his partner William Postlethwaite at St. George's as an apprentice. Sheryllynne Haggerty elaborates on such arrangements: "Apprenticeships were accessed via networks of family and friends, often accompanied by a fee of between £50 and £100. A good apprenticeship would give formal training in accounting and letter writing, wharfside and Custom House procedures, as well as access to contacts which could be used for development in the future."[45] Margaret and Samuel's return to Grenada was not only a welcomed event but also a carefully anticipated one, so that their transitions would prove comforting and productive.

For the next two years, from November 1789 to June 1791, mother and son would spend their longest time living in proximity, with Samuel apprenticed at St. George's on the western side of the island, and his family on the eastern side, near Grenville Bay, on the Simon estate, approximately fifteen to twenty miles away. Their home at Mount Pleasant in St. Mark's Parish was about twenty miles northeast of St. George's. Sarah and the children would stay at Mount Pleasant in "the unhealthy months, which was during the wet weather from September to December," as Margaret later explains, and Samuel Cary Sr. would join them on Sundays from Simon. There was also a plantation manager on the estate. Margaret describes Mount Pleasant as situated "on the slope of a high hill, backed by mountains still higher, and on either side the hills rose high; but the view in front was of the ocean, and all the vessels coming from or going to Europe passed before it, and were looked down upon." There were two rows of coconut trees, "planted by my dear father," lining the lawn, and a house with wooden shutters for the windows facing out to the sea: "The only glazed window in the house was in my mother's closet. She often read or wrote there of an evening in the frequent absence of my father; for his superintendence at Simon obliged him to make that at all times his principal residence." Other structures included the sugar works, a hospital, and "the negro-houses on another rising, to the south." She also notes, "There were about eighty negroes." Regarding her father's purchase of this plantation, Margaret explains, "When my father first owned it, it was coffee. At considerable expense it had been brought into sugar."[46]

There was "very little society in the vicinity. Madame Lamellerie, a French widow, with her family, was the chief person," and despite language barriers, there was a "kind feeling, and, from being next neighbors, occasional dealings in the way of barter and so forth." Adjacent to the Carys' property were Samuel Sandbach at the Respect estate and David Barry and his wife, who owned "an estate joining on the north side. . . . They were very pleasant people, and a very friendly intercourse was established with them, dining at one another's houses alternately, at which times all the children accompanied their parents." Margaret also notes that "Simon, on the contrary, was not only in a pleasant neighborhood, but there was a church and clergyman; and strangers generally who came to the island liked to visit the plantations, and would come with letters of introduction and depended on being hospitably entertained for a week or more."[47] Simon may have offered more social interactions, but Mount Pleasant allowed Sarah more frequent contact with Samuel at St. George's, as they exchanged letters and notes via messengers.

In early 1790, Sarah and Samuel initiated what would become a twenty-year correspondence. They wrote on a range of topics, from everyday matters to philosophy and literature, including the classical orations of Cicero, references to William Shakespeare's plays and poetry, the contemporary poetry of Edward Young and Alexander Pope, and the works of Jonathan Swift and other writers. From nearly a dozen letters and notes that have survived from their initial correspondence on Grenada, mother and son were, in many respects, getting to know each other for the first time. For Sarah, their exchanges and meetings allowed her to influence his moral and spiritual upbringing. In doing so, Sarah would mentor Samuel and later her other sons by giving them advice and encouragement. Her sons, in return, would feel the weight of their mother's charge to live a moral life and to help sustain the family's prosperous lineage, and they would respond with both compliance and resistance. Sarah may not have spoken out against slavery directly in her letters to her sons, but her insistence that they adhere to a higher moral and spiritual code than was prevalent in the West Indies signaled her disapproval, however genteelly it may have been stated.

And while separations between parents and children during this time were not unusual, Sarah Cary's relationships with her oldest sons, Samuel, Charles, and Lucius, would be sustained primarily through correspondence. As such, long letters exchanged months apart supplanted everyday interactions that would have allowed mentoring by example. These circumstances lent their relationships a different kind of contemplative, reflective quality, at times more formal than a physical conversation might have been, and at others, more revealing and confessional than might have been possible, or comfortable, when sitting across a dining table or chatting in a parlor. As with many letter writers, especially women, letter writing was contingent on having the time to write and varying degrees of privacy. For Sarah, who wrote after long days attending to household duties or in brief, often interrupted sittings during the day, letters allowed her to nurture friendships, as with Mary Gray Otis and Mercy Otis Warren, and to maintain family connections, as with her sons. Whether she was discussing motherhood, sorting out domestic concerns, engaging in financial planning, or commenting on social issues, Sarah Cary belied any stereotype of female passivity or naiveté. Instead, she was intimately involved in her family's welfare and finances and spoke her mind confidently. The intensity and directness with which she gave advice and provided consolation, along with social commentary, not only reinforced the importance of letter writing as a means of expression, but also allowed Sarah to keep her identity intact during these extended separations.

Within the tradition of polite letters in which a parent offers instruction and guidance, Sarah's letters to Samuel, and later to Lucius, provide a new perspective in that letters between mothers and sons have received less attention than perhaps those between fathers and sons and between mothers and daughters. Letters between Sarah and her sons also reflect conventions of their day, with details about the previous letter received and by what conveyance, along with ship and captain's name, to preserve the narrative thread of the correspondence and to verify that letters had indeed arrived. These notes were often followed by expressions of pleasure or reprimands, depending on the regularity of the correspondence. Knowing such conventions helps in sorting out tone and intention, for what might be mistaken initially for either an overly crafted, formulaic response or a hyperbolically affectionate reply with an equally effusive closing and signature is understood as a style conforming to a prescribed norm. Letters also reflect the expectations of discourse in polite society. Elizabeth Hewitt, for example, explains how letters in writing manuals, such as *The Complete Letter-Writer* (1790), "served as models for epistolary intercourse between persons stationed along a range of social positions: letters from daughters to mothers; apprentices to employees; lovers to betrothed; poor relatives to benefactors." Sarah M. S. Pearsall finds that letter manuals were "clearly popular and in wide circulation on both sides of the Atlantic. Between 1755 and 1768 alone, for example, twelve editions of *The Complete Letter-Writer; or, Polite English Secretary* appeared in

Great Britain." Kevin J. Hayes makes this connection between letter writing and social behavior: "*The Ladies Complete Letter-Writer* (1763), a work which could be found from Boston to Williamsburg during the last decade and a half of the colonial period, differed from other advice books in both format and focus. While it sought to teach women how to write letters for every occasion on a variety of subjects, the collection, taken as a whole, also could be read as a conduct book." Eve Tavor Bannet, in turn, addresses writing style in regard to epistolary practices: "Conversation and correspondence were supposed both to reveal and to mask: they were to seem 'natural and simple,' even sincere, in order to more successfully guard their secrets. Letters must show ease and not be 'too highly polished,' but they must pay careful attention to those conventions bearing on subject, style, self-representation and decorum, which constituted worldly polish."[48] Letter writers were thus expected to follow guidelines, even as they adapted their styles to circumstances and made important emotional connections.

In keeping with epistolary conventions, the first of Sarah's letters, dated simply "Mount Pleasant, Saturday Morning," begins with an acknowledgment of Samuel's letters: "I received your favor of Wednesday noon, and also that of Thursday morning, with peculiar pleasure." She then advises him to choose acquaintances carefully: "Your very becoming reserve will secure you from what is certainly most to be feared,— a set of companions whose gross manners and way of life are a reflection upon human nature." Noting that she is "not afraid of your descending so low," Sarah adds this portrait: "But there is another set of people who call themselves, and have really the appearance of, gentlemen, but who, although perhaps more refined in their manners, are no less criminal in the sight of that Being whose eye is ever upon us, and who, whatever fashionable doctrine may say to the contrary, will be just as wise as merciful, and who will not, *cannot* be offended with impunity." As this letter indicates, Sarah directed her advice with an eye for Samuel's future and often within the context of a higher, divine judge. The letter ends with a list of household goods, a reference to their "friend Cato," presumably a slave, and a reminder to Samuel to look after his own health: "I send you as follows: 2 pairs of smallcloaths, 2 waistcoats, 3 pairs stockings, 3 pocket handkerchiefs, 3 cravats, your slippers, and a counterpane, lest our friend Cato should not have accommodated you. Send back whatever you think proper. Say how you do. I fear nothing so much as your not keeping your health." With householder matters duly noted, she concludes with these instructions and questions: "I have only one word more to say,— study economy. Do you come on with your Spanish? What time do you appropriate to study?"[49] With letters that served as part memorandum and part advice, Sarah covered several topics in these dispatches.

Another instance of a letter that addresses multiple topics, as if in a conversation, is this note from Simon, dated "Wednesday Morning," in which Sarah comments on Samuel's health, reading selections, and career: "I'm very sorry to find you have been indisposed, and, I'm told, look pale, owing probably to the sedentary life you lead. You should take as much exercise as your business will allow of; and if you could use the cold bath *once a week,* I should think it would be highly salutary to you." She then shifts to literary matters: "I cannot but congratulate you upon your philosophical sentiments communicated in your letter before the last."[50] A discussion of Roman authors Seneca, Cicero, and Pliny follows. Margaret Cary later elaborates on the family's literary pursuits, noting, for example, that her father "sent to England for a library, and had a valuable collection," and that "a part of every day was given to reading, and my mother's voice lent a charm to whatever she read. Men of sense and information visited intimately at the house; and though they lived in the country, there was no feeling of solitariness."[51] Books were thus integral to the family's intellectual life and helped alleviate their isolation.

In Sarah's "Wednesday Morning" letter, she also comments on what would become a recurring topic—Samuel's career plans and his desire to return to America. Her responses are supportive, yet measured: "Nothing gives me greater pleasure than your looking forward to America, yet I cannot but agree in part with what your father proposes, which is, if anything very highly advantageous offers when you come of age, to remain in this country for three or four years longer, it should not be rejected, if it will furnish you with a sufficient capital to sit down afterwards in business in America." Just a few months into his apprenticeship, Samuel was already considering his return to Chelsea, a signal perhaps of his displeasure with clerking, if not with living at Grenada in general. Sarah's advice was thus both practical and encouraging, especially when setting a finite period for his time at Grenada. She then notes her husband's view on these matters: "Yet, after all, I know your father's wish would be to see you there as soon as you come of age, were he to consult only his own inclinations; but every good parent is ready to sacrifice his dearest wishes for the advantage of a beloved child." Samuel Cary Sr. appeared to understand his son's desire to make a path on his own as well as the advantages of remaining in the West Indies. Sarah then reassures her son of his father's approval: "You grow every day upon the affections of your father. The more he sees and knows of you, the more dear are you to him." The repeated reassurances of their confidence in Samuel were punctuated by an underlying assumption that Samuel's career would be determined by family concerns rather than by his personal desires. Shifting to her role as instructor, Sarah adds, "I am told to observe that your letters, bills, parcels, etc., never contain a good S̲. the only bad letter you make. I mention it because I know how easily you can rectify such a trifle."[52] As she moves seamlessly from one topic to another, Sarah again illustrates the conversational quality of these letters. Her direct, at times emphatic tone also suggests anticipation of yet another inevitable separation.

Along these lines, Sarah's letters frequently addressed philosophical, moral, and religious topics. For example, in another letter to Samuel from Mount Pleasant, in 1790, she begins with a lengthy passage about religion: "I cannot but approve of your sentiments of religion, because they correspond with my own. Confined to no particular form of worship, it is enough for me to know that my dear boy adores and reverences that greatest and best of Beings who, according to the inimitable Doctor Young, surveys naught on earth with equal pleasure to a grateful heart." Tending more to the philosophical than the specifically doctrinal, Sarah has paraphrased lines from Edward Young's popular poem *The Complaint: Or, Night-Thoughts on Life, Death, and Immortality* (1742–1745), a meditation on life in nine books, with 10,000 lines in blank verse. More specifically, she paraphrased from "Night the Eighth. Virtue's Apology; or The Man of the World Answered": "Th' Almighty, from his Throne, on Earth surveys / Nought Greater, than an Honest, Humble Heart." She then remarks on the value of private reflection: "As to stated times for private devotion, I cannot but think it highly acceptable to the Deity; and this I am sure of: that secret prayer conduces more than can well be imagined to the propriety of our outward behavior, softens and polishes the manners, and gives us a firmness of mind to withstand every temptation of doing what the judgment disapproves." Again, Sarah appears to be referencing the lines from *Night-Thoughts* cited above, which continue: "An Humble Heart, *His* Residence! pronounc'd / *His* second Seat; and Rival to the Skies / The Private Path, the secret Acts of Men, / If noble, far the noblest of our Lives!" Moreover, *Night-Thoughts* holds particular significance, as Margaret explains, in that William Gray, Sarah's brother, "interested himself very much in her improvement, and gave her something, I forget what, for every page of Young's 'Night Thoughts' that she learnt by heart."[53] Sarah then elaborates on the importance of "private devotion" and the need for commitment in doing so: "Yet, if the heart cannot regularly engage in this duty, I think, with you, that it must be omitted. Any other than sincere devotion seems to me to be mere mockery, and I believe religion has suffered more from false pretenders than from the most open infidelity." After making these distinctions, she notes, "The Judge of all the earth will do right," and reflects on larger concerns: "One thing let me recommend to my dear boy: your principles of religion once fixed, keep them within your own breast and avoid any disquisitions upon the subject."[54] By internalizing his principles, Samuel could safeguard them against challenges, with which she apparently had some experience.

Elsewhere in this letter, Sarah notes the passing of Charles Spooner, who died on May 12, 1790, which suggests that she may have been writing around July 1790: "The death of Mr. Spooner, I assure you, shocked me very much, and, notwithstanding it will certainly accelerate our voyage to America, it is an event which gives me some pain." Because Charles Spooner was part owner of the Simon estate, his death would now renew attempts to sell the property, which in addition to establishing their son in business on the island would precipitate their return to Chelsea. In this context, Sarah notes, "I am very glad Lucius did not go to England, and am quite contented to give him an American education." Other considerations for their return included Samuel Cary Sr.'s health: "Your father is by no means as well as I wish, although much better; for his sake more than my own, I wish to quit this country." Another concern is Sarah Tyler Gray's advancing age: "My mother, too, whom I most tenderly love, requires my attention, and wishes once more to see, what she must hold very dear, her only child. Oh, my son, if it please Heaven to allow her a sight of you before her death, I think she will die satisfied. After a painful journey through life, she has yet the expectation of some felicity, of which she says she has tasted very little, although sixty-seven years old."[55] As if to soften the trauma of their pending departure, Sarah presents these reasons on behalf of the family, rather than, for example, her own personal desire to return.

With the Carys' departure less than a year away, letters between mother and son continued with their now typical mix of topics, from housekeeping to literature and career. Sarah thus begins an undated letter in 1790 on "Wednesday, 11 o'clock," with a list of household items followed by a note about books: "Mrs. Beatty is arrived. She will therefore call for her books. Have you not two more volumes in town? Cicero's Orations, I think. You may return them by the bearer." She then turns to his work situation: "I hope my dear Sam is perfectly well. I wish for nothing more. In regard to everything relative to business and the pleasing of Mr. M., I have not a doubt." Although she understands that Samuel may have larger ambitions than clerking for Thomas Morris, Sarah tries to console him in her next letter, dated "Wednesday, 12 o'clock": "I'm half inclined to suspect that you think book-keeping tiresome; yet, if you do, I do not wish you to tell me so, for I could not prevent it, and besides it is wise to seem to like what is for our benefit, if the mode is not perfectly agreeable to us. I know you are closely confined, but there is a method of making every business light and easy. I hope you have found that method." In an attempt to encourage him, she also offers practical advice: "I hope you find time to take a little fresh air either in morning or evening. I fear nothing but your want of health." Having attended to her son's work and health, Sarah then reports that her husband has "set off, along with the President, this morning for Marques," a reference to Samuel Williams, president of the Council for the Island of Grenada, 1789–1793. And, in a note from late 1790 that begins with her "disappointment" on not seeing him on Christmas Day, Sarah includes details about her own health: "Of late I am a great invalid, and never well a whole day together. This you can say when asked. I am now so much indisposed as to be unable to write you what I intended." Sarah's references to being "a great invalid" and "much indisposed" appear to be in regard to her recent pregnancy. Sarah then turns to literature and includes this critique: "I began your Tasso's 'Jerusalem' last evening, when I read his life and the first book. One can scarcely read the former without being prepossessed in favor of the latter. The happy concurrence of philosophy and poetry can hardly fail making an amiable character. The appearance of the angel to Godfrey, his submission and reverence to the heavenly messenger, etc., etc., is truly elegant and beautiful."[56] Shifting from advice to literature, Sarah supported her son and encouraged his plans.

In the first of three letters before his family departs, Samuel writes from St. George's on Tuesday, May 19, 1791, beginning with a note about housekeeping matters: "Jean Philip comes upon me now-a-days at an hour when I am more busy than any other in the day. — As he is to return by the canoe I cannot now send you the useless cloaths I have here, but the following is a list of the Things I want next 1 pr Sheets. 3 towels. 1 pillowcase. 1 large bag to hold dirty linen." Although irritated by the unexpected interruption, Samuel takes the time to include a request for books that range from history and biography to poetry: "Sallust, Cornelius Nepos, Quintus Curtius, Gil Blas, Roman history with the things ordered before." Samuel's reading materials thus show his varied interests, from an epic poem about the First Crusade by Italian poet Torquato Tasso, *Jerusalem Delivered* (1575), and volumes on Roman history to Alain R. Lesage's picaresque *The Adventures of Gil Blas of Santillane* (1700–1730), which was translated from the French by Tobias Smollet in 1782. To explain the hurried nature of his letter, Samuel adds, "I did not expect the Boy till this evening."[57]

As the day of the Cary family's departure grew closer, messages between Sarah and Samuel became increasingly emotional, with references to household items and books included alongside speculation about the future. Caroline Curtis explains these final exchanges, beginning with one dated "*Friday Evening,* 7 o'clock": "This was written upon the eve of sailing for America when Sam was to remain in the West Indies. He had been with the family for two days; and his mother being in delicate health, her husband had been unwilling that she should risk the agitation of a parting interview."[58] As this letter begins, Sarah struggles with her composure: "Oh, my dear child, you have deprived me of all my fortitude! While you were with me, I would not allow myself to think of our separation; and as I saw you in excellent health and seeming spirits, I thought of nothing but the happy moment when I should embrace you at Chelsea." In trying to contain her emotions, Sarah already imagines their reunion, even as she reflects on their recent meeting: "I felicitated myself upon my good behavior on Tuesday night, after I got into my room; and though I dropped some tears, as there was no witness, I hoped all would pass over, and no one would suspect that I quitted you with reluctance." By maintaining a stoic, genteel composure, Sarah also allows Samuel an emotional distance as befits a young gentleman: "I felt calm and resigned. My mind felt no disturbance, and I encouraged none but the pleasing idea of being possessed of the finest boy in Grenada, who I was very sure was quite capable of taking proper care of himself, and who would be an honor to his father and mother." Noting the pressure on Samuel as the family's representative, and the "honor" that he must uphold, the weight of this pending separation on both mother and son is clear. Sarah then seeks perspective: "I confess, when I got up in the morning, my spirits failed. I heard you walk and talk, but had determined not to trust myself with seeing you. I held my resolution, and notwithstanding your message suffered you to depart. I knew my own feelings too well and was afraid you would have caught the contagion." As if in a state of self-imposed quarantine, Sarah tries to prevent "the contagion" of emotions. Still, she reaffirms their bond: "You love me. I see it with pleasure, and no mother ever loved a son better than I love you. Let us then, my dear boy, mutually endeavor to show that firmness so necessary upon the occasion. Your gently upbraiding me in your letter for not permitting you to see me convinces me now that I have acted right. I should have lost myself and unmanned you." Sarah thus justified her actions with a concern that she not "unman" her son. The letter ends with a plea to write and an indication that this separation might prove longer than either wants: "Write me, if it be but two lines. I will leave a letter for you. We sail on Sunday. The little folks all love you, and wished to have seen you again. We will take care they never forget you."[59] The tender language speaks to her deep regret for the pending departure, and by taking care that his siblings will "never forget" their brother, she acknowledges that this separation will last for at least three years, as per the terms of his apprenticeship at St. George's, if not longer.

The next day, Saturday, May 28, Sarah sent notes from Mount Pleasant, dated from three different times. At "5 o'clock," Sarah writes, "I had a secret wish that my dear Sam might accompany us here and remain until we sailed, but to what purpose? Could I love and admire him more than I now do, or if I could would it not have been wrong? Are we not forbidden to place our affections upon earthly objects? No, my son, it is well I did not solicit your stay, for the same reason that I would not, dared not, trust myself with seeing you last Wednesday." Four hours later, at "9 o'clock," she adds, "I'm this moment favored with my dear Sam's letter of today. You ask me to make you some request. What can I make you? Have you not promised me all I wished?" She then prefaces a quotation from Alexander Pope's "Universal Prayer" with the admonition to "Remember those lines": "What conscience dictates to be done, / Or warns me not to do, / This teach me more than hell to shun, / That more than heaven pursue." Urging Samuel to become his own guide and to follow his "conscience," Sarah acknowledges, "Why point out to you a path of virtue? You are capable of judging. May you never feel the remorse attendant upon an ingenuous mind, or rather may you never experience a guilty moment!" Appealing to a sensibility of balance and moderation, Sarah also reminds Samuel to "be temperate" for "upon this virtue perhaps depends all others. One moment of intoxication is sufficient to overthrow every good resolution. I have never, my dear boy, discovered any propensity to intemperance in you, but I've chosen this channel to convey my sentiments of everything else." The next morning, Sarah sends one last note: "Sunday, 6 o'clock. Farewell, farewell, my dear son; take care of yourself."[60] With mixed emotions—sorrow for leaving her son and anticipation of returning home—Sarah made final preparations for their departure. And although both

Samuel Cary Jr. to Sarah Cary, St George's, Wednesday, June 1791. Cary Family Papers III, Collection of the Massachusetts Historical Society.

St George's Wednesday

   Why, my dear madam, was I denied the pleasure of bidding you Farewel this morning? — Is this, think you, a custom Friends should not observe?— Surely they of all others should observe it most.— What are our Ideas at parting but a recollection of every little act of tenderness every past testimony of fondness & Affection? Ideas which rush upon our minds & collect our whole force of Love.— Does not the falling tear at parting imprint a scene upon our memories which neither time nor absence can wear away? What though the scene be melancholy, does not the remembrance of it relieve the mind in the hour of thought, & should we meet again, [. . .]

parents looked forward to returning home, they clearly found it difficult to leave their son behind.

Their parting was also hard on Samuel, as noted in a letter from St. George's, Wednesday, June 1791. He begins with a reprimand: "Why, my dear madam, was I denied the pleasure of bidding you Farewell this morning?— Is this, think you, a custom Friends should not observe?— Surely they of all others should observe it most." And though his mother had been trying to control her emotions, Samuel had wanted this contact in order to impress the moment on his heart, as he then explains: "What are our Ideas at parting but a recollection of every little act of tenderness every past testimony of fondness and Affection? Ideas which rush upon our minds and collect our whole force of Love." Samuel would rather experience the range of emotions, even the sadness of their parting, than withdraw. In this regard, he continues with a series of questions: "Does not the falling tear at parting imprint a scene upon our memories which neither time nor absence can wear away? What though the scene be melancholy, does not the remembrance of it relieve the mind in the hour of thought, and should we meet again, does it not inspire us with redoubled Affection? Do we not feel twice the pleasure from it?" Having established the importance of experiencing the emotions of departure despite the potential for pain, Samuel continues his questions: "But was there nothing to say to me?; no last request to make? Why I would have observed it with all the strictness an oath could bind me to.— Oh there is something so tender and affectionate, so pleasingly melancholy, so exquisitely fond in the parting of friends — why was I denied it?"[61] Drawing on the language of sentiment to express his regret about being "denied the pleasure of bidding [her] Farewell," Samuel frames the scene as a "parting of friends," perhaps to signal a new phase of their mother-son relationship.

The Cary family left Grenada on June 1, 1791, with seven of their children, ages one to fifteen—Harriet, Edward, Ann, Henry, Lucius, Sarah, and Margaret—with Charles still in England for school.[62] Accompanying them were "three of their black servants," as Caroline Curtis explains: "Two of these, Charlotte and Pompey, grew homesick and returned to Grenada; but one, Fanny Fairweather, ended her days in Chelsea."[63] Mellen Chamberlain adds that Samuel Cary had "acquired what he considered a competent fortune," which suggests that Samuel had confidence in the family's future prosperity.[64] The Cary family would arrive in Boston on July 2, 1791, to what they anticipated would be a joyful reunion.

CHAPTER THREE

Relocating and Adjusting

A Family Separated, Chelsea and St. George's, 1791–1794

Upon returning to Chelsea in July 1791, after an eighteen-year absence, the Cary family began extensive remodeling of their house, a two-story mansion with thirty-one windows. Flush with funds from their Grenadian enterprises, they appeared to spare no expense with the renovations, including costly white pine paneling imported from England. Caroline Curtis recalls, "One of the family remembers finding an account book of my grandfather's, showing that he himself had spent twelve thousand dollars upon it, — a large sum for those days." In *The New England Historical and Genealogical Register* (1891), Augustus Thorndike Perkins remarks, "Many of us remember with keen pleasure, the stately old colonial mansion house, under Powderhorn Hill, with its fine wide hall, and spacious staircase." Mellen Chamberlain describes similarly ambitious landscaping projects for the 365-acre farm, which included planting a garden; elm trees, "which became majestic"; and "hawthorn shrubs, which grew to trees," as well as building "a dyke across Chelsea Creek." By planting elms, chestnuts, oaks, and Lombardy poplars, Samuel Cary created tree-shaded lanes for his working farm, which also included cherry and pear trees and an apple orchard. The intent, as Margaret Cary explains, was that her father "hoped to cultivate it so as to bring it into good order, by hiring help and superintending himself, after the present year." These efforts appear to have succeeded, for as Chamberlain reports, "in due time this place, named The Retreat, on the southeasterly slope of Powder Horn Hill (whose summit belonged mainly to the estate, commanding prospects that, once seen, are never forgotten), became one of the most beautiful in the vicinity of Boston." Walter Merriam Pratt, in turn, notes that Samuel Cary "proceeded to enlarge and embellish house and grounds to a degree that made it one of the most fashionable rural seats Boston has ever known." From these accounts, Samuel Cary appears to have not only "acquired what he considered a competent fortune," as Chamberlain notes, but also fulfilled his intentions of nearly thirty years earlier, when he first left Boston for the West Indies.[1]

Meanwhile, back in Grenada, Samuel was in a state of despair over his family's departure. On May 31, 1791, the day before they set sail, he wrote to his grandmother Sarah Tyler Gray: "I am here now to bid adieu to them. — this is the last day I remain with them. — when I see them again — but what an improbable idea! perhaps I shall never see them again." His anxiety is somewhat muted in his next letter, written to his mother on June 11, in which he imagines their joyful homecoming, with "all the sweet hurry of unpacking, Grandmamma above stairs, mamma below, papa and Margret admiring the place, the little folks making all the riot they can." Still, the sorrow of their departure remains, even as he offers reconciliation—"Come you must forget our parting now. — that matter is over. — for my part, I do not think of you but with a joyful heart"—and encouragement: "Enjoy the present, is a very good maxim and one I intend to adopt; so true it is that they who place their happiness on future prospects in this world seldom fail of being deceived . . . but as I well know there is philosophy enough in the family to prevent your being cast down at a disappointment." The letter concludes with questions directed to his grandmother: "And how is Grandmamma? What between the care of the little ones and the hurry of business I am much mistaken, if she has not her hands full." Filled with nostalgia for his boyhood home and regret for having to remain behind, Samuel fondly remembers Chelsea as "the pleasantest place I was ever in."[2]

For the Cary family, however, their return to Chelsea was far less ideal than Samuel had imagined. On July 14, Sarah begins her letter to Samuel with a direct response to his reminder to "enjoy the present" and to not be deceived by placing "happiness on future prospects." Taking a cue from this advice, Sarah writes, "Where has my dear Sam, at so early a period learned to know the proper estimate of human life, not surely from experience. How truly did you prognosticate that we promised ourselves too much pleasure in our return to Chelsea." What begins as an ordinary account, however, soon changes to a tale of sorrow: "Ah my dear Son my Tears flow while I write you, that my excellent Mother died 3 weeks before our arrival, — I had not even the satisfaction of a last embrace — how difficult is it to submit to the bitter cup." The sorrow is both immediate and far reaching, as Sarah regrets the loss of both her mother and a grandmother for her children: "With so sweet a disposition, so sensible and capable of assisting me in the domestic duties, particularly in forming the minds of my little People to Virtue, I can never cease to regret the loss, and am daily sensible how unfit I am for so heavy a tryal, time only can cure the wound." Clearly distraught, Sarah thus explains her opening reference to Samuel's ability to "prognosticate." She then provides an overview of their return on July 2: "We had a pleasant Passage of 27 days, and were in the greatest Spirits at the thoughts of our landing in Boston," which they had by 11:00 in the morning, when they disembarked and "went ashore."

It was, in fact, soon after they landed that Sarah began to sense that something was wrong. Instead of going directly to Chelsea, the family went to the Harrison Gray Otis home in Boston, a change that Sarah found disconcerting. Although compliant, she tried to reconcile herself to the delay: "Surely the Mind has sometimes a presentiment of its sorrows; for as soon as we got to Mr. Otis's House, a sort of deadly sickness seized upon my spirits, and I fell into a flood of Tears, there shou'd have been nothing but felicitations and compliment on my part." Sarah, who was greeted by Sally Foster Otis, tried "in vain . . . to affect to be gay," but, she confesses in her letter, "My Mind was wholly absorbed in my own melancholy Ideas." These sensations were soon confirmed when "your Aunt Gray with her Daughter Sally, came in, their grave appearance, and being dress'd in mourning, soon inform'd me, without speaking, of the cause of my dejection." She then discovered that her mother had died only weeks before: "The last confinement of only a Fortnight, carried her off, to the inexpressible regret of every one who knew her." Several death notices for Sarah Tyler Gray appeared in Boston newspapers, as in the *Herald of Freedom* on May 13: "DIED. . . . Yesterday afternoon, after a short confinement Mrs. Sarah Gray, relict of the late Rev Ellis Gray, in the 69th year of her age." The notice then provides this portrait: "In her character were combined all the virtues which adorn the Christian and all the qualities which dignify a Lady in the various relations of it. Her uniform and exemplary manners commanded the affections of the aged—her mildness, cheerfulness and condescension, secured the respect of the young—To the former an endeared companion, to the latter a principled friend, she had effectually secured the attachment, and will command the tears of all who knew her." Sarah acknowledges how deeply Samuel will be affected by this news about his grandmother, who had raised him from infancy to ten years old: "You will feel much at this acct but I think it incumbent upon me to acquaint you with all our Joys and Sorrows, you have a right, my dear Son to be acquainted with every thing that relates to us, I know your kind participation in the concerns of your Family, and in this Event your feelings will be greatly interested."

Although the anticipated joyful homecoming was not meant to be, Sarah places the events in perspective with a reminder about moderation and mortality: "Our Journey is strew'd with thorns as well as roses, and that those who have most belief in the unerring wisdom of God, are most able to bear with firmness the vicisitudes of life." Having described their emotional homecoming, Sarah concludes with notes about the "extreme heat of the Weather" and a book that Samuel "so much wished to have, Lex. Mercatorio which the captain will deliver you."[3] From the sadness of her mother's passing to a reference about a business text, Sarah's letter is part reflection and part newsletter, as she relates this unhappy homecoming and prepares for their separation. Sarah M. S. Pearsall provides insights about such strains: "Transatlantic distance, a common feature of eighteenth-century life, was a source of comment and concern for family members. The ability of transatlantic distance to fracture families made individuals worry about how the ties of friends and families could be maintained in such circumstances."[4] This depiction would apply to the Cary family as they corresponded from Chelsea, Massachusetts, the West Indies, and Great Britain.

Margaret Cary provides additional details about their return in her magazine article of July 2, 1791: "We landed at Long Wharf, and filled two hacks. There were twelve of us in all, and we were most kindly received by Mrs. Otis, a young married lady, confined just three weeks with her first child. I went up with my mother into a chamber to take off our bonnets, and my aunt Gray and two of her daughters came up to us, all dressed in new mourning. Before they spoke, like a flash it struck to my mother's heart. 'Is my mother dead?' It was too true; she had died while we were on our passage." Similar to her mother's account, Margaret describes the shock of seeing her relatives dressed in mourning. She then recalls her grandmother's last illness: "The dear old lady had made all the arrangements she could in the Chelsea house, half of which was occupied by the farmers, and had then gone to Boston to await our arrival. There she was taken ill with a bilious colic, and had died." The diagnosis of "bilious colic" refers to a type of abdominal pain.[5] Their homecoming was thus more of an occasion for sadness than a hopeful anticipation of the future.

A Mother-Son Relationship Sustained by Letters:
Sarah and Samuel Resume Their Correspondence

In that letters between Chelsea and Grenada would have taken around five to eight weeks to arrive when conditions were ideal, and longer when storms, wars, or frozen waterways delayed or prevented delivery, the gap between the family's departure, Samuel's first letter to Chelsea, and Sarah's response resulted initially in an uneven, one-sided conversation. On July 30, 1791, for example, Samuel writes to his mother from Simon still unaware of the events in Chelsea and expresses sadness on returning to a familiar place now made unpleasant by the absence of his family: "Once more, you see, I revisit this place I used to delight in. . . . In spite of myself now I cannot drive away the melancholy ideas the place inspires me with. I cannot step but some things or other reminds me of the scenes I have past here. — To be out of the way I have seated myself in the little Counting-room which Margret had, but the prospect from the window which I thought would enliven me serves only to inspire me with its own dullness." As Samuel wanders around the now quiet house, he begins to recall more pleasant times: "Where is the little groupe of innocents which once inhabited here? where is the dear directress of the whole who made every thing smile around her? This house, the sight of which used formerly to make my heart glow with pleasure is now a life-less shell, forsaken by the soul. — But I will not communicate to you my sad thoughts. — they are only a proof of the effeminate enumeration of your son. — Besides it will be said 'it is time he should forget these things.'" As Sarah had insisted before their departure that emotions be contained, Samuel refrains from expressing his "sad thoughts" lest they be judged as "effeminate enumeration." Instead, he fondly recalls these familiar scenes, even as he acknowledges the significance of this moment of transition.

Samuel then breaks from his reflections to address present matters. He is clearly impatient to hear from his family: "It is impossible to say with what anxiety I wait for an account of your arrival." He also affirms his virtuous intentions: "Believe me, my dear Madam, if it be necessary to assure you, I shall always pay the strictest regard to your advice and always, too, give it its full scope and meaning which I have done." Samuel thus sets the tone and intent of their correspondence and, by extension, their newest long-distance relationship, while also maintaining the Chelsea-Grenada connections. Not only would Mr. and Mrs. Horsford hand them this letter, whom Samuel notes will be "unexpected, but I should imagine not unwelcome visitors," but he also imagines that Mr. Horsford "will be so pleased with the country that on his return here he will wind up affairs and go settle with you."[6] Samuel thus continued to adjust, even as he suffered a bout of homesickness for Chelsea. His emotional response is similar to that of other eighteenth-century migrants who, as Konstantin Dierks notes, "strove to come to terms with displacement and change," and as a result, "The letters of transatlantic immigrants and frontier migrants contain all the sentimental expression one would expect of people separated by distance, and missing each other, and sensing the permanence of that separation."[7] Even as Samuel wrote from a familiar setting that encouraged nostalgia, he was also beginning to adapt to this new set of conditions.

Samuel's descriptions of the Simon estate mark distinctions between the family living quarters and the business of the plantation. Although he does not mention the slave housing or the sugar works in general, Samuel does include a postscript with a dictated message from Catharine, who was presumably one of the Carys' slaves. He thus begins: "Enter Catharine," who then asks, "Master Sam, are you writing to Mistress? Give my Compts. — Tell her I am very sorry I could not get any sweetmeats ready to send her. — I will get some next crop. Tell her I want a little pan to make sweetmeats in." With details about sharing food and requesting cookware, Catharine then sends her regards: "Give my Compts to Massa — Miss Margret, Charlotte, [torn page] every body. — Tell Mistress send me some of the [torn] drops she used to give me for pain in the stomach. — Mistress gone, pain come again. — I hope Mistress brought to bed of a fine Boy. — I hope Mistress very well — please God — I will send the preserved pine apple as soon as the crop sets in." Eight months later, on April 20, 1792, Sarah mentions Catharine in a letter to Samuel: "I am quite mortified I can not get a bottle Pepper Mint Water for poor Catharine Jean but it is not to be had in Chelsea just now, I will take care to lay in enough of it next Fall, that I may have an opportunity of sending her some; when you go to Simon say every thing that is kind to her from me."[8] This exchange of items, "Pepper Mint Water" from Sarah and "preserved pine apple" from Catharine, appear to indicate that the connections between Chelsea and Grenada remained active.

Meanwhile in St. George's, Samuel continued his apprenticeship in the office of Thomas Morris and William Postlethwaite, improving his clerking skills. On July 27, 1791, he writes to his father with a report on crops, finances, and plantation management issues and addresses an apparent breach: "I beg, Sir, that in future whenever I recommend any thing of this kind you will look upon what I say as entirely submitted to be controuled by you." Humbled by his misjudgment, Samuel then thanks his father for a recent loan and adds, "but you shall not have any of my drafts to answer for some time — I have sufficient for the present."[9] He also grew more self-assured as he ventured into his own mercantile transactions. He thus writes to David Barry, neighbor to the Mount Pleasant estate and now acting as an attorney, on "Sunday Morning 1791": "I thank you for the Joe you advanced me which I received by George; I am not however in any want of it as you seem to suppose. — If I were I never would suffer a false idea of delicacy to prevent my mentioning it to you, after the expressions you have used." Having asserted his financial independence, Samuel then explains his plans "to invest whatever I can spare, in trade and as the expenses of my person (exclusive of dress and etc.) are almost nothing," as well as the source of his income: "I am in hopes my allowance will prove a growing fund from which I may have it in my Power to draw from time to time. — Five Joes my father told me was the sum he should allow me. — more I do not wish for — less is sufficient. — I do not therefore desire you should be in advance for me at any time, except when something extraordinary happens and it may appear to you necessary."[10] As he began to find his own way in business, Samuel acknowledged that he was beholden to his father for financial support and, if "necessary," to Mr. Barry.[11] As it turned out, Samuel's plans did meet with his father's approval, as evident in Samuel Cary Sr.'s letter to David Barry on September 20, 1791, in which he refers to letters "from Sam to you" that Barry had enclosed and notes that Samuel "promises everything that we can wish — I find by his letter to his Mother that he expects to save something out of his six Joes to put into trade, I wish to encourage his trading and shall be obliged to you to let him have 4 or 5 Puncheons of Rum the next Crop to put into trade — £100 — gain'd by himself will give him more pleasure than 2 guinea given to him, and when a young man has once made £500 there is no fear of his doing well." Samuel Cary was clearly encouraged by his son's interest in trading, expressing confidence that Samuel Jr. would become a successful merchant. He also expresses concern about the "behaviour" of the current plantation manager: "And altho I had great expectations from his always being in the field with the negroes, and not having any desire to be off, or for Company on the Plantation, yet I am by no means so partial to him as to wish his stay if he treats the negroes unkindly." He then defers to Barry to "act as you would do for yourself" and relays this direction: "If he does the like again or the negroes shew any great uneasiness at his being on the Estate pray look out for some careful steady person to put in his place, the pleasantness of the situation and Salary might

I think command a good man, let no one remain there that will not obey you in every thing."[12] Samuel Cary thus tried to exert his influence on the estate while also keeping an eye on his son's career.

Settling in to Chelsea

For the seven children who were all born in Grenada, their new Massachusetts home required its own set of adjustments. In one of Margaret Cary's magazine articles, she shares her first impressions: "Chelsea, on our arrival, presented a strong contrast to the luxuriant country we had left. We went in at a gate, and through two rows of cherry-trees, up to the house, at one corner of which was a pear-tree, another at some distance in front, and a tall pear-tree behind the barn. These were all the trees, except an apple orchard at the back of the house, sheltered by a hill on which were two cedar-trees."[13] While Chelsea was certainly less "luxuriant" than Grenada, Boston would have offered more social and educational opportunities, especially for the younger children, who unlike their sister Margaret or their older brothers, Samuel and Charles, had not been sent to England for school. Along these lines, Sarah told Samuel on November 11, 1791, "Lucius is at school in Boston, which I believe I wrote you. He is very well." Margaret Cary also notes that "Lucius was placed in Mr. Ticknor's family, and attended school." According to Joseph M. Wightman, Elisha Ticknor arrived in Boston [1788] from New Hampshire and "became the principal of the Town Grammar School at the South end, and continued such till about the year 1795." Caroline Curtis adds that Edward, Henry, Sarah, Harriet, and Ann went to "Mr. Woodbury's school in Medford."[14] Their mother, however, tells Samuel that his sisters Sarah and Nancy, a nickname for Ann, are "at a boarding school of great repute," which she later identifies as Mr. Woodbridge's school at Medford, which opened in 1790, adding that "the school is kept by a clergyman, and his sister, the former a little man of strict morals and mild manners, the latter sensible, extremely masculine in her person and manners, and said to be severe and reserved in her disposition, a maiden of about 45 this is not the woman I should have chosen for my little girls, yet you never saw in your whole life two children so much improved, Sarah begins to read very prettily, Nancy [letter ends unfinished]."[15]

On the "Woodbury" school, the *Essex Journal* published this notice on March 23, 1791: "Mrs. Woodbery takes the liberty to inform the public that she will open a BOARDING SCHOOL for misses, the first of April, at her house, near the *Town-house*, where she will teach French and English, Embroidery on Satin, Silk or Muslin, and every sort of Needlework that is useful for Misses to learn. She also teaches drawing. Her terms will be two Dollars per week, those who do not choose to undertake to study French nor drawing, ten shillings." On the Woodbridge school, the *Independent Chronicle* published this notice on April 19, 1792: "Mr. and Miss Woodbridge, Continue their BOARDING-SCHOOL for Misses and Young Ladies, in a very pleasant and healthy situation, at *Medford*, 4 miles from *Boston*. — The principal Branches of Instruction are, *Reading, Writing, Grammar, Letter-Writing, Arithmetick, Geography*, and etc." Nancy F. Cott elaborates on the significance of Woodbridge to education in general and to girls' education in particular: "William Woodbridge taught school in New Haven during his last year at Yale, 1779–80, and offered arithmetic, geography, and composition to girls. He later taught at Exeter Academy (boys only), and then opened an academy in Medford, Massachusetts which had about twice as many female as male pupils."[16] On December 16, 1791, Sarah sends Samuel this update: "Our little School House is now nearly finish'd, which will be provided with a Master, and take some of the young Folks off my hands." On April 20, 1792, she reports, "The finances at Chelsea will not hold out all the year for a man's school, and a woman is now to be substituted for the little children. During the summer those Boys, who do not go to school in Chelsea, will stay at Home to assist their Father in the culture of the land." And on July 10, 1792, Sarah writes, "Last week we sent Henry to join Sarah and Nancy at Medford, Mr. Woodbridge keeps up his reputation as a Master and has now actually 70 schollars upon his list."[17]

The Cary girls were also beneficiaries of recent educational reforms that encouraged female attendance along with presenting an expanded curriculum, reforms that Cott explains were initiated in part by Benjamin Rush's *Thoughts upon Female Education* (1787), which "epitomized the progressive republican attitude on the subject. In good Revolutionary style, Rush wished to erase British models of fashionable womanhood—which he saw as ornamental at best and, at worst, corrupting." According to Mary Kelley, "Benjamin Rush called for schooling that fitted the nation's women for enlarged responsibilities." This call was apparently well received, for, as Kelley explains, "In the decades between the American Revolution and the Civil War, hundreds of newly established female academies and seminaries introduced women to the subjects that constituted post-Revolutionary and antebellum higher education, teaching them natural sciences, rhetoric, history, logic, geography, mathematics, ethics, and belles lettres. Latin and to a lesser

extent Greek were also taught at these schools."[18] The American school curriculum was thus extensive, and the classroom was increasingly welcoming
to women. Sarah, Nancy, Henry, Lucius, and eventually all the younger Cary
children would have access to educational opportunities that not only were
impossible in Grenada but also included subjects and instruction specifically
relevant to the newly formed United States.

In addition to the children's formally structured education, the family
enjoyed books, music, writing, and poetry. Caroline Curtis describes "life at
Chelsea" as that of "a large family with education and tastes which made
them a happy community among themselves." She also notes, "There must
have been a great deal of poetry apparently because it was the custom of the
time to express one's self in poetry, as well as in prose, — with rhymes, if
feasible, but if not, in blank verse. . . . There were hoards of this, written on
scraps of paper and in little blank books, lying at the bottom of the boxes of
family letters." They were also avid readers: "Reading aloud was an institution of the household, — Shakespeare, the old comedies, poetry, and every
new book attainable." To this last point, Curtis relates a story about Sarah
Cary reading aloud a 1794 gothic novel by Ann Radcliffe to an "absorbed audience" in the "intense quiet of those winter evenings" when Samuel Cary
inadvertently frightened the listeners: "They were in the middle of the 'Mys-
teries of Udolpho,' and he, leaving his seat to put a fresh log on the fire, took
the chance to peep through the curtains, and found that a snowstorm had
begun . . . and, as he slipped into his place again, he whispered, 'Harriet, it
snows,' and the shriek she gave was worthy of Mrs. Radcliffe's heroine."[19]
These anecdotes not only illustrate how "reading aloud was an institution of
the household," but also show how the Cary family's literary interest "made
them a happy community," as Curtis has surmised.

A Surprising Turn of Events: Samuel Adopts a Child

Three months after the departure of Samuel's family, he unexpectedly adopted an orphaned boy and then arranged for the child's passage to Boston. Anticipating his parents' surprise upon the young boy's arrival, Samuel
wrote to each of his parents on August 8, 1791. In the letter to his father, he
begins: "This Letter I imagine will be opened with a kind of doubtful haste,
an anxiety to be acquainted fully with a circumstance you may have heard
but confusedly, and of which this alone can give a clear account; — for I suppose that before this is handed you, Capt. Dornell will in some manner have
inform'd you of the passenger I have put on board his vessel." As if hearing his

father's questions, Samuel provides a detailed narrative: "Therefore, Sir, to keep you no longer in suspense, the fact is plainly this — Walking the street, some time in the month of June, I was accosted by a little beggar-boy who asked for alms. — Surprized at an accident so extraordinary, I made several enquires of him relating to his parents, country, and present manner of living. — The openness and simplicity of his answers pleased me very much." Samuel found this encounter "extraordinary" because children were not usually unaccompanied nor found begging on their own. Knowing his parents would also find this situation unusual, Samuel first explains his motive, "thinking it a duty to relieve such an object of distress," and then provides more details: "I hunted out the place of his Living, (which was with a Mulatto Woman upon charity) and from questions put to this woman and others . . . I collected the following account. — His father's name was Edgar, Captain of a Ship at St. Eustatia, who dying, as well as the boy's mother, the little lad was left to the care of an aunt. — This aunt not willing (as I imagine) to be at the expence of maintaining him; had him shipped off and put alone on shore here and left to provide for himself." The now abandoned child "was taken notice of by some sea-fairing people and served aboard the Carriacou-packet for some time as sailor-boy — but not liking the treatment he met with here, he left the vessel and came to the parish."

Having discovered that the child who was living "upon charity" that "allowed him neither food nor cloathing which obliged him to beg," Samuel was prompted to take action. Having explained some of the mystery of finding this young boy on his own, Samuel now clarifies why he decided to informally adopt the child and then send him "off the Island." After consulting Parson Dent about whether "it was necessary to go through any forms," Samuel tells his parents, "He gave me to understand, that as the boy did not belong here he might be sent away with only a note from me to him (Mr. D) saying where he went, when, and in what ship, that if he should be enquired after it might be known where he was gone." Apparently satisfied with these instructions, Samuel proceeded: "On the strength of this I took little Edgar under my care. — I bought him clothes, got him food and lodging, and finally have sent him to you." Knowing that this decision would require additional explanation, Samuel continues, "And now you will no doubt ask me what are my intentions. What I have done, Sir, has been the result of deliberation and reflection. — What I intend to do; so far as depends not on myself is under your direction."

Having explained his intentions, Samuel elaborates on his long-term plan for Edgar, including his education and eventually an apprenticeship. In anticipation of his parents' questions about finances, Samuel reassures them: "Think not that I would heap an additional burden on my mother, or that I would add to the expences of your family." Instead, he plans to help by using the "pocket-expences of Six Joes" that his parents provide and "money from Mr. Barry to pay the expence of making clothes and etc. for the boy, and his passage to Boston." For Samuel, this act is one of benevolence, as he tells his father: "By indulging me you will most effectually prove yourself, the feeder of the hungry, and the clother of the poor, a title Kings might envy you. — Though the reward be not immediate, it will hereafter descend as ten-fold blessings on your family; — and at the close of Life when all your actions will pass before you in review, the reflection on this act will brighten up the scene and dispel the clouds of uncertainty and Death." By this reasoning, taking care of Edgar would reflect on his father's generosity, rather than on the son's judgment. Offering his emotions as a possible excuse for this unusual request and not knowing how his parents would react, Samuel also asks that the matter be kept private: "Let me request the favour of you to let this matter be entirely secret. — My Motive was never an ostentatious one, and it will do no good to any party concerned to have any circumstance disclosed." Writing to his mother on the same day, Samuel again defends his actions: "This is the first time I ever ventured to out-step the boundaries of the beaten track to find satisfaction of mind. — The first effort of the kind I ever made which required any fund of resolution to execute." Samuel thus acknowledges that by acting so independently, he might be testing his relationship with his parents. Sensitive to accusations of irrationality, or that his behavior "appear to you to be bordering on romantic," he emphasizes the charitable nature of his actions: "I cannot close this without asking a question which naturally occurs on the occasion. — Were one of your children ever to be in the circumstances I found young Edgar in, would you not bless the hand which was stretched out to relieve him?"[20] His plans take on an even greater sense of charity as he appeals to his parents' generosity. Although conveyed as a sincere act, this willingness to extend charity to an orphaned boy while working within a system dependent on slavery suggests a tiered sense of benevolence. Notably, Samuel's decision to adopt the child comes at the same time he is experiencing his own separation.

In general, both parents responded positively to Samuel's good intentions regarding Edgar, and they were willing to take on the responsibility of another young child in their growing household. To Sarah's mind, her son's act was a sign of maturity. On October 2, 1791, one month after giving birth to Thomas Greaves Cary on September 7, she writes to Samuel describing Edgar as "active, sensible, and I believe, good, but it is rather early for me to Judge" and reports that Margaret has "under taken to learn him to read." For household duties, Edgar "cleans knives, prepares the side board, waits at Table, brushes away flies, while we are there." Regarding his education, Sarah looks forward to the opening of the Chelsea schoolhouse, when "Master Bill (for that I find is his Christian name) and Henry are to become schollars; writing, reading and arithmetic are I suppose the most you wish for him, and at 14 to be placed with a good Master <u>Mechanic</u>, this will give you vast satisfaction, and unite him to you for life." Regarding Samuel's wish to keep these matters private, Sarah asks, "Why shou'd you be desirous of concealing an action that does you honor, you have done perfectly right. Your Father approves of your conduct, and received the little orphan with pleasure; I discovered the emotions of his mind in his Eyes and <u>know</u> that he congratulated himself upon having a Son, who instead of incurring expenses for frolicking and dissipation, knew how to retrench even a necessary allowance of pocket Money, for the relief of an object in distress." Having praised his modesty, Sarah adds that the news could not have remained "a secret" as "it had flown over the Town of Boston" even before "your Father had seen the Captn."[21] Both parents thus approved of Samuel's actions and praised his good deeds, even while noting the uniqueness of his actions.

Samuel's decision to adopt this child and assert his independence is interesting for many reasons. First, it was Samuel who remained in Grenada while his parents departed, unlike his father leaving his family in Boston when he departed for St. Kitts. Second, the economic situations are different. In Joyce Appleby's discussion of fathers and sons in post-revolutionary America, she describes similar shifts in father-son relationships and how they are affected by economic factors: "The opening of fertile new acres in the national domain greatly lessened that bond that the expectation of a valuable inheritance had forged between the generations." Moreover, even though sons and husbands had often traveled far afield as merchants and traders instead of staying close to home, as with several generations of the Cary family, now there were even more options for sons, which altered expectations of compliance. Samuel's adoption of Edgar, for example, thus suggests an act of independence similar to the acts Appleby observes of sons in early America: "Opportunities to teach school or become a peddler further enlarged the scope of action for restless sons, whose restlessness often precipitated family conflicts. Leaving home at the onset of manhood was more than an economic decision; a strike for personal autonomy involved an emotional struggle as well, intensifying the normal tensions between generations with anxiety and guilt about separation."[22] Although this description more closely aligns with Samuel Cary Sr.'s decision to leave Boston for the West Indies, Samuel Cary Jr. also acted independently regarding his own finances, for example, by choosing to care for a child rather than spend money on diversions.

Samuel's "adoption" of Edgar also suggests a parallel to Sarah's first encounter with Fanny Fairweather, as Caroline Curtis describes: "One day, in walking through the street in St. Kitts, my grandmother saw a little girl about seven years old standing on the sale block with other slaves. She was moved by the child's attitude, with hands folded upon her breast and a very sad expression in her face. She said to her husband: 'I must own that child.' And so Fanny became hers and was brought up by her mistress very much apart from the other servants."[23] Why Curtis places this scene at St. Kitts rather than Grenada is unclear, unless Sarah had accompanied her husband to a slave auction, but the meeting is portrayed as leading to an act of benevolence, as Sarah expresses concern for a vulnerable young child. In emphasizing Sarah's compassion, Curtis appears to convey her own post–Civil War antislavery perspective. If this intention is accurate, it may have also influenced the following passage, in which Curtis describes Fanny's capture and passage to the West Indies: "With the rest of her family she lived in Africa, and one day, while sitting outside the cabin tending her baby sister, men rushed from the woods, seized her and carried her on board a vessel, and brought her over to this slave market, where she was saved from further misery by this kindest of friends." The horrors of being kidnapped and surviving the Middle Passage are placed into a narrative whereby Fanny "was saved from further misery." As previously mentioned, Fanny Fairweather returned with the Carys to Chelsea. Curtis's narrative thus continues, including remembrances from her childhood: "At the west corner of the house a group of pines had been planted just where the ground sloped down to the orchard and at the foot of this slope came old Fanny Fairweather's little red cottage. She had been nurse to my father, who was born the first summer at Chelsea, and when I first remembered her I suppose she had lived there forever with her cat and her parrot and her pipe." Curtis refers here to the birth of Thomas Greaves Cary on September 7, 1791. Seven years later, Fanny married David Fareweather, as noted in the Chelsea town records—"Fareweather, David (of Boston, int.) and Fanny Cary, Sept. 28, 1798. Blacks"—and in the Boston town records: "David Fareweather of Boston & Fanny Cary of Chelsea Cold., Rev. Phillips Payson, Sept. 28, 1798."[24] Fanny continued to live at Chelsea, and as Caroline explains, "Old and young, every one went to say a word to black Fanny, and we children always saw that she was kept supplied with needles threaded, and the thread twisted back and forth to keep them in the needle-book. . . . She lived in her little home till she grew so feeble that she consented to come up to the house, where she could receive better care, and died tended by my aunts."[25] These passages offer some insight into how the Carys, and perhaps others, operated within a contradictory world, condoning slavery while also acting with kindness. Meanwhile, Samuel's concern for Edgar may have, in general, been influenced by his mother's encouragement toward charity and benevolence, even within the context of slavery.

Separations and a Need for Economizing at Chelsea

By the end of the Carys' first year back in Chelsea, their financial situation had clearly not met their expectations. Sarah writes to Samuel on November 11, 1791, with an overview of the family's current living situation: "Since coming here I have hardly had a moment's leisure, and as yet no one of the rules laid down in Grenada, and which you saw, have been put in practice. Mr. Low's Family are here and are to remain during the Winter; the Kitchen in common to us both, and everything as contrary to my wish as possible." The Samuel Low family had occupied the house while the Carys were in Grenada, but Sarah had not expected them to still be there, nor could she have anticipated that they would remain on the Chelsea property for another ten years. Financial concerns are also apparent in Sarah's letter on March 4, 1792, as she responds to Samuel's request for "one of the miniature Pictures," most likely the Copley portraits: "I shou'd be happy to gratify you with mine, but no consideration cou'd prevail upon me to part with your Father's for numberless reasons. He perhaps has the same for refusing to part with mine." She offers a possible alternative, though: "If my purse wou'd allow of a little trifling in that way, I wou'd sit again, and request yours in return." Sarah was reluctant to have another miniature made, however, in part because of the price. Joseph Cooke of Philadelphia, for example, was charging "three guineas each" for a miniature painting "set in gold," as noted in the *Federal Gazette and Philadelphia Daily Advertiser*, April 28, 1791. While Sarah's hesitation is focused on the cost, of approximately £3, the subject of an image as a representation prompts additional reflections: "Altho' absence nor time can efface you from my mind, yet to look on the picture of one we love excites the tenderest and most pleasing emotions and makes them if possible more dear and amiable to our hearts and affections." Pictures also invite favorable reflections on the person's character, as Sarah explains: "In the absence of our Friends, we contemplate only their virtues, those too heightened greatly by the loss of their company and conversation. We look on the little representation, forget their faults and think them all perfection, as such we certainly wou'd wish to appear to one another." While Sarah acknowledges the value of pictures, she also remarks on the idealization of the person they present: "Yet how vain the wish; in another life perhaps when in different pursuits and surrounding objects more calculated to calm and harmonize the human passions, we may appear, what in reality we doubtless shall be, as perfect as Him who made us."[26] For Sarah, a miniature represented an idealized self whose spiritual qualities mirrored perfection, thereby mitigating the pain of separation. Still, the need to economize would delay having a portrait made.

In other discussions about career, tensions arose between Sarah's expectations and Samuel's aspirations, which also raised the issue of finances. For example, Sarah responds on April 20, 1792, to Samuel's letter from February 4, in which he has apparently expressed a desire to try farming, a plan that his mother discourages, at least for the moment. For now, the family needs Samuel to remain in Grenada. Their return to Chelsea seems to have modified any idealized view of a "gentleman farmer," and Sarah reminds him that the farmer's life is not without struggle. They may have differed on this subject, but Sarah still reinforces their connection: "I rise early myself, and in Idea rise every morning now with you, and will you believe me, so far am I from desiring to join you, that I walk softly least I should disturb some fine spun, delicate reflection, and throw into disorder those principles that are to govern your actions."[27] In this poetic passage, Sarah acknowledges their connection, which she is mindful not to "disturb." As the first year of their separation drew near, letters between Chelsea and St. George's took on a routine, with the occasional breaks owing largely to weather and at times to the lack of conveyances. From discussions about portraits to advice about farming, these letters show not only how seriously Sarah took her role as mentor but also the family's need for Samuel to stay at Grenada and keep an eye on their finances.

While letters between Samuel and Sarah address various topics and often evoke language of sentiment and emotion, letters between father and son also offer opportunity for reflection, even as they primarily address business matters. In a series of letters from summer 1792, Samuel kept his father up to date about shipments, payments, and bills regarding their Mount Pleasant plantation. He also awaited the possibility of being invited into the House of Morris and Postlethwaite more permanently and confided in his father the conflict that such an offer might create. Writing from St. George's on July 7, Samuel frames this discussion with an overview of his position: "My principles for my government in the conducting of mercantile business are fixed, and while I continue the same Man, they must not, nor cannot, be altered.— My education, particularly in my earliest years when the deepest impressions are made was, you well know I believe, Sir, of a religious turn; and all of my consequent Actions and Rules cannot but be tinctured with it, if I am willing to preserve my peace of mind." Having asserted that his business practices are founded on principles derived from an education "of a religious turn," Samuel signals that ethical matters will influence his plans: "As I do not believe that great riches are productive of any peculiar happiness, I do not place my mind upon the acquisition of more than a moderate sum, which gained with honesty will be enjoyed without remorse; and as I do not, while I preserve the peace of mind which I have not yet lost, look upon poverty as the greatest misfortune which can befall me I will not avoid it by the sacrifice of what I hold much dearer than riches, my conscience." Samuel's comments not only contrast with the incentives of his father's generation to move to the West Indies, but also indicate that a pursuit of riches may threaten his "peace of mind."

As if to allay any concerns, Samuel again reassures his father: "If it be necessary I will remain in the West Indies and that as long as you please." Having made this commitment clear, however, he notes that he will not engage in unethical transactions: "Whatever offers may be made me, or whatever advantages may be held out, I am determined to prefer a good conscience to every consideration." And though he cannot reveal details in this letter, Samuel hopes that his father will be sympathetic to his concerns: "From what I have said I believe you, who are not ignorant of some customs of the extensive houses in the West Indies, will collect that the place you set your hopes upon here will not, however advantageous, suit me. I am afraid, Sir, the Idea of my possessing it must not be indulged." Without disclosing more details, he does make this promise: "By a vessel which sails from this in a fortnight I hope to be able to write you more clearly, and more positively."[28] Samuel thus expresses discontent with these as yet unexplained business prospects.

In a letter to Samuel Jr. on July 13, 1792, Samuel Sr. reports on a recent visit to Boston, where he dined with his cousin Thomas Russell and "made an offer for your service." He then provides an overview of various transactions and sends these directions: "I must beg you will enquire into this business and write to Mr. Russell, he is not only your relation but is the first Merchant on the Continent, and one of the most amiable of men; I wish you may by your attention to this Business recommend yourself to him."[29] Samuel Sr. might have felt anxious about not being more directly involved in the family business transactions, so by advising his son, he could exert some degree of influence while preparing him for business in general. At the same time, Samuel Cary's own plans for retirement as a "gentleman farmer" appear to have been even more costly and time consuming than previously imagined, which added to the focus on his son as the family's representative in business matters.

Samuel reveals the specific reasons for his previous concerns in his next letter from Grenada, on July 31, 1792. Although he has not yet been offered "a place in this house," he tells his father, "I must beg leave to repeat that I fear I cannot accept the place without making a sacrifice which the place will never compensate for." Samuel is confident that Mr. Morris is "satisfied" with his work as a clerk, but he remains uncertain about working for this house. He again appeals to his father's understanding: "I ask your pardon, Sir, if in the course of what I have written here and in my Letter of the 7th there should appear an obscurity of expression which prevents your comprehending even upon what ground I found the refusal of this place: it is so very delicate a matter that I do not like to touch upon it: — however, as it is necessary to be plain, I must mention that it is, the clandestine intercourse with the French Islands, which I never could bring myself to approve of, through whatever light I received it."[30] The scruples were thus apparently about illegal activity, which he had still not fully disclosed. In Samuel's subsequent letter, however, he would clarify these events and new directions in his career.

In a five-and-a-half-page letter on September 13, 1792, Sarah addresses Samuel's career dilemma while also sending an update about young Edgar. She begins with supportive words: "Tho' my Letters may generally seem to commend my Son, it is because I conceive he means to put in force all those expressions of duty, obedience and affection, perseverance, economy and industry, that he professes himself capable of doing, so often in his Letters, those words are important, not empty names, let your conduct evince that those professions are sincere." Affirming Samuel's good intentions, Sarah then advises him to be patient and to be mindful of his father's expectations: "Your present situation even if you do not approve, should be chearfully submitted to from propriety, as His choice. When you come of age you have the same tie in my opinion, if as you repeatedly declare, your highest ambition and wish is to please Him." Regarding Samuel's concerns about certain business transactions, Sarah offers this advice: "If my love you have scruples concerning particular modes of carrying on business, enquire of those you most esteem, sensible honest men, how they reconcile to their feelings, carrying on an intercourse that seems to you so unjust, Mr. Morris for instance, for whom I know you have a great veneration, Mr. Barry also, and many others, the sentiments of good men should decide you; a young man never need be under any apprehension of doing wrong, provided he has discernment enough to distinguish character." Sarah thus places responsibility on Samuel to make these choices.

In light of Samuel's discomfort, Sarah also conveys both parents' support should he continue to "be unhappy in the line of business that so sensibly affects" him, adding that his father "will give up his expectations (tho' till now very great) rather than your happiness should in any, the least degree be affected— do not determine hastily." This emphasis on sentiment and the description of a job that "so sensibly affects" show her concern for Samuel's unhappiness with clerking in general, if not with this house in particular. Sarah also asks Samuel to consider a longer view of his obligations to the family while reminding him of the potential opportunities that his apprenticeship promises: "You have 3 years before you. It is my private opinion that you will never have so advantageous an offer, but particularly before you are of age — your sentiments in the above mentioned period of time will change, be assured. At present your doing business upon the Sabbath, I take to be the line of your Duty, an unavoidable necessity, which you should do chearfully, in compliance to the custom of the House you live in, and in obedience to those you serve." For now, Sarah advises Samuel to be patient and to complete his apprenticeship: "The wisest way is to be satisfied with our situation, in which there will always be found peace of mind, if we choose to embrace it; happiness is within the reach of most men, and by no means so partially bestowed as many young people are apt to imagine."

In other developments, the family's relationship to Edgar had entered a new, conflict-ridden phase. Sarah begins with this report: "Your Boy Bill is placed with a shoe maker, where he will be fast bound untill 21 years old, he will be taught to read and write; which is perhaps more than he deserves." She then reprimands Samuel for his initial decision to adopt Edgar, while commenting on the general responsibility of parents: "I always thought you wou'd have done better to have found out the Father of the Boy, and insisted as far as you were able, upon his doing his duty towards him; if a man chooses to abandon his child, I don't know that any one is Justifiable in adopting him; it is a bad precedent, laws were made for unnatural Fathers, as well as for those who offend against the community in which they live, in any other way." Sarah may not have remembered that Samuel's August 8, 1791, letter had provided an explanation about Edgar's parents: "His father's name was Edgar, Captain of a Ship at St. Eustatia, who dying, as well as the boy's mother, the little lad was left to the care of an aunt." Still, this is the first indication that Samuel's plan may not have been the best, and where he was once praised for "adopting" Edgar and looking after his welfare, Sarah was now suggesting that Samuel reconsider his actions.

Sarah then relays a series of incidents whereby Edgar's behavior had exerted a bad influence on the younger children: "I must take this opportunity of saying, that you have the best and the most generous of Fathers, or the Boy would have been return'd upon your hands— for my part, the trouble of having him wou'd have been nothing, had he been innocent and good; bad language, indecent behaviour, and lying, have been customary to him from his infancy. Henry and Ned have both been twice whip'd for repeating words that shocked me, learnt from <u>Him</u>." While Sarah has "endeavored to conceal" these developments for "fear of hurting [his] feelings," she now has new concerns about Samuel, as she explains: "I have been led to believe from a certain cast of sentiment in your Letters of late, that you will ere long do some precipitate action that will occasion you trouble." Noting that her fears might be unwarranted, Sarah then expresses a more pressing concern: "I hope, at any rate not to be presented with another Child." Sarah's concerns were thus related to both the situation with Edgar and the objections Samuel had raised about business transactions.

When nineteen-year-old Samuel mentioned the subject of marriage, Sarah's patience became strained. In her letter, she is quick to advise that he wait: "You startled me indeed, when I come to that part of your Letter, where you mention Matrimony, that wou'd be madness in the extreme. I am glad however to find that our sentiments accord there, 25 is a good age, provided there is a sufficient fund to maintain a Family. — Matrimony at 25 in my opinion, is not necessary to restrain from vice or ambition all danger of the former is before that period intirely over, <u>with a sensible man,</u> and from the latter a young man and a sensible one shou'd never wish to be preserved." In dissuading him until he is "of age," Sarah is mindful that his apprenticeship still has three more years. One month later, on November 28, 1792, Sarah writes just before she is about to give birth, which again heightens financial concerns: "I expect to be confined in a very few Days when I shall present you with another little Brother or Sister. You see my dear son with such a family how necessary your steady perseverance in the line you have adopted of business and economy will be."[31] As she tries to console and encourage Samuel, Sarah again affirms the importance of Samuel's role as eldest son.

On November 19, 1792, Samuel writes to his father from Demerary (Demerara), on the northern coast of South America, a Dutch colony that the British seized in 1796 and that the Dutch ceded in 1814. As a follow-up to letters from July in which Samuel expressed concerns about working at the office of Morris and Postlethwaite while they conducted "clandestine intercourse with the French Islands," Samuel thus begins: "You will I dare say be much surprized at finding me here, perhaps agreeably surprized to see that I am allowed to take a trip to this country which must be serviceable to my health." Having explained his new location, Samuel relays disturbing news: "How will your pleasure be damped when I inform you that Mr. Morris is dead, and that I am here inspecting his affairs as an executor! Mr. M. arrived here from St. Vincent, having been taken sick at sea, the 15th Octr. and died the 18th — To say that this loss is severely felt would be hardly doing justice to his memory.— surely the trite term of <u>universal regret</u> could never be more properly used than on the present occasion." He continues with kind words for Mr. Morris and notes that his death "will naturally cause a revolution in the house of T. T. and Co." Here, Samuel is referring to the firm of John Abraham Tinne and Philip Frederick Tinne. He then summarizes the events from the past month, in which "Mr. Postlethwaite, about ten days after the death of Mr. Morris, made me a proposal of offering me to Messrs Tarletons and Backhouse to join him in the agency here." As Samuel notes, John Tarleton, his son Thomas, and Daniel Backhouse from Liverpool were wealthy West Indian merchants. Samuel had thanked him for the proposal but, reiterating previous concerns, "told him that my notions of the illicit commerce with the French islands were an insuperable bar to my acceptance of it. He laboured to convince me of the propriety of this commerce, but his arguments had little effect." To emphasize his response, Samuel informed Postlethwaite that he was awaiting his father's assessment "relating to my ideas of clandestine trade." About the proposal, Samuel has "not a doubt that it would have been refused by Messrs T's and B. for reasons I will communicate to you when we meet." Samuel then conveys his plan to stay in Demerary for the next month to help settle Mr. Morris's estate. He also defers to his father whether he

should remain an apprentice to Postlethwaite, which he assumes is determined by their contractual agreement, noting that he will stay "if you desire
it." Alternatively, Samuel notes that if his father thinks it "proper," he is willing to "enter into business myself."

In closing, Samuel observes, "Were I to prefer a planter's to a merchant's
life I know no country I would sooner wish to lay the foundation of my fortune in than in this Demerary. — This however I speak merely from the success the planters have met with here, not because I think it superior to the
islands; for in my mind there is no doubt that a country divided into hills and
vallies is more pleasant than an entirely level one." Samuel also notes "the
town of Stabrook is pretty well filled with merchants like all other places."[32]
Kit Candlin and Cassandra Pybus corroborate Samuel's observation: "By the
end of the century Demerara and its two neighbors had grown rapidly. Huge
merchant companies moved their offices there, and legions of factors, agents,
bookkeepers, and managers came with them."[33] And although Samuel continued working for Postlethwaite, these letters suggest a change in attitude
about his future as he imagines the possibility of venturing out on his own.

Samuel Cary Jr.'s Continued Search for
Mercantile Opportunities, 1794

That Samuel was still not quite settled would be evident two years later when
Sarah recollected with nostalgia their time together in Grenada and raised
concerns for the future, as their separation entered its third year. On May 24,
1794, for example, she includes this remembrance: "I look back with pleasure upon the time you and I pass'd together, and recollect many conversations as we walk'd together in the front Gallery at Mount Pleasant, and
at others when we were alone in my chamber." She then recalls her role as
counselor: "How seriously did I recommend you to abate of that impatience
and warmth of temper I had discovered in you, and to submit to your situation." Having noted his shortcomings, Sarah adds, "I reflect with pleasure
upon your tender and dutiful attention to all I said, you promised to be all I
wished you, and I believe you have faithfully performed it, as far as it is in
your power." Hopeful that Samuel has since cultivated the virtue of patience,
she further advises him to "pray when you have nothing else to do." Here,
as in other letters, Sarah also remarks on the potential dangers of living in
the West Indies: "I well know the common routine of people in your part
of the World, but do you fall in with the habits and manners of those with
whom you converse, or have you firmness to mark out for yourself a line of

conduct irreproachable to your conscience, an important witness." To emphasize her point about his conscience, Sarah references Edward Young's
Night-Thoughts: "As the inimitable Young expresses it 'that sly informer who
stands behind the scene and marks down every fault.'" Here, Sarah paraphrases lines from "Night the Second: On Time, Death, Friendship," in which
"Conscience" keeps a watchful eye: "Unmart;—See, from behind her Secret
stand,/The sly Informer minutes ev'ry Fault,/And her dread Diary with
Horror fills." She then reflects, "I should perhaps apologize for asking the
question to one of your sentiments, and excellent principles, <u>such at least
when we parted</u>, did I not know the temptations, which beset a young person
in the part of the World you are destined to reside, don't therefore my dear
Boy be offended at my suspicions." And though Sarah is not asking "for an
exact account of the employment of time destined for amusement," she still
offers advice. Then, almost as a deflection for her serious tone, Sarah notes, "I
write carelessly and without Study to you; the thoughts that occur, I commit
to paper without any nice reflections about consequences or giving pain; I
flatter my self that your pleasures as well as your business are regulated by
reason and propriety."

As their separation continued, Sarah's efforts to parent and advise from
afar were both encouraging and pointed. After affirming Samuel's good judgment, she turns to the latest developments with Edgar, who despite their
well-intended actions had left the Boston area on his own accord. In this
same letter from May 24, 1794, Sarah thus tells her son, "He has absolutely
decamp'd (as we all believe) to the West Indies." A week later, however,
Edgar "misbehaved and returned home," after which he ran away and returned once more. Sarah then notes, "You may think probably that I congratulate my self upon the child's escape, it is very true that to be rid of him was
my most ardent wish, but not in such a way, my feelings are hurt more than I
can express." And while they had intended "to bind him to some good Man at
a little distance from us that we might now and then see how he went on," she
concedes, "no Boy can be bound without his own consent untill arrived to the
age of 14 and he was by his own account only 12 and without being bound no
one would take him, for this reason we cou'd not continue him with the Shoe
Maker, of whom I wrote you in a former letter." These developments then
prompt Sarah to remind Samuel of his responsibility for his own conduct in
addition to cautioning him should "he ever see" Edgar again. In light of these
events, Sarah discusses Samuel's future within the context of "ambition" and
happiness: "I have seen enough of the world to convince me that probity,

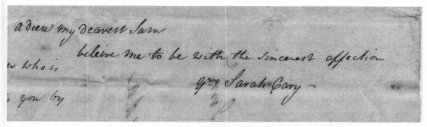

Sarah Cary to Samuel Cary Jr., Retreat, Chelsea, May 24, 1794. Cary Family Papers III, Collection of the Massachusetts Historical Society.

Adieu my dearest Sam
believe me to be with the sincerest affection
Yrs Sarah Cary —

honor, and honesty, are not confined to particular places, and that happiness is in a man's own mind, and the rectitude of his own conduct."[34] From her perspective, remaining in the West Indies held more promise for Samuel than returning to Chelsea, with the underlying presumption that the family would also benefit if Samuel remained in Grenada.

Three months later, Samuel responds from Trinidad, on September 4, 1794, offering a thoughtful portrait of a young man finding his way in the business world while addressing similar concerns about life in the West Indies, in terms of the climate and the absence of a moral standard. He thus explains, "My present life is a roving one, not having been settled when I expected it, and continuing to do the Out business for Mr. Postlethwaite till another plan less precarious be ripened for my establishment." Now, one month shy of his twenty-first birthday, Samuel reflects on his overall situation: "The business among the islands which I am employed in being confined to no particular hours leaves me a deal of leisure time often, — as much as two or three years ago I used to consider enough to make a man happy, if he had a mind to be so." In retrospect, Samuel has revised his earlier assessment: "This time I spend partly in reading, in riding, partly in a State of indolence or unemployed, and a great deal in thinking of America and etc. The Company I keep is rather general than particular, and upon the whole I spend my time nearly as I should three years ago had I had so much to spare. I am commonly pretty well received in the different islands where my business calls me, notwithstanding the reservedness of my disposition, which makes me not forward to recommend myself." Partly as a defense and partly as an autobiographical narrative, Samuel describes his life as a work in progress.

In doing so, his candor and self-reflection suggest yet another level of confidences in their letters. As he continues, Samuel appeals to his mother to keep her expectations realistic. More directly, Samuel responds to Sarah's previous letter and her concerns about "the temptations" in his "part of the World": "You fancy, perhaps, that it must be difficult for me to have remained so long in the West Indies without being tinctured with the vices and follies which prevail here, to increase in years at my time of Life in the islands, and preserve the niceness of feeling which I brought here." In this regard, Samuel notes, "You may suppose that my being engaged in the active Life may have turned my ambition from aiming to excel in points of morality to a desire of perfecting myself in the duty of my employment." Samuel thus evokes philosophical discourse and addresses prevailing presumptions about life in the West Indies regarding negative, corrupting influences, such as "the vices and follies" that make it difficult to "preserve the niceness of feeling." These references might have been to slavery at some level, if not a general comment about the "State of indolence" that results from being unemployed or otherwise not productively engaged.

Samuel's initial enthusiasm for the promise of his apprenticeship had since faded, while the absence of any firm business direction contributed to his discouraged attitude. In this mood of reflection and disclosure, Samuel continues his self-assessment: "I could not send you any but a character candidly drawn, and Candour would oblige me to confess so many imperfections and would allow me to set so little against them, that I fear I should be ashamed of myself though represented in my own colours. — I wish, therefore, you would undertake me yourself." As he asks his mother to accept him for his apparent shortcomings, he provides additional perspective: "Think what I was when we parted, think what I have been exposed to, . . . think what faults I was likely to fall into — think what excesses I would scorn to indulge in, be candid, make allowances, and you may come near the mark. — I do not wish you to think better of me than I deserve for I should be sorry to disappoint you." Although he does not go into detail about what specific behaviors might warrant her disappointment, Samuel is also aware that his image and position may have been exaggerated: "I have perhaps been represented too favourably to you since you have been in America. — A desire to recommend himself to you and my father, and an ignorance of the minutia of my character, may have induced a man to speak better of me than he thought, or better than I merited." Claiming to be essentially the same person that they knew in 1791, upon their departure, Samuel presents himself in an understated manner, all the while deferring his own aspirations on behalf of the family's welfare. As he turns his attention to Edgar, there is a sense of resignation, if not acceptance of these events, and an understanding that his initial good intentions may not have been fulfilled as planned: "What you tell me of little Edgar does not surprize me much. — The character you have given me of him in your Letters led me to expect that he would never come to any good."[35] Still, in noting his business travels and plans, Samuel describes productive and valuable transactions with local managers and his father's business associates. Confidence thus mixes with regret, even as he imagines returning to America and to his family.

Around the same time that Sarah was writing to Samuel and trying to smooth out his discontent, she received a letter from her friend Mercy Otis Warren, from Plymouth, dated June 24, 1793. Warren apologizes for not having visited Chelsea yet because of "unavoidable circumstances" and encourages Sarah to visit her instead: "I will expect you. Let me know when I may with probability calculate on the pleasure of seeing you at Plimouth."[36] With Sarah's epistolary companion within a two-day's journey of around fifty miles, Sarah may have found solace in this invitation in the midst of maintaining her large household and counseling her son. In her correspondence with Samuel, moreover, Sarah expressed growing concern over the political struggles for control of Grenada and the potentially negative effects of the West Indies on one's character of the West Indies. On December 14, 1794, in addition to discussing family matters and business affairs, Sarah responds to Samuel's recent letter expressing his discontent with his current situation and offers cautious support: "Your last letter is that of a man of sense who thinks and acts properly; You reason thus, My situation is not what I admire, those I am obliged for want of other society to make friends and companions of, are not to my taste, nor of my way of thinking, but I cannot help it." Having acknowledged his situation, Sarah then surmises Samuel's understanding of his father's perspective: "My father who loves me would do anything to make me happy, but it is not in his power; he has 8 sons of which number I am the eldest, if by my industry and economy I can make a little independancy, I shall not only make myself respectable without distressing my father's feelings but be able to lend my assistance in bringing my Brothers forward into life. This shall satisfy me and from henceforward this shall be my pleasure and my ambition." As Sarah paraphrases Samuel's attempts toward accepting his current situation, she also praises his character and his devotion to the family.

Having dispatched her advice, she reports on daily life in Chelsea, holding out the possibility that Samuel, too, may one day enjoy the benefits of his father's hard work. Still, she adds, farming is difficult, and after three years, she now has a more realistic perspective. She perhaps offers hope in the line "as you are the eldest this spot will probably be yours." And in a reversal from her earlier reaction to the idea of Samuel marrying, Sarah reflects, "At the decline of life a retreat is agreable to a man of sense and reflection but more particularly so if after the storms of life are over he can meet with a woman of the same taste and way of thinking. I believe I was wrong once when I mentioned your not thinking of retiring untill you were sixty I would rather it shou'd be forty or even sooner if you make a Capital sufficient to live upon your income." This amended time frame is then followed by a few additional words of caution: "Retiring to a farm is by no means retiring to be idle, your Father is always employed in overseeing and directing his workmen in planting Trees, running out fences, ditching and etc." Sarah retreats from her earlier comments meant to discourage Samuel from considering the life of "a gentleman farmer," now allowing that it may be an attractive possibility in retirement. She notes that a genteel life will require additional income and includes very specific conditions in terms of both finances and labor: "But still a farm alone is not sufficient of itself to maintain a family genteelly so you see there is something to be done before a man can set quietly down with propriety, the life of a farmer is laborious and full of care[,] the high price of labour run away with the profits and he must himself become one of those labourers unless he has a resource beyond what the farm can give him." Having dispatched this dose of reality, she then points out, "If therefore my dear Sam you can make 8 or 10,000 sterling he will be intitled to retire to any spot that is most agreable to him. I hope it may be in this Country not far distant from Town and I think you may enjoy all the happiness this life is capable of bestowing."[37] The idea of returning to America is thus set forth as a reward to follow all his current storms and travails. As 1794 drew to a close, Sarah summarized in this nine-page letter their current state of affairs at Chelsea and offered a revised scenario for Samuel's future, as the family's representative at Grenada, even as plans for their own retirement underwent reevaluation. The candor and intimacy of these exchanges show not only Sarah's skills at mentoring but also her insights into her son's current difficulties.

~

The family's return to Chelsea in 1791 had, in turn, coincided with several civic projects to gradually improve transportation. When they had first arrived, traveling from Chelsea to Boston had been a half-day journey, over land

and water, but by 1800, a ferry between Chelsea and Boston had shortened the trip to one hour.[38] In 1803, as Mellen Chamberlain notes, the opening of the Chelsea Bridge and Salem Turnpike "gave the Cary family easier communication with their Boston friends as well as with what is now Revere, where they worshipped . . . which was about two miles distant from The Retreat."[39] The town also grew. According to the 1790 census, Chelsea had 472 people, 60 houses, and 81 families, while Boston was a bustling city with 18,038 residents, 2,376 houses, and 3,343 families. By 1800, Chelsea's population had grown to 849, including the outlying islands.[40] And even though the Carys' financial prospects had not altogether met their expectations, The Retreat was still a destination for many visitors: "To this place, though not easily accessible before the building of Chelsea Bridge in 1803, came people from Boston, attracted by the beauty of the situation, or as relatives of its occupants, whose talents, culture, and intimate knowledge of strange lands and life, made their society interesting."[41] Moreover, when Sarah and Samuel were living on Grenada, the implications of declaring independence from England were considered primarily economic rather than ideological. Not until they returned to Chelsea were they able to process and assess the radical changes that had occurred during their eighteen-year absence. And though they assumed that they would be able to maintain their level of wealth based on profits from their Mount Pleasant plantation, supplemented by their working farm, Samuel and Sarah could not have imagined at this point how tumultuous the situation in Grenada was about to become.

CHAPTER FOUR

Slave Revolts and Shifting Fortunes

Grenada, 1795–1797

As renovations to the Chelsea estate continued into 1795, it was slowly becoming The Retreat that Samuel and Sarah had imagined upon returning from Grenada nearly four years earlier. As Caroline Curtis recounts, "Everything now seemed to promise a life of ease for my grandparents, the best education for their children, and good business prospects for the elder sons." This promising picture was altered, however, "when a sudden change came."[1] This "sudden change" was news of a slave revolt that had broken out in Grenada in March 1795. The Carys were certainly aware of the potential for instability in the West Indies, but they were not prepared for a violent rebellion that would place their son Samuel in harm's way as well as jeopardize their property. In this chapter I trace the origins of this revolt and discuss Samuel's subsequent attempts to save the family's Mount Pleasant estate. Tensions on the island between the British and French had, in fact, been building since the end of the Seven Years' War in 1763, when the Treaty of Paris ceded Grenada to the British. Andrew Jackson O'Shaughnessy elaborates: "Following the formal acquisition of Grenada in 1763, a maroon population of six hundred to seven hundred escaped French slaves began guerilla campaigns. They intimidated the planters, who only traveled in small, well-armed groups and left guards at their houses because 'the terror was so universal, and the danger so great.'" The American Revolutionary War had also contributed to general instability in the West Indies. Bryan Edwards provides this perspective: "The hopeless and destructive war in North America had drawn to its vortex all the powers, resources, and exertions of Great Britain. Already had Dominica and St. Vincent become a sacrifice to that unfortunate contest; when it fell to the lot of Grenada to experience her share of the general misfortune."[2] In 1779, the French recaptured the island

and were in control until 1783. At that point, the Treaty of Versailles returned Grenada to the British. In addition to these territorial struggles, ideological forces, such as the French Revolution (1789–1799) in general and the Haitian Revolution (1791–1804) more directly, contributed to this instability while also inspiring change. Regarding the former, William Spence argues, in *The Radical Cause of the Present Distresses of the West-India Planters Pointed Out* (1807), "In the year 1792, the French revolution extended its baleful influence from Europe to the West Indies. The mad introduction of 'liberty and equality,' those watch-words of anarchy and devastation, into the island of St. Domingo, at first diminished, and at length, in a few years, totally annihilated, the supply of 114,615 hogsheads of Sugar, which France and Europe had been accustomed to draw from thence." David Patrick Geggus, in turn, notes, "By 1789 angry colonists and alarmed officials were complaining that antislavery literature and artifacts were circulating in both the French and the British West Indies and were attracting the excited attention of slaves."[3] The revolts were thus the consequence of several factors.

In addition, antislavery societies in both England and America advocated for an end to the slave trade and ultimately for the abolition of slavery itself. In doing so, antislavery efforts challenged assumptions about slavery as a viable economic system and exposed it as a morally corrupt institution. To these ends, in June 1787, the London abolition committee decided Thomas Clarkson "should go to Bristol, Liverpool and elsewhere," as Marcus Rediker explains, to " 'collect Information on the Subject of the Slave Trade.' " Subsequently, Clarkson gathered testimony from sailors and seamen about the harsh conditions of the slave ship. Clarkson's *An Essay on the Impolicy of the African Slave Trade* (1788) refuted economic justifications of the slave trade and brought attention to the captains and merchants who enacted misery on both slaves and seamen. In Rediker's compelling account of Clarkson's efforts, he describes the influence of these investigations: "He would use these stories to make the trade, which to most people was an abstract and distant proposition, into something concrete, human, and immediate."[4] An image of the slave ship the *Brooks*, depicting the cramped, stifling conditions of the ship, was published in Plymouth in November 1788 and in Philadelphia in May 1789. In the lower deck, as Rediker explains, the startling image shows "294 Africans tightly packed and arranged in orderly fashion in four apartments," for girls, women, boys, and men. The impact was far reaching. In William Wilberforce's speech to the House of Commons on May 12, 1789, "On the Horrors of the Slave Trade," as Rediker notes, he "coined a memorable phrase when he observed of the slave ship, 'So much misery condensed in so little room is more than the human imagination had ever before conceived.' " James A. Rawley cites Wilberforce's speech as "a masterly display of rhetorical power and eloquence," one that "opened what turned out to be the long war against the slave trade." Rawley also reports, "Charles Spooner, a London merchant 'of considerable respectability' and agent for St. Kitts, presented a petition against abolition on behalf of Grenada and the Grenadines."[5] As the debates intensified, the French and British continued to vie for dominance and power in the West Indies, and tensions between British and French landholders escalated. Thus in 1792, as Michael Duffy explains, "the British colonists finally pressed the Privy Council to enforce the original British-based constitution of 1763 and to disallow concessions made to the French in 1768. Many French-speaking coffee planters and smallholders, white and colored, were therefore willing to make contact with Victor Hugues," on Guadeloupe, who was a commissioner appointed by the French National Convention.[6] Hugues was also in contact with Julien Fédon, a "mulatto of French extraction," as Edward L. Cox explains: "By 1794, he owned in the town of Gouyave a house and his 360 acre Belvidere estate with 96 slaves engaged in the cultivation of coffee, cocoa, and sugar."[7] As plans were made to protest the British measures, the stage was increasingly set for confrontation.

Fédon's Rebellion on the Island of Grenada, 1795–1796, and the Cary Family's Estate

On March 2, 1795, Julien Fédon initiated a sixteen-month rebellion on the island of Grenada with a dramatic nighttime attack. The anonymously penned Grenada Planter's *A Brief Enquiry into the Causes Of, and Conduct Pursued By, the Colonial Government, for Quelling the Insurrection in Grenada* (1796) provides these details: "The insurgents, in two parties, commenced their operations about the same hour, in the night between the 2d and 3d of March, upon precisely opposite sides of the island." Gordon Turnbull's *A Narrative of the Revolt and Insurrection of the French Inhabitants in the Island of Grenada* (1795) describes the confusion of the events following March 3, including the capture of Alexander Campbell and Lieutenant Governor Ninian Home. Of particular concern for the Cary family would have been this passage: "It ought to be mentioned here, that the insurgents had made prisoners several managers and overseers of plantations in the neighbourhood of Charlotte Town, and carried them to their camp, along with those they had taken in the town itself."[8] Not only was the Mount Pleasant estate located just north of Charlotte Town, but, as Edward L. Cox explains, "the militia was very unevenly distributed parochially"; consequently, Cox notes, "The irony is that the outlying parishes, where the disproportion between white and black population was greatest, remained virtually defenseless while most of the available military was concentrated around St. George's. Fedon was, therefore, able to plan the rebellion with minimal interference from local authorities and chose for his headquarters a portion of the island far removed from the capital."[9] With Fédon's stronghold in Belvidere, the Carys' estate was especially vulnerable.

This vulnerability is also evident in the opening lines of General Kenneth Francis Mackenzie's report to the Duke of Portland on March 28, 1795: "I have a great concern in acquainting Your Grace that a General Insurrection of the French Free Coloured People broke out in this Island on the night of the 2nd instant, and commenced by the massacre of the English white Inhabitants at Grenville Bay, and the seizure of the persons of the English white Inhabitants at Charlottetown and on several Estates in the Country." Prominent in General Mackenzie's report is the framing of the conflict as a French-aligned resistance, rather than, for example, as a revolt of slaves. The report also includes as a separate document Lieutenant Governor Ninian Home's comique letter of March 6, 1795, from "Camp at Belvidere," which reiterates Julien Fédon's request for "Fortifications" and lists the names of forty-three prisoners. The British were thus on the defense. Many of the names listed in this letter are those from Samuel and Sarah's correspondence, which emphasizes the personal component of the revolt. With Samuel on the island and a member of the St. George's militia, the revolt was especially terrifying for the Cary family.[10]

As the rebellion continued, violence escalated quickly on both sides, as Michael Duffy describes: "On Grenada, McKenzie and the British colonists hanged captured rebels without mercy, and Fédon slaughtered his captives likewise: during the attack on his Belvidere camp on 8 April he had forty-eight of his fifty-one prisoners, including Governor Home, shot, one by one." These events lead the Grenada Planter to remark, "The result will be long deplored by all men connected with this devoted Colony." Gordon Turnbull halts his *Narrative* before discussing the death of the prisoners to comment: "At this period of the unnatural rebellion, the author is forced to pause. The mind is struck with horror, and recoils at the recollection of an event, which, for its atrocious barbarity, has not, perhaps, been paralleled in the history of the most savage nations." Focusing on the "horror" of "its atrocious barbarity," Turnbull continues without describing further details of the attack. In John Hay's first-person account of April 8, 1795, *A Narrative of the Insurrection in the Island of Grenada* (1823), he describes how the thirty-two guards shot the prisoners, with Fédon giving the orders: "He gave the word *Feu* [fire] himself to every man as soon as he came out; and, of fifty-one prisoners, only Parson M'Mahon, Mr. Kerr, and myself, were saved. They all bore their fate like men and Christians, and, except a young boy of twelve years of age, I did not hear a word from one of them."[11] Like Turnbull, Thomas Turner Wise, in *A Review of the Events, Which Have Happened in Grenada* (1795), also omits the details of the attack and focuses instead on the intent and effect of the events: "I now turn with Horror to a Scene, at which my Blood runs cold, the Moment it presents itself to my Recollection. Fain would I drop the Curtain here, and not attempt to describe a Scene so truly tragical indeed, —a Scene at which I shudder myself, and at the Recital of which every one of my Readers must stand aghast, —a Scene, which my languid Pen has not Powers to give suitable Expression to." Having established his hesitancy to commit gruesome details to paper, Wise continues by describing "a Scene, which for it's diabolical Atrocity, it's barbarous, savage Cruelty, equals, if not exceeds, any Thing, as I believe I have already said, that has yet been exhibited on the Stage of the World." With language derived from the theater, Wise evokes a stage, with actors committing a "diabolical Atrocity."[12] From these dramatic accounts of the events, biased as they are toward the British perspective, the emotional impact of the revolt resonated more strongly than the justifications. For British plantation owners, the revolt threatened their estates and their future livelihoods. For the free colored planters, French landholders, and slaves, these events appeared to promise reclamation and freedom.

Samuel Cary Fights in the Militia and
Defends the Mount Pleasant Estate

Amid this turmoil, Samuel Cary sent dramatic eyewitness reports to his family in Chelsea and to business associates in England. On May 6, 1795, he writes to Joseph Marryat, "Affairs in this island wear a bad face. The estates are almost every one burned, either wholly or in part. The Negroes are more in awe of the enemy than of us, so much so that they dare not venture amongst us, lest on their return to their estates they should be massacred." He then describes plans "to prevent the enemy's receiving a reinforcement and to starve him out," though he doubts whether the plans will be successful. Samuel also reports on divisiveness in Fédon's camp: "They are numerous and have amazing strong holds in the mountains, but they disagree amongst themselves, and must certainly run out their provisions before long. We have about 1,700 men, and we have the insurgents hemmed in, but we are not equal to them in vigilance or energy and they may perhaps be reinforced in spite of us."[13] In fact, the rebellion would continue into the next year. From Samuel's account, the "insurgents" wreaking havoc on the island were clearly leading an unjustifiable revolt.

A week later, on May 12, Samuel writes to his father about the "unhappy unsurrection," describing the British failed attack on the "main Camp," and this outcome: "Immediately on the day of this attack the rebels shot the prisoners, 54 in number, Gov Home & Mr. Alexander Campbell being at the head of the latter." The letter also reports, "I went up the other day with McCarthy and a few negroes to Mt. Pleasant to see if I could save anything. I found the dwelling-house and the negro houses burnt. They also burnt your papers. But the works were all standing." Samuel was able to recover "Seven Hhds of Sugar (all that was left of nine hogsheads made when this business broke out) and 3 small Casks of rum." He then shifts his narrative to describe slaves who were displaced by the rebellion: "The negroes came running to us from different Bushes and Canepieces and informed us that the enemy had been there two days before and had killed four stout men and mangled a fifth shockingly, who, however, will recover. Of the negroes I brought 65 to town, 6 being hiding about whom I could not find. I am going to place these negroes on Gahangan's estate of the Hospital where they will get fed for their work. Your negro man Joe behaved very steadfastly."[14] Samuel's descriptions of the destruction of their estate and the displacement of their slaves identifies another aspect of the rebellion and the various factions attempting control. As Kit Candlin explains, "This was not a slave-inspired rebellion. Indeed, littered throughout the three main sources and countless letters written are repeated references to slaves found cowering in their plantations or discovered aimlessly wandering the island's roads, unsure of what to do or who to side with." Candlin also notes that Samuel Cary's letters and "views provide an important extra source of detail," for example, "Cary also writes about the difficulties experienced in the capital over the housing of refugee slaves picked up wandering the roads or fleeing into the town."[15] These comments reinforce the importance of Samuel's eyewitness accounting.

As the transatlantic world learned of the revolt, various newspapers addressed its larger consequences. On December 4, 1795, Baltimore's *Federal Intelligencer* reported "via the brig Peggy, B. Fox, master" newly arrived in

Bermuda from Grenada and St. Vincent's on November 7, 1795: "By her we have accounts from those islands up to the 15th of October, which inform that Grenada is still in a dangerous situation; that the French have taken Guave, and in it were left between 30 and 40 persons, sick at the time, who no doubt, all fell by the hands of the assassins." Additional accounts were published throughout the following year: "West-Indies. St. George's (Grenada) March 19, with a summary of the 'attack,'" *Oracle of the Day* (Portsmouth, NH), May 19, 1796; "Extract of a letter from a gentleman in Grenada, to his friend on their island, dated April 3," *Independent Gazetteer* (Philadelphia), May 18, 1796; "'Antigua' St. John's, April 7, and 'Norfolk,' May 7, taken from 'papers' that arrive from 'St. John's (Antigua),'" *Connecticut Courant* (Hartford), May 23, 1796. An article titled "Grenada, July 25," appeared in the *Minerva and Mercantile Evening Advertiser* (New York) on September 6, 1796, and in the *Independent Gazetteer* (Philadelphia) on September 9, beginning with the following announcement: "I have the pleasure to inform you that we have, thank God, at length returned to a state of tranquility and quiet, having some weeks since, got possession of all the posts occupied by the infamous and execrable brigands, so long opposed to us." As these reports circulated, they may have provided some relief, even though they brought the events closer into focus and, as with letters from Grenada, were cause for alarm.

Attempting to understand the motives of the different participants and leaders further complicates these events. Michael Craton provides this assessment: "More than 7,000 slaves were actively involved, half of the island total, but the leaders were undoubtedly the 150 or more French-speaking Catholic coffee planters and smallholders who, like Fédon himself, felt oppressed by the British regime and looked to the French Revolution for redress and revenge." Edward L. Cox offers this perspective: "Moving from covert day-to-day resistance, Grenada's free coloreds and slaves demonstrated to the world in 1795 that their apparent inaction in the preceding years represented not acceptance of the system but simply an alternative form of resistance within the whole range of possibilities available to them." Regarding this larger view, Kit Candlin observes, "The Fedon Rebellion is not about slave resistance so much as it is a story of free coloured planters and disaffected whites who saw the French Revolution as a force for social mobility rather than as a mechanism for freeing the slaves."[16] Women also played a significant role in the rebellion, providing supplies and support. Nicole Phillip notes, for example, "There was evidence of women involved in transporting weapons, plundering provision grounds of plantations, property of planters, and taking part in the cultivation of food crops on small plantations of the leaders of the rebellion. A number of free coloured women were supposedly involved in sending supplies to Fedon's troops." Kit Candlin and Cassandra Pybus provide additional details, including information about Marie Rose Fédon: "Free women of color, particularly the wives and family members of the revolutionaries, became a specific target for the governor and his council, who believed, correctly, that women of color had been complicit in the organizing of the rebellion. Marie Rose Fedon had actively taken part, and so had some other women."[17] As both contemporary and historical accounts attest, several factions were involved in the rebellion.

As the revolt continued, Samuel reported on plantations that had been damaged and destroyed, including David Barry's Soubise estate, south of Grenville in St. Andrew Parish. He writes in his May 12, 1795, letter to his father that "Mr. David Barry has had the mortification to see the works of Soubise burnt down and the ground smoking from a recent fire when we went round to Labay. He hardly knows where to put his head. He and his family however are well." This destruction leads Samuel to conclude, "In short, altho' we are not so fortunate as a few, we are far more so than many, many others who were richer than ourselves. The negroes will I hope be preserved at all events and if the reinforcement of veteran troops, which is daily expected arrive, as indeed they must, altho' we shall be thrown back in the world a little, we may still hold up our heads and hardly feel the misfortune." Having noted the financial implications of the revolts, Samuel remains optimistic about the family's ability to recover, noting his own self-sufficiency and that of his brother Charles: "For my own part I am young and able to take care and provide for myself, so is Charles, and I think it must go harder yet indeed if we cannot do something for the little ones. I shall think it my duty as I have hitherto done, to expose myself to any danger from which I can reap service to you or the Colony, and shall trust to providence for the rest." Amid this chaotic situation, Samuel affirms his role as eldest son and speaks with a newfound confidence: "I beg of you always as much as possible to keep yourself at ease in this Business. The lighter we think of this misfortune the more able we shall be to bear it. You will at all events, I think, be able to keep the American estate."[18] By minimizing "this misfortune," Samuel reassures his parents of his commitment and of their future security.

When Samuel joined the St. George's militia to help defend the plantations on the island, he became even more directly involved. Gordon Turnbull, for example, records that on March 6, "Captain Gurdon, and Captain Park, who commanded the St George's militia, with greatest expedition formed their troops, and marched to support the piquet. In passing the works, to ascend the hill near the dwelling-house, they were fired on by a large party of the enemy, which obliged them to halt and return the fire; and after a few rounds the insurgents retreated." As these events unfolded, Samuel Cary's troop, "defended themselves with great steadiness and resolution. In a short time the enemy fled in great confusion, leaving twelve dead on the spot; and it was afterwards said, that twice that number were wounded. On our side, three of the regulars were killed, and one was wounded; together with two of the militia, one of whom, Mr. Barry, soon after died." Turnbull refers here to William Barry. He then concludes this account with praise for the militia's actions: "Both regulars and militia (except for a few who had got drunk), behaved with great intrepidity on this occasion; and, for a *first essay*, the St George's regiment may be said to have performed wonders! They were mostly picked men, and had come forth voluntarily on this service, very firmly attached to, and having the most entire confidence in their leader, Captain Park."[19] Regarding Samuel Cary's participation in particular, D. G. Garraway notes in *A Short Account of the Insurrection of 1795–96* (1877), "We are told that, in the course of the action, a young gentleman in the name of Cary, a non-commissioned officer, in the Light Company of St. George's Regiment of Militia 50, remarkably distinguished himself, by his noble and spirited behavior," upon which the president was "pleased to promote him to a Lieutenancy."[20] In Margaret Cary's recollections, she notes, "My dear brother belonged to the militia, and went through great exposure. For a long time he did not take off his clothes, and was exposed to great hardships, several of his friends dying in his arms." Margaret also describes Samuel's actions toward the slaves: "My brother, with the manager of the plantation, — who had hastened at the first alarm to St. George's, — went in a sloop, and took the remainder of the negroes, about seventy, to St. George's, where they were placed on a plantation and merely worked for their living."[21] Samuel's direct involvement brought the turmoil into sharper focus in both economic and human terms, even within the context of the preservation of their estate.

Sarah and Samuel's Response from Chelsea: Caution and Concern

As Sarah and Samuel read about the events of April 8, 1795, in newspapers and letters, their anxiety for Samuel only intensified. After months of waiting, Sarah Cary was relieved to learn from Samuel's May 6, 1795, letter to Joseph Marryat that he was unharmed. Still, she remained anxious about his situation, especially after various reports arrived from Grenada and else-where. Sarah thus expresses a range of reactions when she writes to Sam-uel on July 14, 1795, recounting a letter from Mr. Jones, which "has given us inexpressible pain," and another from Mrs. Horsford and Mrs. Rose, which she describes as "giving us a detail of the insurrection in your island; think my dear Boy of our anxiety for you, which is not lessen'd by the receipt of your Letter 12th May, nor can it be while we value your life beyond the loss of property." News from her former neighbors has only heightened her sense of the danger Samuel is in: "While in reading the account given me by Mrs. Horsford, and of the ardour and bravery you shew in aiding to sub-due the Mulattoes and other insurgents, and of your being perfectly well, I confess I am highly gratified." Although Sarah appreciates Samuel's actions, she then reconsiders: "But a moment[']s reflection cools my ambition, and makes me regret those qualities that before I so much commended, it is the fear of losing you, and I am ready to submit to the mortification of your being charged with cowardice, and rendered unfit for the use of arms, so that your life may be spared; which is now made doubly valuable by the danger to which you are daily exposed." Praise for Samuel's bravery is tempered by the dangers that remain, leaving Sarah to hope for a quick resolution: "Heaven grant the next Letters may be what we so earnestly pray for, which is first your safety, and next an intire subjugation of the insurgents, the rest we must endeavour to submit to." The full scope of the revolt has not yet registered, as she assumes that "the insurgents" will be subdued and the island will even-tually return to its former state. And even when Sarah and Samuel call upon higher powers for strength and guidance, they cannot hide their fear: "We set in our chairs, our eyes often meet, and we are each conscious that our thoughts are the same, but know them to be too terrible to communicate to one another; you are the subject, and who can venture to express even to the partner of every pain and pleasure what the mind can scarcely bear to think on, one consolation Heaven has allowed to every reflecting mortal, that a Su-preme Being governs the universe, and that this lord of all the earth will do right."[22] Placing the situation in the context of providence allowed for some relief and understanding. The upheaval clearly underscored the sacrifices Samuel had made on behalf of his family.

On another topic and in response to the destruction of their property, Sarah reassures Samuel in this same July 14 letter that the family has begun economizing: "You will see by your father's Letter that he has taken every possible precaution to lessen our family expenses. The children are all at

Home, and Charles is learning Navigation." Mellen Chamberlain affirms these adjustments, noting as well the new school in Chelsea: "In 1795, when the news of losses in the West Indies arrived, the children were recalled from the boarding school in Medford; and the youngest received the rudiments of their education in this little schoolhouse."[23] Sarah also relates her concern that her husband will need to leave for Grenada: "Your father talk'd seriously of quitting us, a more deliberate and cooler reflection convinced him of the in-utility of such a step; I thank God for it; and rejoiced to see that part of your Letter, wherein you say that you do not see any necessity for his presence." She then conveys their gratitude for his actions: "I am happy to tell my dear Sam that his father approves intirely of his conduct; your securing the sugar and rum, shipping it, sending the Bill forward, and securing the safety of the poor negroes, as far as it was in your power, are steps that prove to him he has a Son, in whom he can confide, and who would in every point act as well as if he was on the spot himself." Struggling to understand the magnitude of the revolts, Sarah adds a note two days later: "16th July upon looking over the above, I am dissatisfied with it all, if however you are in as bad a situation in your island as my fears represent, to my imagination, my letter will be in unison with your feelings, if otherwise you will make allowance for my fears and the gloominess of my letter, the result of my anxiety for you— farewell, my dear Sam, Heaven bless and preserve you, and allow us at least the hope of meeting in some future day together."[24] Although these events were far more indicative of a radical change than just a momentary disruption, Sarah intuited the grave dangers Samuel faced, even as she offered hope.

Throughout this unstable situation, Samuel continued to reassure his family of his safety while also charting the chaos that ensued. On August 12, 1795, he begins a letter to his father from Grenada on board the "Schooner Wilmington" by noting, "Opportunities from this are so rare that I cannot write so often as I wish," then proceeds to explain that the "rebellion" has not yet been "quelled": "We have remained at our posts on the sea coast & except for a skirmish or two of no consequence, & cruising to prevent a supply of ammunition getting to the Brigands, no measure have been taken which lend to quiet the Commotions in this country." He also notes, "Sickness had carried off immense numbers of the Militia & Regulars" and their expectation that "reinforcements" will arrive. Reflecting on the effects of the revolt on the slaves, Samuel writes, "What I look upon to be the most unfortunate Circumstance attending this business next to some of the negroes joining the Brigands, is the idle state the rest of the negroes are in, for if we are successful in getting back the island they will be so much at cross purposes with us that it will be a long time before we shall be able to discipline them again." Consistent with his previous comments, Samuel assumes that Grenada will eventually return to its former state, and he worries about how the revolt will affect disciplining the slaves. He then provides another similarly distressing report: "Several of your negroes have died since I brought them to town, & Gahagan finds himself unable to feed them for their work. I have therefore got them over at our wharf & employ them in bringing grass to support themselves for I can persuade no proprietor to take them & feed them."[25] In the context of protecting the family's property, Samuel appears to interject some level of humanity by noting the deaths of some of the Africans and attempting to find some means of support for those who survived.

The Cary family, meanwhile, continues to gain perspective from their home in Chelsea. Sarah thus writes to Samuel on November 13, 1795, "Our last accounts from you were 12th August among other anxieties attending our situation think what we suffer upon your account not only in regard to your personal danger, exposed as you have been, and for ought I know still are, but because you are not engaged in any particular line of business satisfactory to yourself and us." Whereas earlier discussions of Samuel's discontent had brought philosophical responses about submission for the sake of future benefits, Sarah now considers Samuel's wishes in a new light, especially with the possibility of Grenada no longer being a viable source for his employment. "You tell us to be easy upon your account," she continues, "that you shall not only be able to fix yourself in business, but assist your brother, this is acting the part of a good Son, and Heaven will doubtless reward you for it. Could you know all we suffer, the sleepless nights, and hours of unavailing anxiety that your father passes in thinking of you, you would allow that your own Idea of his feelings falls far short of the reality." This admission of their own fears reveals a shared burden on both parents and son, especially now that their plantation may fail altogether. Sarah acknowledges that the family's economic future is in jeopardy: "Add to this the situation of Mt. Pleasant, hitherto our whole dependance, and a fund as we thought, and had reason to think, for education, and some little fortune for our Children." She now sees the serious repercussions of the revolt and begins to understand that their fortunes have been significantly reversed. Still, Sarah tries to find some hope while remaining realistic: "Altho by your last Letter the works were still standing, yet it will be a long while before things come into their old channel, the loss of Negroes, the still more certain loss of Mules Cat-

Sarah Cary to Samuel Cary Jr., Chelsea, November 13, 1795. Cary Family Papers III, Collection of the Massachusetts Historical Society.

Nov. 13th 1795 —
My dear Sam

The last letter I received from you was dated 4th Sept. 94 — do not think I mean to upbraid you for letting so long a time elapse without writing me again, you have written your father & that is the same thing as writing to me, but if I were disatisfied with that the situation of the times in your island would sufficiently exculpate you from any blame, Our last accounts from you were 12th Augst. among other anxieties attending our situation think what we suffer upon your accot not only in regard to your personal danger, exposed as you have been, & for ought I know still are, but because you are not engaged in any permanent line of business satisfactory to yourself and us, over and above this, the pain of not being able to give you any assistance, this you are fully sensible of, & endeavour in all your letters, in imagination at least, to become yourself a father, that you may know what He feels in having a beloved Son situated as you are, you tell us to be easy upon your account, that you shall not only be able to fix yourself in business, but assist your brother, this is acting the [. . .]

tle, and etc.: and destruction of the dwelling and negroe Houses; with the loss of the last Crop (excepting what my dear Sam at the risque of his life secured for us) and necessary expense which must attend the next, with many other similar circumstances that are yet to come to our knowledge."[26] Although her immediate response to the revolts was shock and dismay, Sarah now tried to see forward to a better situation.

Aftermath: Evaluating the Mount Pleasant
Estate and Waiting for Reinforcements

With Samuel Cary Sr. now fifty-two and Sarah forty-one, the prospect of having to start any new enterprise was daunting, and their dependence on Samuel Jr. only increased. To avoid the possibility that her husband would "be obliged to go to Grenada," Sarah hoped instead that they might retain Mr. McCarthy, who "seems to be a good man in whom we may place a confidence." In her letter to Samuel, she offers an assessment of the manager's role and advice about McCarthy's salary, which, she argues, "ought to be raised so as to make it an object to him to go there again, when things are reinstated as formerly; Managers will be scarce after the loss of so many good Men." If Samuel and McCarthy could contain the damage, Sarah thus suggests, they might prevent the need for her husband to make the journey to Grenada: "At any rate do all you can to retain McCarthy. He knows the disposition of the Negroes, and from his so readily accompanying you to the plantation in such a moment of danger, shew him self attach'd to your father's interest, and by his writing and manner of speaking of the Negroes, in his former letters, I judge him to be a humane man a qualification of the highest importance." In a passage that echoes sentiments of the plantation manual Samuel Cary had written twenty-one years earlier, in 1767, Sarah notes the importance of a humane manager. She is also aware that should their plantation revenue collapse, they will need to survive solely on the Chelsea farm, which has yet to yield a substantial profit: "This is our third year of managing this farm, and probably by living upon it and attending to the direction ourselves, we shall secure a comfortable livelihood when other resources fail."

Aside from Sarah's immediate concern for the Carys' finances and for Samuel's safety, she had larger concerns about the family's overall direction. Along these lines, in the same letter, Sarah again notes the family's efforts to economize: "We have a small school house close by where the children are taught reading, writing and arithmetic. While your father and I remain together, superintending their education together with the business of the farm <u>the whole will flourish</u>." As Sarah continues to worry about her husband returning to Grenada, she tells Samuel, "Should a separation take place, <u>I know not the consequence</u>, His loss <u>would be irreparable</u> if the whole devolves on me I doubt, <u>greatly doubt</u> my ability to discharge so important a trust." As she once again acknowledges the family's indebtedness to Samuel, she holds on to the possibility of a better outcome at Grenada: "Think of this my dear Sam, should you be so fortunate as to quell the dreadful rebellion in your island." Still, she acknowledges, "There is a stagnation to all business, and since writing the above, your father has seen Mr. Stewart from there who has given such a deplorable account of the destruction of property, want of provision and etc., that I am almost tempted to throw aside my pen, and indeed I must, for what can I say— our apprehensions are greater than I can express, and still encreased by our not hearing from you." She remains hopeful that the British reinforcements will arrive: "We are told of troops having gone out and being immediately divided between Grenada and St. Vincent. Heaven grant this may be true." From her perspective in Chelsea, Sarah tries to process all these various reports while maintaining a larger view that will help her family through the uncertainty. She then expresses concerns about both Samuel and his brother Charles, who is about to head out for the "east Indies": "Thus you see how the feelings of a parent[']s Heart are exercised, after ten thousand cares in bringing them forward to manhood, and the flattering expectation of their society as a compensation, duty, inclination, or necessity steps in, and by a separation precludes the most pleasing hopes."[27] Sarah's reactions to these events thus went from fear to recognition, and in the process, she conveyed deep respect for Samuel's efforts.

Any hopes for resolution, however, were soon dismissed, as Samuel's reports exacerbated their concerns. In the same week that Sarah was writing to Samuel, he sent a letter to his father, on November 18, 1795, with this dire account: "Misfortunes are come thicker upon us, and this insurrection which a vigorous effort would have quashed in its infancy is likely to deprive almost every proprietor in the island of half his fortune." He then expresses his disappointment and frustration with the lack of reinforcements: "The troops expected from Gibraltar mentioned in mine of the 12th August passed by to St. Dominigo and those from England instead of the seven thousand expected amounted but to 2400, — of which about 1800 were sent to St. Vincent, some kept in Mtque, and 300 sent here to strengthen our posts till the arrival of General Abercrombie who is now looked for with 25,000 men for these islands and St. Domingo. — At St. Vincent they have done almost nothing, either from the timidity of the Commanding or their Inexperience." Nine months after the revolts began, Samuel thus relays a bleak situation. Even when troops do arrive, the situation appears overwhelming: "After the landing of the men from the Brig the enemy projected an attack upon Gouyane, and, although the hill above Gouyane House was fortified, and that above 200 effective men were stationed on and about it, it was taken in the night without a dozen shot being fired." Adding to this loss is a general sense of vulnerability and an alarming lack of security: "The Officer commanding at that post had warning the day before of the preparations making by the enemy, yet he placed only 36 men on the hill, the rest slept below at the Gouyane house and in the town." Samuel's account not only parallels the historical record about the lack of adequate defense and the haphazard retreat, but also provides specific details from his eyewitness perspective: "So shamefully precipitate was the retreat, that 100 sick men were left in the hospital; and even after they left Gouyane so fast did 200 men armed and accoutered hurry to town that several women and others who attempted to follow them were left by the way, and some were killed by the negroes, and some taken up along shore by the Cruisers." As a result, the "100 sick Soldiers" became "prisoners of war." Amid this disarray, Samuel notes additional frustrations: "Fedon still continues in his command in the mountains and the whites are it is said stationed at Gouyane which they are fortifying the hills about."

As they waited for reinforcements from General Abercrombie, questions prevailed. Samuel addresses his uncertainty to his father: "We are yet to know how far the force of arms will succeed in laying this unquiet Spirit of Insurrection." In expressing disapproval of the "Insurrection," he again conveys the prevailing attitude that these events were not only unwarranted but potentially disadvantageous for the slaves: "Those negroes who have tasted the charms of a Life of Indolence free from controul will return with bitter reluctance to their former Subjection." This could be read as either a justification for or a criticism of slavery, and either way, it would seem unlikely that the Africans would willingly return to slavery after experiencing some degree of freedom. Even if this passage is read as a lament to a former time and order, it seems impossible for Grenada to be restored to its previous state. Samuel then tells his father about the current condition of the slaves: "Your negroes are still in town and continue to feed themselves except a few, but I am sorry to say that we have lost since we got them to town a proportion of 1/6 of them by death. — The unhealthiness of the Hospital estate carried off some, and the Change from an active Life to a life of indolence made them sick afterwards." The Africans have suffered not only from the "unhealthiness of the Hospital," but apparently from "a life of indolence" as well, whereby slavery is depicted as "an active Life," even though the reference to "Your negroes" identifies the slave as property. In relaying this report to his father, Samuel's conjectures about slavery, however justified, seem out of place in the larger context of the rebellion.

Regarding his own heath, Samuel notes, "I fell sick myself (tho' I thank Heaven I am partly well now)." He also comments on Mr. McCarthy and the slaves' situation: "McCarthy who is much changed from that attentive man he was on the estate, neglected them." That McCarthy, who was once an "attentive man," now "neglects" his duties suggests another effect of the revolts. Samuel then remarks on a general indifference and describes his attempt to provide medical treatment for the slaves: "A Spirit of military emulation for a long time pervaded all ranks of people and made every one in some degree remiss in his attention to his business, and amongst others the medical men equally, so that altho' I hired a Doctor they did not receive that Care that was necessary." Having critqued the inadequate medical attention to the Africans, Samuel notes, "Those who remain, however are faithful and well-inclined, which is a thing very few men can say of theirs and there is reason to hope from the good health they have been long in, that we shall lose no more." Again, a sense of concern is expressed alongside a confirmation of ownership. As he praises the slaves' faithfulness, Samuel draws a comparison to other slaveholders that may imply some degree of criticism. He then adds an overview: "Indeed we are far from singular in our loss, — every man who has been able to get his negroes in hand lost some more, some less. — Mr. Webster had got most of his negroes in at Gouyane, but was obliged to leave them at the evacuation. — Mr. Barry found by a list of one of the enemy's companies taken at one of their posts that at least twenty of the Soubise negroes had taken arms at that Company alone." The rebellion had thus led to a general state of confusion and a widespread loss of life and property. Samuel then reports directly on the family's plantation: "Mt. Pleasant works are still standing and there is no fear now of their being destroyed. — I am endeavoring to get the accounts together from the merchants, that I may see how we stand— the day book was saved." So, even though the houses were destroyed, that the sugar works remained suggested the possibility of restoring their plantation.

Though Samuel had yet to grasp the far-reaching effects of the revolts, he held out hope for restoration of some sort. He also considered how these events would potentially affect his family's financial and social standings and their subsequent need to adjust accordingly. In doing so, he anticipated that Bostonian society may not be as welcoming as they had been when the Cary family first returned from Grenada. But Samuel remained calm even as he took on yet more obligations. Thus, in a postscript to his mother, he writes, "We shall see better times soon I hope and when this Storm is over, we shall enjoy ourselves the more, although our fortune be reduced." He also tries to console his sister Margaret with this perspective: "In these hard times when misfortune obliges us to retrench our expences, and flattery turns her back, how do I feel for you who have been so little accustomed to adversity.— The deprivation of amusements, the omission of those little attentions so flattering I fear you undergo, and if to these is added any neglect from those who a few months ago would have thought themselves honoured in your Society it must require the greatest exertion of your Spirit to spurn at such fortune." Here, he again notes the long-term effects on his family, whose status will no doubt be dramatically altered. Still, he remains confident that Margaret will adapt: "But I confess I am in the wrong to doubt you. — Your long Society with your dear mother, added to your own Sweetness of disposition, will certainly enable you to bear up against the times, and bury all mortifications in the consciousness of your own rectitude of Conduct."[28] Now, it was his turn to provide moral support, as the family's financial resources were threatened and prospects dim. In providing solace, Samuel also acknowledged the difficulties that lay ahead. As a result, the pressure on Samuel as the eldest son only intensified, and he would thus continue to defer his own ambitions and desires for the sake of his family.

Meanwhile, as the British waited for reinforcements, which would eventually arrive in June 1796, economic development in Grenada had been significantly interrupted, as crops were destroyed and planting suspended. Edward L. Cox elaborates on the losses: "Sugar-works, rum-works, and other buildings on sixty-five sugar estates and thirty-five coffee estates perished, about 7,000 slaves died in action, were killed for complicity in the rebellion, or were deported, while island losses reportedly totalled upwards of £2,500,000 sterling between 1795 and 1798." The revolts not only disrupted the Grenadian sugar trade but also anticipated future antislavery efforts. Michael Craton calls the rebellion "the most remarkable episode," one that "paralyzed Grenada for almost two years." David Brion Davis underscores historic significance of the events: "The major revolts in British St. Vincent and Grenada in 1795–96, which were part of the Anglo-French struggle for the Caribbean following the French edict of emancipation in 1794, destroyed more British lives and property than any other slave uprising in the history of British slavery."[29] With production curtailed and the settlements in disarray, the island's sugar trade would continue to struggle.

Assessment and Recovery:
The Cary Family, Grenada and Chelsea, 1796–1797

In the years immediately following the slave rebellion in Grenada, the Cary family focused on their financial recovery. With Mount Pleasant out of production for the next few years, they immediately began imposing a set of restrictions to further reduce expenses at home in Chelsea. Caroline Curtis summarizes some of the changes: "The losses in Grenada changed the whole aspect of life at the farm. The children were recalled from school, and strict economy was practiced from this time. Aunt Margaret's English education enabled her to serve as governess to the younger sisters, and also to the boys as long as they could remain at home." The children's education was thus curtailed, and Samuel's and Sarah's lives were similarly altered, as Curtis also notes: "My grandfather returned from his expedition to the West Indies a poor man, and so remained till his death. From this time the heads of the family remained stationary at Chelsea, two absolutely devoted people one to the other, and having their interest with the outside world maintained by the coming and going of their children." Once secure in their finances, the Cary family was now faced with living on a far more modest income. Curtis remarks on Samuel Cary's difficulty in adjusting to these changes: "With our grandfather's character and previous life of prosperity and importance on a plantation, the change to reduced means and to all the sacrifices necessary in such a great family of children must have required him to exercise a constant restraint upon himself."[30] For Sarah, the desire to have the family nearby was often at odds with the need to shore up their finances, which meant that the eldest sons would most likely be away in search of new avenues for income. Throughout, Sarah Cary continued to manage a large household, with eleven of her thirteen children still at home, their ages ranging from one to twenty years old.

In April 1796, Samuel returned to Chelsea from Grenada to recuperate for one month before relocating to Philadelphia. Margaret Cary provides additional details about Samuel's departure from Grenada and pending business venture, noting that he "commenced business there in company with a friend whom he had known in the West Indies who was related to the gentleman who discovered Sam in one of the islands, I think Tobago, after the insurrection in Grenada, in which Sam had an active part in a regiment under government, and lost his health." Exactly how Samuel arrived at Tobago is not clear. Margaret simply notes, "This kind friend gave him the means and sent him home to Chelsea, and afterwards encouraged his going into business at the South."[31] On May 11, 1796, Sarah writes to Samuel about his recent visit, the first since the family had left Grenada five years earlier, and describes his stay as "a pleasing dream" that has "left a sweet impression." She especially values his visit considering the dramatic events that preceded his return: "To enjoy luxuries we must endure hardships, had I never known the pain of absence, I could not have been susceptible of so exquisite a delight as your return afforded me." Regarding Samuel's move to Philadelphia, Sarah notes, "Even your departure has occasioned no alteration in the calm serenity of my mind, now that I have seen and conversed with you, and know that you are engaged in transacting Business agreable to yourself, and that your Health is fast approaching, you have left me nothing to regret but that I did not accompany you down to the ferry along with your Father; a satisfaction from which I should have derived much pleasure." Additionally, she commends his decision to forgo the Boston social scene: "You were lucky not to be troubled with feasting at large parties, by residing all the time at Home, and so escaped invitations; these would have delayed the progress you were making in the recovery of your Health, and besides but ill suited I believe with your inclinations, which I wish you may be as able to follow at Philadelphia." She also hopes that his health will continue to improve: "The perfect recovery of your health depends on temperance and regularity . . . your Health is of the highest importance to yourself and us." Overall, Sarah is optimistic about Samuel's prospects, despite the family's financial uncertainty, and she concludes by once again noting his important role in the family: "By your care of yourself, you make your own fortune, and remake (if I may be allowed such an expression) that of your Fathers; besides what is of more consequence, save him the trouble of going to the West Indias, and me the pain, the inexpressible pain of parting with him."[32] Even as she worried about her husband's potential return to Grenada, Sarah remained supportive of her son's endeavors.

Samuel was also hopeful that the business venture in Philadelphia would prove successful. On May 1, 1796, he writes to his father from New York about his journey, beginning with the first stop in Boston, where "there was a petition signing to Congress the object of which was to obtain an accomplishment of the B. Treaty, to which amongst the most respectable names of Boston I added your's, thinking you would not be willing to go over for that purpose merely." Samuel refers here to the Treaty of Amity Commerce and Navigation between His Britannic Majesty and the United States of America of 1795, also known as the Jay Treaty, which was being widely debated prior to Congress passing an appropriation bill. Of particular concern for merchants were the limitations placed on American trade in the West Indies. The fears of war with England, however, contributed to its passage. In Boston, Samuel also visited several of his father's business associates, including Mr. Codman, Mr. Kemble, and Mr. Hays, who provided him with "a most handsome letter to Anthony and Co. of Philadelphia," accompanied by a recommendation: "You may place the highest confidence in whatever Mr. Cary offers, and which I will guaranty in its fullest extent." In New York, he set about organizing his finances but was only "able to draw but 2000 dollars in Gold from the Banks. . . . In Philadelphia I am informed there is more gold, — but the Banks are so wary I am much afraid I shall make a losing voyage.— If I find that I can do nothing at Philadelphia I shall be off directly."[33]

A month later, in June 1796, Samuel left Philadelphia for the West Indies, where he turned a profit by trading various goods. On his return voyage, he writes to his father on August 7, recapping his journey: "I got to Barbados after a passage of 37 days, on the 8th July, and took the first opportunity for Mtque." Financially, the trip appears to have been successful, "I bring with me near three times the Sum I had before, to be employed various ways, and when it is expended I shall go out again." He then describes the beginnings of a new business partnership: "I have an offer to make to Mr. Bennett a gentleman formerly in business in Mtque, now unemployed in Philadelphia whose interest is equal if not superior to mine, to take half of the Business. — As our remittances go out to Mtque we shall have our Supply kept up so that it is likely a very large Sum may pass through our hands in a short time, upon which our Coms is 2 1/2 per cent, we paying our own expences." Knowing how any trade venture might go, he is cautiously optimistic: "The present is but a temporary business; but it may be the means of setting B. and myself up in America."[34] Samuel's guarded optimism speaks to the volatility of trade in the post-revolt years. Still, he remained confident. On this trip, moreover, Samuel did not travel the nearly two hundred miles to see Mount Pleasant: "I was not at Grenada,— not thinking it necessary to lose any time as it is not yet safe to return to the plantation." He then summarizes what has remained an unstable situation: "Fedon is not yet taken.— On the arrival of Genl. Abercrombie, troops were sent to Grenada which took and destroyed all the Camps of the Insurgents:— the Guadeloupe people surrendered and

Fedon fled into the thickest of the woods with a parcel of desperadoes who knew their death would be inevitable if they fell into our hands — These are not yet taken altho' parties have been out continually and a reward of £500 Stg. is offered for Fedon, who if we do not mind will give us the go-by yet." Having conveyed the uncertainty of Fédon's whereabouts, Samuel adds, "The rainy season being come on is in his favor, and people are apt to slacken in such a search after having looked for him a long time in vain."[35]

Various theories have been posited to explain Julien Fédon's disappearance. "It was rumoured that he drowned while trying to escape in a canoe to Trinidad," Duffy writes, "but there was another subsequent rumour that he was at Trinidad when Abercromby landed there in 1797 and that he escaped again." Craton notes, "Popular legend placed Fédon in Trinidad or Cuba, living incognito and waiting for his chance to return and lead the ultimate rebellion." Steele describes similar accounts of Fédon's movements, adding, "There is now some evidence that he hid sometimes in the mountains, and sometimes in Carriacou and in Petit Martinique before making good his escape by rowing out in a canoe to meet a vessel in the open waters off Grenada. This vessel took him to Cuba, where he lived for the rest of his life." Kit Candlin's assessment suggests another likely scenario: "Given the interconnectedness of relatives in Trinidad and Grenada, though, it was far more likely that he made his escape to Trinidad and lived there among his relatives and friends." Regarding both Fédons, Candlin and Pybus conclude, "No one can be sure what happened to him because his body was never found. While Marie Rose Fedon may have died in the fighting, there is circumstantial evidence to suggest that her husband escaped their defeat on Grenada in 1796 and moved to Trinidad to be with his relatives already living there."[36] Given the questions surrounding Fédon's disappearance, Samuel's hesitation to return to a still unstable Grenada made sense. In his August 7 letter to his father, he notes additional disruptions: "Just as I left Mtque a report was spread that some soldiers of a French sort of Emigrants lately from England had been tampering with the Negroes at Grenada.— In short although the Insurrection is nearly quelled, the tumult is not subsided,— nor tranquility so well established as that a man would be willing to go alone through the country." Considering this ongoing instability, Samuel decided not to risk the journey and instead contacted various associates, managers, and owners: "I therefore did not go down — but I wrote to Mr. Webster, Cooper, McCarthy, and Snagg, enclosing your letters and the power.— I told Snagg that I should want the Negroes when Grenada should be at peace— and if that should be the case before my return to deliver the Negroes to the other Attorneys upon their requisition."[37] Samuel thus postponed buying additional slaves as he continued to monitor the situation.

Samuel Cary Sr.'s Adventurous Return to Grenada, 1796–1797

Three months after receiving his son's letter, Samuel Cary left Chelsea for Grenada, in November 1796, to evaluate the family's plantation and to assess the damages. On November 11, while in New York waiting for passage, he writes to Sarah about the family's finances, with instructions to sell off their livestock: "In the memoranda left with you, please observe that there are three cows to be sold in the spring or summer. They are, I find as I came along, worth from forty to fifty dollars without the calf. I mention this as there is no price fixed to them, and as we sold them this year for twenty-five dollars I did not know but Mr. Low might think thirty a good price; but all kinds of stock have risen. All the calves are to be kept." He also mentions his sons' plans to do business in Philadelphia: "The more I think of it, the more I am convinced it is best for Lucius to go to Philadelphia, if sent for, and all of the boys, as they grow up, to go from home, painful as it is to part with them."[38] Samuel thus weighed the importance of his sons' contributing to the family income against the value of family unity.

Meanwhile, as the family awaited news of Samuel Cary's arrival in Grenada, a dramatic turn of events unfolded. Just three weeks after his departure, his ship was intercepted by the French and redirected to Guadeloupe. In his letter on December 26, he explains the delay: "I wrote to Sam on the 19th inst., informing our being brought into this island by a privateer on the 14th; and, as there is a vessel going in a day or two to Newburyport, I have obtained leave to write to you, thou dearest and best of women." He then describes their capture: "After being out twenty days from Philadelphia, we met with a small schooner that brought the vessel here; and here, except the being confined on board a guard-ship, we met with very kind treatment. The officers are all gentlemen, who have made our confinement as agreeable as it is in their power." Now taken captive by the French and temporarily detained, he optimistically adds, "We expect leave to go from this island in a few days; and before this is handed to you it is most likely I shall be at Grenada."[39] Albert J. Gares explains why in 1796–1797 Guadeloupe was especially dangerous: "The French continued their seizure of American vessels in the Caribbean. An *arrêt* by Victor Hugues, the 'tyrant of Guadeloupe,' on February 1, 1797, declared neutral vessels and cargoes 'good prize' if destined for

Windward and Leeward Island ports captured by the British." There were political implications in addition to financial motives: "In March, 1797, it was further reported that Hugues had not only announced a French declaration of war on the United States, but that the 250 American prisoners allegedly held at Guadeloupe were treated 'far worse' than British prisoners because 'it was a favorite maxim with Hugues that the British were enemies, but the Americans were a pack of double-faced rascals.'"[40] The seizure of Samuel Cary's ship appears to have been a prelude to future danger.

Thus caught in these struggles for control of the waters, Samuel Cary managed to stay calm. Perhaps as a way to cope with the situation, in his December 26 letter to Sarah, Samuel cites and paraphrases passages from various plays that express his emotions and mirror his dilemma, including Thomas Southerne's *The Disappointment, Or, the Mother in Fashion: A Play* (1684), "Oh, let my arms thus press thee to my heart, / That labors with the longings of my love, / Struggles and heaves, and fain would out to meet thee" (4.1); William Shakespeare's *The Tragedy of Othello, the Moor of Venice* (1603), "How poor are they that have not patience! / What wound did ever heal but by degrees" (2.3.376–78); along with quotations from David Mallet's *Mustapha: A Tragedy* (1739) and Nathaniel Lee's *Mithridates, King of Pontus, A Tragedy* (1678), which Samuel prefaces with "When I think of you I cannot help saying": "Tell me, O ye Powers, — / For I'll be calm, — was I not worthy of your care? / And why, ye gods, was Virtue made to suffer, / Unless this world be but as fire to purge / Her dross, that she may mount and be a star?" (4.1). Samuel also adds a message for his eldest daughter: "Tell my dear Margaret that every day at twelve o'clock, and many times oftener, I view her heart, although she has never made known its contents," which is followed by quotations from Sir William D'Avenant's *The Fair Favorite* (1638): "Who is it that will doubt / The care of Heaven, or think immortal / Powers are slow, 'cause they take the privilege / To choose their own time when they will send their blessing down?" (5.1). By drawing on plays based on classical and historical figures who question their own fate and seek guidance, Samuel Cary tries to shore up his strength. In a few closing remarks, he writes, "*28th.* We are still waiting to hear from Basseterre, where the general is. *29th.* We were sent here last night, and are now ordered to Basseterre. I have not time now to write to Sam; let him know the contents of this letter. From Basseterre we expect to be sent to Martinique. I am, best of women, yours most affectionately, Samuel Cary."[41] On this hopeful note, he awaited his release.

Meanwhile, Sarah writes to her son Samuel on December 23, 1796, addressing his insistent request that Lucius join him in Philadelphia as his apprentice, noting his "impetuosity" in making such a demand: "You express, also a sort of <u>astonishment</u> that Lucius had not come on, it is very true that you mentioned it, yet not positively, otherwise I should not have replied that 'I hoped not till spring' <u>you now</u> in your last, request that he may be sent on immediately, and immediately he shall be sent on, for painful as it is to me, to part with him, I am too sensible of the advantage he will certainly derive by being with you, to think of a refusal." Considering that Samuel had not spent much time with his brother except for the two years in Grenada, when Lucius was between seven and eight years old, Sarah also provides background notes on the younger brother's personality:

> Lucius has many fears, you will find him extremely reserved also and it is from <u>me</u> only that you must learn, that he thinks himself very ill calculated to serve you in capacity of a clerk; his advantages you know perfectly well have <u>been few</u>, he has perhaps received more information from your father the short time they were together, than at school; He has however, with this diffidence from which arise his fears, a <u>strong quick resentment</u>, and exquisitely tender feelings; such as he is I send him to you, be a father as well as a Brother to him; and believe I am perfectly satisfied with the Idea of resigning him intirely to your care, in short make him like yourself, I rejoice at your agreable prospects.

Sarah's description of young Lucius and directions to the elder Samuel communicate both her concern and her trust. She is confident that Samuel will take care of his brother, who needs only reassurance to dispel his "diffidence." With still no letters from her husband, Sarah adds, "I am in hopes your Father had a pleasant Voyage, there is nothing now that I wish for, but a letter from him; when I know he is safe arrived in Grenada, I shall be tranquil, and hope the <u>best consequences</u>, will arise from his being on the spot; that alone can calm my fears, and resign me to so painful an absence." She concludes by expressing relief that although Samuel could not return for the Christmas holidays, she is "now happy to find" that his business "is likely to be confined in good part upon this continent."

The tone of Sarah's letter apparently surprised her son, for in her reply on February 4, 1797, to Samuel's letter from January 6, she writes, "I was rather hasty perhaps in my condemnation of you the other day and like many other <u>irritable people</u>, the pain recoils at last on myself. Your apology so handsomely written, and so much what I wished and expected to receive from you, I feel myself the offender and am tempted in my turn to apologize to

Sarah Cary to Samuel Cary Jr., Retreat, Chelsea, December 23, 1796. Cary Family Papers III, Collection of the Massachusetts Historical Society.

I rejoice at your agreable prospects, I include you always in my prayers, I hope you do the same for me; I am convinced there is no satisfaction without religion; it gives a relish to all our rational pleasures,— & I am fully persuaded you never allowed yourself any others.— I am in hopes your Father had a pleasant Voyage, there is nothing now that I wish for, but a letter from him; when I know he is safe arrived in Grenada, I shall be tranquil, and hope the best consequences will arise from his being on the spot; that alone can calm my fears, & resign me to so painful an absence— we go on very well here, in want of nothing, altho it is pleasing to me to receive so kind an offer of yours I shall most certainly apply to you, if there be occasion; farewell, my dear Son let me hear often from you I intreat you, I shall pay the postage with pleasure. Margaret says she shall write you a long letter by Lucius.— We had talk'd of your passing XMas with us, but we were too sanguine in our expectations, it seems, you can never be more beloved & admired certainly in any house than you are in this, we must however submit to your time, & give up pleasure for the sake of your business which I am now happy to find is likely to be confined in good part upon this continent. —

Yr most affect Mother Sarah Cary —

P S

when you see Mrs. Breck & Mrs. Williams present my remembrances to them—

you." Having acknowledged their differences, she adds, "You have my fullest pardon therefore, and in future a hasty expression of yours, shall never give me pain, at least shall <u>never excite my anger</u>," then returns to the subject of Lucius: "You acted certainly right in preparing to receive Lucius, the moment I conceived that you earnestly wished to have him, I set all hands in motion around me; being convinced that when you found it necessary to have an apprentice, if Lucius was not ready, some one else must take the place." Finally, she addresses Samuel's specific comments: "'I presume you do not expect that by putting him with me, now he is of a warm temper he will leave me <u>tame</u>,' believe me my dear Sam I do not <u>wish</u> it and much less expect it, but <u>with you</u> and <u>by your example</u> I expect he will learn to <u>command</u> that warmth of temper which makes you and will make him so much more estimable for possessing it." Sarah also repeats concerns about her husband's silence: "I know I have no right yet to expect a letter from your Father, yet I have scarsely patience to wait that 3 or 4 weeks longer that you tell me of, before I can have a letter, from him; it is 3 Months this Day since his departure, but in my mind at least <u>3 years</u> and I fear it is not improbable he may be absent as many, <u>for one year</u> I would gladly compound, but am ill prepared for more."[42]

As Samuel Cary awaited release, he wrote to Sarah on January 4, 1797, from Basseterre, Guadeloupe: "We still remain prisoners, and when we shall be exchanged or get away it is impossible to say. We have met with civil treatment, but being confined here is painful; it is attended with a heavy expense, and how I shall pay it I at present know not." The situation is clearly discouraging: "Thus are all our plans frustrated, and at the time I am most wanted on the plantation I am kept from it, but I will not complain."[43] In 1797, as Michael A. Palmer explains, "Of more than 280 merchant vessels seized in the Caribbean that year, over 200 were taken by privateers based around the approaches to the straits between Cuba and Hispaniola. Over 60 were seized in the Lesser Antilles, virtually all by corsairs operating from Guadeloupe."[44] As Samuel's letter indicates, this disruption was already evident in early 1797. He provides more details about his situation on January 5: "We are allowed to walk about the town, and are boarding in a very good house. Our health and spirits are good, considering our situation." Next, he comments on meeting a friend of Samuel's and the ongoing interest in Demerara: "There is nothing that gives me so much satisfaction as that our son is fixed in America. I met a friend of his named Brummell, who has made a purchase at Demerara, and, he thinks, a fortune. He was at sea, bound to Liverpool for his health, poor young man. I wish he may reach the land. For all Demerara, I would not see Sam in such a situation." A similar scenario had drawn him to St. Kitts in 1763 in search of wealth, but he now understood the larger picture, the sacrifices of health for the promise of fortune. Samuel Cary then turns to his son with praise and includes notes about his family: "Sam is all I could wish. Heaven will bless him for his attention to me. Let all my children know how kind he was to me. If the prayers of a father are heard, he will be blest. I want a letter from you, to hear something of the school, the dyke, the farm, Mr. Low, etc., etc." Samuel thus expresses frustration for being held captive, gratitude for his son's help, and interest in household matters. In closing, he describes a chance meeting of their former slave Pompey: "I was much surprised when the commissary ordered us on board a small sloop at Point Peter to come to this place, to meet Pompey. The poor fellow was glad to see me, but soon showed his pain when he found I was a prisoner, and he was suffered to stay but a few moments. He has promised to go to Chelsea as soon as he arrives." In Margaret Cary's later recollections, she also describes this encounter, whereby her father "recognized a former negro servant, Pompey, who had come from Grenada with the family, and lived some years at Chelsea." She then interjects, "It was to Pompey's violin that the children had often danced in the west parlor." Returning to Samuel Cary's narrative, Margaret reports: "His master signed to him not to approach, but in his walk, passing near him, said, in a tone and manner only to be observed by Pompey, 'When you reach America, go at once to Chelsea, see your mistress, and tell her I am a prisoner, but hope to procure safe release.' Pompey executed his commission faithfully."[45] Samuel's encounter with Pompey, in turn, shows an interesting change of their situations, with Samuel a prisoner and his former slave volunteering to relay his situation to Sarah at Chelsea.

These experiences continued to prompt Samuel Cary toward reflection, as he again cited various literary and historical works. On January 21, 1797, he begins with a passage from Donald Campbell's *A Journey Over Land to India: Partly by a Route Never Gone Before by Any European* (1795), which Campbell addressed to his son Frederick as a series of letters recounting a four-year adventure. At one point, he was shipwrecked in the Indian Ocean and subsequently imprisoned. Cary quotes from "Letter XXI," in which Campbell is traveling from Bavaria through Tyrol Country: "Here Providence seemed to speak in language most persuasive: 'Come, silly man, leave the wild tumult and endless struggle, the glittering follies, the false and spurious pleasures which artifice creates to seduce you from the true. Dwell here, and in the lap of Nature study me. 'Here, oh here!' exclaimed I, in a transport which bereft me for a time of every other consideration, 'here will I dwell forever.'" Having heard this voice, Campbell reflects, "I hung my head in sorrow, offering up a prayer to protect my family, strengthen myself, and bring us once more together."[46] With this passage about a change of attitude toward adventures and dreams of fortune, Samuel appears to reflect on his own reversals of fortune. Without commenting directly on the quotation, Cary later adds, "I began with a sentiment of Mr. Campbell's from his 'Journey Overland to India,' which I have in one of my letters requested you will give our children an opportunity of reading."[47] Samuel's capture also appears to have affected his attitude toward the rebellion. For example, he references his remarks on January 4 about being "met with civil treatment" while captive: "I have, perhaps, in some of my letters, said too much in favor of Citizen Hugues for those that are sore with losses; but depend on it I have wrote you no more than the truth, but remember the truth is not always to be spoken. You'll therefore keep what I have wrote to yourself. I will, when I get from this, write my son Sam a letter that he may make public." Then, after a month and a half, Samuel Cary is finally able to report: "We are told that a flag is to be sent from this to Martinique the day after tomorrow, in which we prisoners are to go."[48]

For Sarah, the stress of not knowing her husband's fate weighed heavily. In her letter on February 4, 1797, to son Samuel, for example, she comments on the attraction that the West Indies has for merchants in general: "Yet I know how rare it is for a man to prescribe limits to himself in regard to his stay in the West indies and altho' I have lived there so many years I cannot account for that fascinating power that leads and so misguides the Judgment. They are all birds of passage, and always say they shall quit the Country the next year, yet years roll on and their resolution not put in practice." Referencing a misleading "fascinating power," Sarah thus characterizes this attraction as a form of addiction, one that tests "resolution" with a promise for riches. From Sarah's point of view, the family's ongoing connection with the West Indies continued to be problematic. Two weeks later, on February 17, she includes this postscript: "Long since the above was written you must have been informed of your father's unfortunate Capture— I have just received a second letter from him dated 21ˢᵗ Janry informing me that he was to be sent in a Flag to Martinique, the very next day— He writes in spirits and is very well, but laments the cruel delay to his affairs." She also notes that his father "has written you several times," and that "Mr. Bennett sets off Monday— and we shall most impatiently wait your coming after he gets Home."[49] In a letter that began with an apology for "hasty" criticisms of her son and expressed anxiety over her husband's absence, Sarah now tries to remain optimistic.

Samuel Cary's capture, trial, and release were subsequently reported in several sources. Margaret Cary notes that her father was "tried for his life by Louis Fedon, an upstart into whose hands was placed temporary power" and pressured "to declare himself a subject of the United States, in order to save his life; but this he refused to do, knowing that he was a British subject owning property in Grenada, though born in Massachusetts, not having become naturalized since the Revolution. But happily, as nothing could be found against him, and probably the firmness of his spirit was respected, he was allowed to depart in an exchange of prisoners." A similar account appears in Mellen Chamberlain's *A Documentary History of Chelsea*, with additional commentary: "The negro insurrection of 1795 in the West Indies imperilled and chiefly destroyed the value of Mr. Cary's property in Grenada. To rescue it he went thither; but on the voyage he was taken prisoner by the French, and only with great difficulty saved his life. On his return to Chelsea he was obliged to accommodate himself to new circumstances."[50]

Samuel Cary finally arrived at St. George's in Grenada on January 30, 1797, and sent Sarah a report in a letter on February 4: "Left Guadaloupe the 24th, and after two days and two nights with 60 prisoners got to Martinique was kindly received by Mr. Higgins, left that at 5 o'clock in the afternoon the 28th in an armed schooner and at one o'clock the next morning was attacked by a privateer which we expected would have carried us back but after firing and receiving our fire until 7 the next morning left us to pursue a Brig coming out of St. Vincent." Having described his uneasy escape, Samuel turns his attention to the Mount Pleasant estate: "I don't know what to say to you about the Plantation, nothing can be made this year and I fear very little the next, we have lost 30 Negroes and have only 50 left." He then reports on the current cost of food and supplies: "The island is in want of every thing fish at 8 dollars and Mules from £40 to £45 Sterling, the fleet not arrived yet from England." After noting that he had converted a mule pen into temporary housing, he speculates on their future: "I hardly know what to write, nor can I tell you just my situation, the Large Estates will soon do well who have money to buy stock." In search of an owner, Samuel "mentioned to young Sandbach the buying of our Plantation but he has nothing nor will he do any thing while his uncle lives for fear of offending him," young Samuel is Samuel Sandbach's nephew. Cary then provides an assessment: "Industry and economy may do great things, but we are weak not having one Mule left that I have my doubts, if I could see Sam we might come to some determination, at present we are weeding the lanes for next year that is for 1798." Despite a two-year interruption of income from the estate, Samuel adds words of encouragement: "But you must keep up your spirits and go on with your attention to the Children and be assured I'll do all I can to get back." He also acknowledges Sarah's role in maintaining the farm at Chelsea: "It gave me great pleasure to find the dyke was completed and that you so easily settled, you must take all on yourself." Regarding the potential departure of Mr. Low the next summer, Samuel advises that he attend to the colts and cattle, repair walls, and put up fences. In relaying these orders, Samuel is again confident that Sarah will carry out the plans: "I am sure you will do what's right and I am and always shall be pleased with whatever you do."[51]

A month later, Samuel writes to his wife, on March 15, 1797, with an overview of the plantations and an assessment about the general state of affairs in Grenada, which he finds discouraging: "The plantations are coming about again though slowly; next year there will be good crops." In addition to the slow return of crops, "the prospect of peace seems done away, therefore my return is now very uncertain; and the price of everything is great. The expense is beyond anything I thought of; and it was expected that at Trinidad we should find plenty of mules and cattle, but there is not any to spare; indeed, there never was a country in greater want of everything than this is." Regarding his own health, Samuel notes, "I have been down with a fever for fifteen or sixteen days, but by being brought to town, with the attention of my friends, I'm as well as ever." Anxious for the future, he again reinforces their dependence on their eldest: "If our dear son should come to this part of the world, I hope I shall see him, that we may come to some determination. If he is not sailed, keep him informed of what I write." The younger Samuel would set sail for Grenada on April 1 to assist his father. On the subject of the farm at Chelsea, Samuel Sr. expresses concern about Sarah being without assistance: "As to the farm, do the best you can. I hope Mr. Low will not leave you; but this I am sure of: that no one will do better than you can, and act yourself. Do as much as you can by shares; the less money you have to pay the better. Mention how the dyke land comes on." He then includes specific instructions about their crops, harvest, labor, wood, hay, and horses, and affirms his faith in Sarah regarding financial decisions: "I leave all to yourself."[52] With their plantation at Mount Pleasant in disrepair, the need for the Chelsea farm to

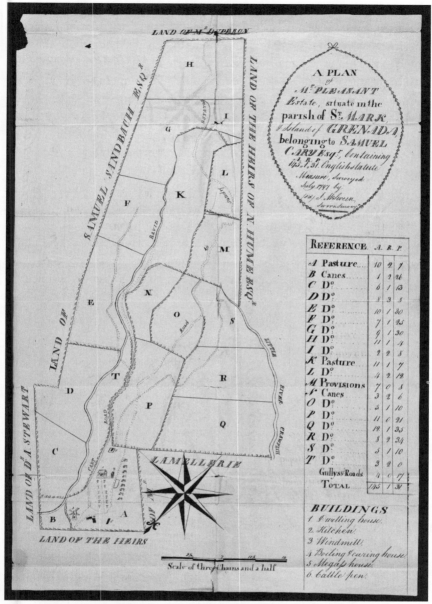

"A Plan of Mount Pleasant Estate; surveyed July 1797." Samuel Cary Papers, Collection of the Massachusetts Historical Society.

be profitable, if not solvent, was even greater. The increasing probability of selling their estate may have contributed to Samuel Cary's decision to commission a survey of the estate before he left Grenada. The title of the map, noted in the upper-right corner, reads: "A Plan of Mt. Pleasant Estate, Situated in the parish of St. Mark & Island of Grenada, belonging to Samuel Cary Esq., Containing 145.1.31, English statute Measure, Surveyed July 1797, by (s. d) J. McSween, Sworn Survey." Directly above the numbers "145.1.31" are the letters "A.R.P.," which stand for acres, rods, perches. In addition to listing rivers and roads, the map shows the neighboring estates of "Duperon; H[o]me (Waltham estate), Lamellerie, Sandbach (Respect estate), and Stewart (Industry estate)"; the survey map shows nineteen sections of "Pasture, Canes, and Provisions." Also included is a legend that shows six "Buildings: 1. Dwelling house; 2. Kitchen; 3. Windmill; 4. Boling & curing house; 5. Begass house; and 6. Cattle pen," which are all neatly delineated on the survey map.[53] Having completed his examination of the Mount Pleasant estate, Samuel Cary Sr. finally returned to Chelsea in June 1797, after a seven-month absence.

CHAPTER FIVE

Recovery and Renewal

Grenada and Chelsea, 1797–1810

In the aftermath of the slave revolts, the Cary family continued to regain their financial bearings. With Samuel Sr. and Sarah committed to their farm and household at Chelsea, Samuel Jr. and Lucius established trade throughout the West Indies and the Caribbean at Grenada, Martinique, Demerara, Barbados, and Bermuda. For the brothers, seeking their fortune would be challenging, and their struggles would mark a definite contrast to the assumptions about wealth that had drawn their father and grandfather to the West Indies in the first place. Samuel and Lucius would also encounter a new maritime reality, in which they faced not only the risk of wars interrupting trade, but also the constant threat of their ships being captured by privateers, as their father's recent experience illustrated. And though they generally conveyed a positive outlook, Samuel and Lucius continued to make sacrifices on behalf of the family. Any disappointment was always masked, however, by their strong sense of duty to their parents and siblings, which inspired them even as their own dreams of returning to America continued to fade. During this time, the family showed the strains and stresses of separation as they once again tried to sustain connections while living oceans apart. Throughout, Sarah Cary maintained a steady correspondence with both Lucius and Samuel, acting as mentor and confidant. This chapter follows the family's efforts toward recovery as they adjusted to their new financial situation.

Soon after Samuel returned from Grenada, he entered into business with Samuel Bennett in Philadelphia, where fourteen-year-old Lucius would then join them as an apprentice. On January 23, 1797, Lucius writes to his mother with an overview of his arrival and reunion with Samuel: "He received me very kindly and carried me to my Lodgings at the house of a Mrs. Baker — a Quaker — where I shall stay till Mr. and Mrs. Bennett come from Boston which will be in a month." Samuel Bennett and Ruth Dobel had married on November 23, 1796.[1] Lucius's daily routine included opening the store each morning and copying letters. Once Samuel "comes down about eleven," Lucius writes, "[We] go about business till one when we go to dinner— and come back at two— at night— we shut up store and go home." Summing up, he tells his mother, "Now I call this a very lonesome life — I have not a single acquaintance," and then as if to punctuate his dismay, he adds, "I have found no Circulating Library yet." James N. Green, librarian of the Library Company of Philadelphia, explains why Lucius could probably not find a library in January 1797: "The Philadelphia directory for 1797 shows two circulating libraries, John Chalk, circulating library, 75 North Third and John M'Donald, broker and keeper of a circulating library, 14 South Fourth St. . . . The directories show these businesses to be very short-lived. Chalk appears in the 1796 directory only in a supplement, and M'Donald not at all. There is another library in the '96 directory that appears in the removals listing at the front, meaning it had gone out of business since the directory was compiled."[2] Without books or friends, Lucius found the move disheartening: "I have been quite wretched since I left you for want of society but I have exerted all my philosophy and have almost conquered it."[3]

For Lucius, letters to his mother provided an anchor, and he was also more direct than his brother in seeking his mother's counsel and subsequent approval. On February 25, for example, he writes, "I shall mind what you say about acquaintances but my dear dear mother don't I beg be too frugal with your advice— don't suppose that I am one of your fine fellows that hate advice— I love it dearly, especially when it comes from such a mother as has not her equal in the world." On March 10, he shares a story about his visit to the theater: "I have also had the pleasure of seeing General Washington, Mrs. W, and Family, I could hardly believe my eyes when I saw this long wished for sight. I am now quite satisfied, for I was afraid they would go away before I could get a sight of them, but I was determined to see them if it cost me ever so much." Having established the scene, he elaborates: "It was not one of those momentary sights, it was a good long view, it was at the play. I had heard that they were going for the last time, so I thought I would go too, and it was very lucky for me that I did, 'tho if I had been ten minutes later I should not have been able to have got in, however I sat very near them."

There had been various announcements, for example, in the *Gazette of the United States*, on January 9, "the President of the United States, and Family, will honor, the Theatre with their company this evening," and in *Claypoole's*

American Daily Advertiser, on February 27: "We are informed that the President of the United States will be at the representation of the new comedy, *The Way to get Married*, this evening, at the New Theatre." This was most likely the performance that Lucius attended, for as he notes, "The play was called 'The Way to be married.' I liked it very well. I have also seen one called Columbus, which is a very good one." Thomas Morton's *The Way to Get Married: A Comedy, in Five Acts* (1796) and *Columbus: Or, a World Discovered: An Historical Play* (1792) were both advertised in the *Gazette of the United States*, as on February 27, 1797: "New Theatre. By Particular Desire. This Evening, February 27, Will be presented, (for the 4th time) a celebrated New Comedy. (written by the author of *Columbus, The Children in the Wood*, &c.) called The Way to get Married."[4] In such esteemed company, Lucius relished his play-going experience. He also reports on making "Acquaintances," and though he is pleased to have met the other "young Apprentices about our store," he also notes, "As for the female sex, I am such an awkward fellow and make so little impression on them, so that I have almost given them up." On July 1, 1797, he returns to this comment: "In one of my former Letters to you I said in the latter part of it 'that as I could make no impression on the fair sex, I was resolved to give them up,' this, no doubt carried a great appearance of levity with it and you might perhaps wonder what I meant, it was quite a mistake, for I meant to say that they could make no impression on me, for you know, being in Company would serve to take off that diffidence which I have, hanging about me."[5] Lucius was thus adjusting to his new life in what appears to have been an exciting environment, lack of female companionship notwithstanding.

While Lucius was in Philadelphia attending to the store, Samuel had departed for Grenada to assist their father. Lucius relays this information to his mother on June 1, 1797, adding this optimistic note: "We shall certainly see happier days yet My dear Mother, the Sun will shine as bright as ever and every thing will look as it used to.— We cannot expect to have all sweet we must have some bitter. The Roses wear thorns therefore my dearest Mother do not let your spirits fail you but look forward to that time when my Father will be with you and all your Children settled round you, for I am persuaded that time will come." As Lucius established his epistolary relationship with his mother, books were a frequent topic. On July 1, he includes his recent reading list: "the Lives of Mahomet, King of Prussia," "Voyages of Cook and Anson," "Travels of Hunter," "Histories of France by H. M. Williams, of Charles 12, Danish Masacre," "Letters of Chesterfield," and novels such as

"Montalbert, Fool of Quality" and "Charlotte or Tale of Truth."[6] Thus, after six months, he had apparently found a source for books.

Lucius's "Letters of Chesterfield" refers to *Letters Written by the Late Right Honourable Philip Dormer Stanhope, Earl of Chesterfield, to His Son, Philip Stanhope, Esq* (1774), which includes 410 letters, written between 1737 and 1768, and is part conduct book and part social commentary. *Letters* was controversial for what many deemed was a promotion of debauched behavior and for derogatory comments about women. These elements appear to have been lost on Lucius, who instead found inspiration, as noted in a letter on June 1: "Chesterfield somewhere says and very justly too I think that 'Of all the pleasures of which the human Mind is sensible there is none equal to that which warms and expands the Bosom when listening to Commendations bestowed on us by a beloved Object when we are conscious of having deserved them' this now is exactly my thoughts— but in another place he says 'Praise underserv'd is Satire in disguise.'" Although Lucius attributes the first quotation to Chesterfield, he is actually citing the narrator in Susanna Rowson's *Charlotte, A Tale of Truth* (1791): "Of all the pleasures of which the human mind is sensible, there is none equal to that which warms and expands the bosom, when listening to commendations bestowed on us by a beloved object, and are conscious of having deserved them."[7] As Lucius had also been reading "Charlotte or Tale of Truth," he appears to have confused his sources here. The conflation is interesting particularly because the two texts address such different audiences: one to a son who aspires to be a "gentleman," and the other to a female reader to warn of rakish intentions from male suitors. The other quotation that Lucius attributes to Chesterfield is actually from Alexander Pope, as Chesterfield writes in "Letter 38": "Mr. Pope observes very truly, that 'Praise undeserved is satire in disguise.'" Moreover, in Pope's *The First Epistle of the Second Book of Horace, Imitated* (1737), this line appears as a quotation from Horace, followed by a second line: "'Praise undeserv'd is scandal in disguise:'/Well may he blush, who gives it, or receives." Still, Lucius understood the main point, for he concludes: "I hope I never shall have any of this sort of Praise I shall always desire and expect to have my faults told me as well as my good Qualities and I know my Dear Mother will let neither escape, to obtain her good Opinion shall always be my Aim and to maintain it my Object, and if I can possibly deserve it I shall think myself happy." One month later, on July 1, Lucius catches his mistaken attribution: "I meant to have said that that line 'Praise undeserved is Satire in disguise' was taken by Chesterfield from Pope and by me quoted from Chesterfield,

C is certainly a good writer but I can't say that I understand all I read of his Letters."[8] Style over substance, then, had drawn him into *Letters*, which marks an interesting parallel to a comical scene in Royall Tyler's play *The Contrast* (1787), in which Billy Dimple's servant, Jessamy, also reads from the *Letters*.

In other developments, Lucius responds in his July 1 letter to the news of his father's return to Chelsea, which prompts both "rejoicing" and reflections "of the loss sustained in the West Indies." Perhaps related to these thoughts, Lucius's sensitivity about his financial obligations leads him to explain why he sent only "a ¼ of a Dollar" to be distributed among his siblings. Although his brother Samuel had been giving him "half a Dollar per Week for pocket money," it was inadvertently suspended when Samuel left for Grenada. Still, Lucius remains hopeful that when Samuel returns. "if I get the whole amount due for the time he has been absent, I shall have about eight or ten dollars, this however is a secret between you and I." Lucius thus acknowledges the expectation that he would be sending money home and conveys his sincere attempts to fulfill that obligation. On October 9, 1797, Lucius wrote from Bristol, New York, three hundred miles northwest of Philadelphia, where he had gone to avoid the yellow fever epidemic. Two months later, the epidemic had subsided, and by January 4, 1798, he was back in Philadelphia, writing, "The City is now perfectly cleared of the Yellow Fever and Philadelphia looks as bright as ever."[9] Lucius's first year in the city had thus proved eventful in both business and social spheres. Meanwhile, regarding the Mount Pleasant estate, Samuel Cary writes to his son, Samuel, on June 1, 1798, from Chelsea, enclosing a copy of a letter from John Campbell Sr. and Company, which now manages the plantation's debt: "My bill on them is still laying unsold and I know not how to raise $500." On a related financial matter, he notes, "If St. Domingo is declared independant as we are informed it is, or will be, sugar and etc. will be very low here and more than ever shipped for England." In closing, he describes ongoing preparations for Lucius to join Samuel in Martinique at some point: "I am to give the Captain a Bill on you for forty Dollars for Lucius's passage."[10]

Seeking Fortune, Again: Transatlantic Voyages and West Indian Ventures

In June 1798, Samuel Cary Jr. departed Martinique for England, an event that Sarah anticipates in a letter on August 25, 1798, directed to Lloyd's Coffee House in London, in which she refers to England as "the scene of your youthful Hours." Her letter opens with a question: "Is there then no period of our lives we can retrace without a sigh? alas no!" Regarding his career, she notes, "but I know you think a great deal, and untill you are fixed in some permanent way of business have much room for serious reflection." Sarah then comments on the West Indies in general, admitting, despite the drawbacks, "There is no way of life in which a gentleman and man of honor, may not lay up more useful reflection, and more substantial fortune." Perhaps as a counterpoint to these matters, she adds, "I congratulate you upon the progress I suppose you to have made on the Violin upon your passage." After noting that he has "a taste for music," Sarah offers advice: "Cultivate it as much as leisure from more important business will admit— it will sweeten in your journey through the rugged path of life, many a bitter Hour." Sarah also reports that his brother Charles "accepted a Birth as second Mate on board the Ship Newport Capt. Tube . . . bound to Virginia for freight, and from thence to London." Directly below Sarah's signature, Samuel Cary Sr. adds, "There was no keeping Charles at home and yet I fear his being taken as we are now at war with the French."[11] Samuel is referring to the Quasi-War (1798–1800) between France and America. Albert J. Gares elaborates: "During 1797 to 1798, relations between France and the United States were exceptionally inharmonious. French seizures of American vessels continued unchecked during 1797, with the result that in May, 1798, Congress empowered American cruisers to capture all French vessels that interfered with American commerce." This situation led Congress on June 13, 1798 to approve An Act to Suspend the Commercial Intercourse between the United States and France, and the Dependencies Thereof, whereby, as Gares explains, "Congress authorized American merchant vessels to defend themselves against search, restraint, or seizure by any armed vessel flying the French flag." Consequently, "American cruisers were directed to seize all French vessels wherever found. There began, therefore, an undeclared naval war between France and the United States which was to last for two and one half years and to cause the capture of several score of armed French vessels in West Indian waters."[12] As a result, trade was once again interrupted.

Samuel Cary Jr.'s return to the West Indies was delayed for reasons other than privateering, however, for his "ship sprung a leak," forcing him to wait for another vessel to Martinique along with "a change" of wind, as he explains from Lisbon on February 3, 1799. His delay caused the family to fear the worst, especially as others in his traveling party had found another vessel: "Mr. Stewart, Mr. Cumming and the ladies got into another ship some days before we quit the fleet, — and I have to regret, if regret were of any service, that I was not equally prudent." With letters crossing in the mail and reports of his ship now missing, Sarah writes to Samuel on March 29, 1799, directed to Martinique: "We are become impatient to hear from you, one of your vessels is said to be missing, the rest of the Fleet safe arrived." She then offers several possible scenarios: "The mind ever busy in creating trouble for itself, we have only one conjecture, which is that your Vessel is the one missing, for my part I am willing to hope for the best, and not to despond altho' the Vessel you may be in should be lagging behind, which is often the case in a Fleet, where one or more I know, often sail more heavily than the rest." This situation has made Sarah particularly reflective: "This morning looking over some letters of yours received during your apprenticeship in Grenada, and others after I quitted you and left that Island all strongly expressive of the tenderest and most exalted love, together with the neat small ring 'to filial affection' has 'awakened all the Mother in my soul' . . . how amply you have fulfilled my wishes respecting your conduct and manners since that period when by your letters it appears I express'd some doubts at leaving you at so early an age, yes, I know you incorruptible, and that to God and your own Conscience you will ever acquit yourself." Sarah thus affirms her love for Samuel and acknowledges her "doubts" about her June 1791 departure from Grenada. Samuel Cary Sr. writes on the same day that the family is "impatiently waiting for a letter from you." After a summary of various business transactions and notes, he adds, "Thanks for the papers, they gave me many particulars that did not appear in our papers."[13]

When Samuel finally arrived in Martinique on March 28, 1799, and did not find any letters waiting for him, he speculated that his father disapproved of his return to the West Indies and possibly of the dissolution of his recent Philadelphia business venture. The next day, Samuel thus reassures his father: "I will confess to you now another reason for coming here which you have not been aware of — I thought it might have been supposed that B and I were engaged in an improper business.— This misfortune might confirm the idea,— but my coming to Mtque must do it away entirely." He then elaborates on these new developments "of my accepting an Office which in two years must place me in a situation I might not attain in a long course of years in America. I am acting in company with Badge for Mr. Ross Jr. the Contractor for provisions for the prisoners of war here and in Barbados." In the same letter from March 29, Samuel adds a note on April 1 that he is relieved to receive his father's letter from Chelsea dated January 12, 1799, with his "approbation" regarding business matters. Samuel Cary Sr., in turn, sheds light on these issues, having just learned that: "Mr. Bennett had been sending gold to Martinique and had lost it all" and that "there was an end to the partnership and that you were not interested." He thus advises his son: "Bennett is no more to be trusted than a child and it will be a heavy Tax on you if you are still to be connected with him." Samuel Jr., in closing his March letter, comments on Lucius's pending journey to Martinique, and after weighing the merits of Boston with the potential dangers of the West Indies, he concludes, "Leave it to himself."[14]

Sarah is of mixed emotions regarding Lucius going to the West Indies. She thus writes to Samuel on June 21, 1799: "When I know that Lucius is in your hands I shall be reconciled to his absence; I see nothing equally eligible for him here, for separate from the difficulty of getting a place in Boston, should the Fever return there again, he must have come home, and should it not, the extreme rigour of the winter season would prevent my seeing him frequently." Having justified his departure, Sarah also makes a plea for family unity: "Those Mothers are happy who have their children always near them, and those who have not must submit to the necessity of their absence." Noting the "necessity" of her sons' absences, Sarah relays her husband's sentiments in this letter to Samuel: "The Business you have confided to him, has thrown his thoughts into a new channel, he is form'd for business, which he always undertakes with ardour. I am certain it will be serviceable to his health and spirits." These remarks, in turn, prompt Sarah to review her husband's career:

> Why did he leave it off? as you are not by me I will answer my self; His fidelity, punctuality, and honor, were too rarely met with amongst young Fellows of his age, and therefore seized upon by those Gentlemen of St. Kitts, and Friends of your Grandfather, and converted to their own use; in return therefore, and to fix his attention to the spot where their interest lay, they assisted him in the purchase of a plantation, in Grenada; for which piece of service or <u>disservice</u>, I am the last that ought to complain, because it was the means of bringing us together for life.

From Sarah's perspective, Samuel was "seized upon" by others rather than pursuing wealth solely on his own behalf. Sarah thus frames these beginnings as a test of Samuel Cary's "fidelity, punctuality, and honor." What had appeared to be a generous act to the young Samuel Cary in 1769, when John Bourryau arranged for him to purchase the Mount Pleasant plantation, is now, thirty years later, considered suspect, if not a "<u>disservice</u>." Sarah then concludes, "I will seal my Letter, before my good Lord reads it, for you men are apt to be vain of the good opinion of Ladies, and it is bad policy in a wife to let her Husband know to the full extent her good opinion of him, and so farewell!"[15] From Sarah's view, her husband acted courageously as he made his fortune, even though the islands bore heavily on his health and tested his character. As the third Cary son now sailed for the West Indies, Sarah would try to keep them all on the right path.

On June 29, 1799, Lucius arrived at Martinique. He reported from St. Pierre on July 3 that his passage of twenty days was "ten days shorter than any vessel now here has had from America." The journey had not been without some drama, though, as their ship, the *Sally*, had been under frequent threat of attack: "We were terribly frightened several times, every sail we saw was a privateer and we gave ourselves up for lost whenever one of them approached us, twice did I go below and put on all the Clothes I could, and put Citizen Beaujean's letter with Six dollars which I had left into my Shoes, however we got clear and are now safe at our destined port." Travel in the West Indies clearly remained subject to disruption. As Gares elaborates, "The prospect for American trade to the West Indies during 1799 to 1800 was not bright. The undeclared war between France and the United States was still in full swing, and depredations upon American vessels were committed persistently by both France and England."[16] Once safely landed, Lucius describes his reunion with Samuel as one "with all the kindness and affection I could possibly have wished or expected." While Samuel conducted business in Fort Royal, about twenty miles south of St. Pierre, Lucius stayed with Mr. and Mrs. Brady for the next two weeks and explored his new surroundings, describing them to his mother: "Saint Pierre is a pleasant place and about the size of Boston and contains 25 thousand people the streets are all paved with a gutter in the middle thro' which there is always a stream of water running." Lucius adds, "I now feel quite contended and happy and if I can only please my brother which shall be my utmost endeavor, and hear often from my dear parents I shall be perfectly so." He then turns nostalgic: "Now and then I feel a kind of regret and think how many happy days I have spent at Chelsea but I always stifle it with reminding myself how much it is for my good, how lucky it was for me that I went to Philadelphia, had I never left home I should now no doubt be indulging a foolish weakness." From this perspective, the West Indies appeared to be a more virtuous and industrious place for a young man than Massachusetts. On July 14, from Saint Pierre, Lucius sent more details to his mother about his arrangement with Samuel, who had returned to St. Pierre from Fort Royal: "My brother called me into his room this morning and told me that One hundred and twenty Pounds would be placed to the Credit of my account at the end of twelve Months beginning from the day I arrived, as an Allowance for Clothes and pocket money which he said I should find quite and not more than sufficient." Lucius is pleased with this arrangement and proceeds to explain how this money will be allotted: "This is exactly what I wished, it appears to me (at present) and will no doubt to you that £120 (267 Dollars) is a great deal too much but clothes here are very high; for the clothes I have had made here cost as follows — a coat (but a very handsome blue one at 5½ dollars per yard) Sixteen Dollars — 2 waistcoats, 3 shillings apiece and overhalls three dollars.— I am very well fitted now I think for Six or Eight Months."[17] Lucius also notes, "My brother goes to Barbadoes in about a week and I am to remain during his absence with Mr. Badge at Fort Royal." His next letter to his mother would thus be dated "Fort Royal, 4th August 1799."

Meanwhile, in his July 14 letter, Lucius describes a network of transatlantic merchants from London, Scotland, and America. To illustrate, he shares an anecdote about a tea at Mr. and Mrs. Brady's house, where he was introduced to Mr. and Mrs. Duncan Macintosh: "Mr. McI after asking me what part of Boston I lived in and being told in Chelsea inquired if I knew Mr. Cary there, I told him Yes and that he was my father— 'Mr. Cary your father, is it possible! — Ah! —You Mr. Cary's son.— Ay ay.— indeed!' he then began a long account of his reception at Chelsea, and of his little friends there, and among them his sweetheart Nancy." Lucius then adds, "It seems he got very little by his Grammars here, for he put them at 6 dollars apiece and no one would buy 'em." Duncan Macintosh and his two daughters were authors of *A Plain, Rational Essay on English Grammar*, a 239-page examination of the English language, from *"Martini'co, the 4th of July, 1797."* Having addressed several topics in one letter, Lucius remarks, "I am very sorry this is not written very well but there is a frenchman playing the fiddle in the house opposite and I cannot help keeping time with him." As he continued adjusting to his newest home, Lucius wrote again, from Fort Royal, on August 4 and thanked his mother "for mentioning the little incidents which happen in Chelsea," as they helped allay his homesickness: "I do indeed look back to the happy days which I have passed there and not only that but anticipate those of the future, of which I do not doubt there are plenty in reserve for us." Although it was difficult to leave home, he credited Samuel and Charles for their "behavior . . . in similar situations": "I was determined that the third Son should never be wanting in that fortitude which his brothers had so frequently shewn before him."[18]

While Samuel traveled to Surinam and Barbados, Lucius remained at Fort Royal and continued to ponder his future. On October 4, 1799, he responded to Sarah's August 30 letter containing career suggestions: "As for a Physician nothing would have been more opposite or more foreign to my feelings.— I cannot help thinking that there is always a fatality attending these things and that all we are to do in the whole course of our lives is determined long before we come into the world." Citing a degree of providence regarding his career path, Lucius remains firmly connected to his family's success. Meanwhile, he looks forward to visiting Grenada "to see how my father's estate comes on there," and yet he fears that scenes associated with "Innocence, Happiness and good humour" will be "too much altered." On December 3, 1799, Lucius provided his mother with a summary of his daily routine in which he rose at five, worked "till sunset," and ended the day: "Six to eight, Walking, eight to nine, Contemplating, Nine to five sleeping." He seems pleased with his job as a bookkeeper for Mr. Badge and has "lately been made Cash Keeper and received the key of the Iron Chest in due form; (which, (between you and I), I think shows a little confidence)."[19] He also notes that Samuel has gone to Grenada, which postpones Lucius's trip.

During this time, Mercy Otis Warren wrote to Sarah, on June 8, 1799, after recovering from an illness, and affirmed their friendship: "As I should have told you before that few things in this world would give me equal pleasure as an interview with my dear Mrs Cary." She then tries to convince Sarah to visit as a break from her domestic duties: "Then Come on my dear *Sally*. Leave the cares of Domestic education for a short time: and spend a few days with perhaps as affectionate a friend as any one you have on this side of eternity out of your own little family circle." She also sends regards to "Margerette," with whom she apparently shared an affinity regarding spiritual matters, as Margaret Cary was a follower of the Swedish philosopher Emanuel Swedenborg. On August 18, Mercy remarks on Sarah's character in response to a recent letter from July 13: "This like all I receive from Mrs Cary is replete with that tender interest that marks the mind of true friendship." Warren then provides an extended reflection on faith, death, politics, religion, and philosophy, followed by this remark: "How have I strongly verged to a subject totally out of my mind or design when I took up my pen to address my mild, domestic, pious, amiable friend. It would have been more natural for one to have discanted on your observation that 'the frequent absences from our children severly try the feelings of the mothers heart' but *mine* has been so often wrung[?] by the circumstances of separation—*final separation* from the most amiable of sons." Mercy refers here to the loss of her "middle son Charles," who, as Jeffrey H. Richards and Sharon M. Harris explain, had died on "November 30, 1785." In bringing Sarah into her confidence, Mercy's characterization of Sarah as her "mild, domestic, pious, amiable friend" provides a view of Sarah outside her family circle.[20]

Mercy again indicated that Sarah was an important confidant on August 23, 1800, following the death of Mercy's youngest son, George. After sharing her grief, Mercy portrays Sarah as a guiding influence: "I rejoice that your numerous family still remains unbroken. Go on my dear madam in the charming work of instilling those principles of virtue that may deter the youthful circle from slipery paths of vice or the dangerous errors of opinion that remarkably hang around them in this day of deviation from the pure principles taught in a sacred code which if not *burlesqued* is too generally neglected in the fashionable world."[21] Noting a larger difficulty of "instilling those principles of virtue" in a generation that lives "in this day of deviation," Mercy affirms Sarah's dedication to her family. She would do so again on February 7, 1802, after noting her own health issues: "But you have cares, lovely cares, a family who I hope, promises to reward every attention that occupies the time of so good a mother." Mercy also includes a note of appreciation for their friendship: "You my dear, Mrs. Cary are almost the only female friend I have left, to whom I can without restraint pour out the flow of thoughts as they arrive, amidst the chequered hue of my span of life."[22] According to Richards and Harris, "Mercy Otis Warren continued to correspond with Sarah Gray Cary, and her last known letter was dated July 14. Shortly after a visit from that epistolary friend, Warren died at home on October 19, 1814, in the presence of her surviving sons."[23] Sarah's friendships with women, and especially with Mercy Otis Warren, thus provided her with an expanded view of her world at Chelsea, even as Sarah focused on her family and her sons traveling throughout the transatlantic world.

Sarah was pleased by Samuel's reports from May 1, 1799, on the improving state of affairs in Grenada, and responded on November 12: "Your successful business raised us to a pitch of happiness and pleasure unknown to us since the insurrection in Grenada." Still, she worries about Mount Pleasant and about her husband returning to Grenada: "He is undetermined what step to take . . . He grows impatient to hear from you, and seems to place his whole happiness in you, and blesses God every Day for having as he says bless'd him with a Son in whom he places such confidence and delight." With Samuel in a state of indecision, Sarah puts forth her own assessment, however bleak it may be: "I flatter myself for my part that Messrs. Cs may be prevailed on to wait untill the plantation holds up its Head again." Having referenced the Campbells' firm, Sarah then speculates, "If your Father could transact any business, upon commission or otherwise, so as to prevent any demands upon Mt. P. more than its own expenses, that there would be some good pickings yet, and it would be able to free it self of the present load of Debt." Despite their precarious financial situation, Sarah closes with a reminder of Samuel's importance to both the family and his father: "And amidst the pangs your Father suffers is it amongst the least think you that He looks to you for assistance now who ought to expect it from him."[24] While noting this shifting relationship between father and son, Sarah was again grateful for her son's assistance.

In May 1800, Lucius Cary finally made the trip to Grenada, arriving at Saint George's "with introductory letters for Messrs. Orr, Campbell, Naghten and Sandbach." Writing from Mount Pleasant on May 8, he tells his mother, "Behold me at length in Grenada after Ten Years absence, visiting the place where I spent my earliest youth and so many happy days. . . . You may easily imagine what I felt when I arrived on the plantation, I recollected everything, The Works, Negro houses and Gully, even the Rock at the corner and bottom of the Hill did not escape me, I could turn my eyes nowhere that I did not meet with some object which put me in mind of former times." The familiar physical landscape and buildings appeared welcoming though altered, and when he describes seeing the slaves again, there is a strong sense of an old order that now appears to have faded: "The Negroes came up one by one and introduced themselves, there were however very few which I recollected.— They were all surprised to see me and particularly Old Constance the Cook who expressed much wonder at seeing me grown so tall. — They all inquired after all the family, very particularly one by one and, desired me to remember them to you, Charlotte and Fanny."[25] Lucius thus frames this scene as a reunion that evokes memories of his childhood, rather than, for example, as an acknowledgment of the changes wrought by the 1795–1796 slave revolts, which is perhaps implied.

When his family had left Grenada in 1791, Lucius had been between eight and nine years old, so his recollections seem more influenced by his childhood perspective than by antislavery discussions in 1800. He not only draws

Lucius Cary to Sarah Cary, Mount Pleasant, Grenada, May 8, 1800. Cary Family Papers III, Collection of the Massachusetts Historical Society.

Mount Pleasant 8th May 1800

My dear Mother,

Behold me at length in Grenada after Ten Years absence, visiting the place where I spent my earliest youth and so many happy days. — I arrived in Saint George's, on Tuesday last, with introductory letters for Messrs Orr, Campbell, Naghten and Sandbach. — Soon after my arrival I waited on Mrs. Horsford with a Book from my Brother.— As I went up the hill to the house where she lives I was thinking how I should introduce myself, however I had scarcely opened the door when the Old Lady came up to me and addressed me by my name and then introduced me to the Mrs. Rose's. — I recollected them all quite perfectly particularly Mrs. H.— I received an invitation to come and visit them, on my return to Town, which I shall comply with. —

You may easily imagine what I felt when I arrived on the plantation, I recollected everything, The Works, Negro houses & Gully, even the Rock at the corner and bottom of the Hill did not escape me, I could turn my eyes no where that I did not meet with some object which put me in mind of former times.— The Negroes came up one by one and introduced themselves, there were however very few which I recollected.— They were all surprised to see me & particularly Old Constance the Cook who expressed much wonder [. . .]

a contrast to the family's former prosperity but also notes a way of life now in retreat: "The Country, you may easily suppose is very much altered since you were there; On every Estate appears Old Walls etc. and all the remains of former splendor." He then notes that he is "at present on the Resource Estate with Mr. Sandbach," adjacent to Mount Pleasant, and describes a similar state of repair. Three weeks later, he continued this letter from "St. George's 20th May": "I arrived here this morning from Maran (Estate) where I had been spending a few days with Mr. Alexander Campbell by his particular invitation." Here, Lucius refers to Alexander Campbell Jr., whose father had owned several plantations, including the large Tivoli estate just north of the Simon estate. Lucius then visited with neighbors: "I dined yesterday with Mrs. Horsford and family and spent the day very pleasantly. She inquired after a great many people in America, and gave me a long history of the Insurrection." Rather than refer to the events of 1795–1796 as a revolt or a rebellion, the term "Insurrection" signals not only that the rebellion was unjustified but that the prevailing narrative was one of landholders defending their property. As Lucius explains, he intends to leave St. George's the next day for Martinique "in a Small Schooner having finished all my business and received every civility from all whom I was acquainted with."[26]

Sarah's Letters to Samuel and Lucius: Adapting and Responding Accordingly

With both Samuel and Lucius now in the West Indies, Sarah responded to each according to their respective ages and concerns. With Samuel, she gave advice and brought him into her confidence, as on June 17, 1800, when she acknowledges, "I envy you, nor deprive you of a moment's consolation especially that derived from so noble a source as comforting the declining years of your dear Father that you are thus instrumental to his happiness." Reflecting on her husband, Sarah then recalls, "the character he sustain'd in the W.I. and the undeviating rectitude he pursued in his conduct while there and thro' life ... may be said in great measure to have been derived from him self." Then, directly addressing Samuel, she writes, "But the Merit, the inclination, the honor is all your own altho' the delicacy of your Mind is such as makes you unwilling to allow it." Sarah thus draws a parallel between Samuel Cary Sr.'s "undeviating rectitude" and their son's "honor" and humility. On October 28, Sarah confides in Samuel about Charles and family in general: "We have not heard yet of Charles— I hope he will succeed this time, now or never, it may be said— for his Character will be this Voyage too firmly fix'd to alter." This anxious note leads her to comment, "I tremble when I look abroad and see children of one Family so totally opposite in their disposition and actions, as we frequently you know do— and ask my self what right I have to expect that my nine Sons should all turn out in life and sustain their parts equally well."[27] With Lucius, Sarah also provided advice and reassurance. On July 4, 1800, Lucius thus expresses appreciation for "the endearing manner in which your instructions and advice are so happily blended, and the kind and lively interest which you show for the success of all my private plans," and then promises, "it shall be the study of my life never to give you one moment's pain, or cause one uneasy thought." His enthusiasm and optimism about his potential, however, also met with his mother's more realistic assessment of his financial potential, which he acknowledges: "You observed very justly the great improbability of my assertion that I should be worth £30. by the 1st. July and £100. by the 1st. Janry."[28] As Sarah carried on correspondence with her sons, the changing content and concerns offer an interesting view of family life and the aspirations and obligations of these two young men embarking on their own careers.

The sons, in turn, monitored each other and offered their own advice. Lucius thus writes his mother from Martinique on October 22, 1800, "My Brother has no doubt acquainted you with his intended trip to England in January, he will not I suppose be longer than three Months absent." And in reference to the economic prospects of Martinique and the West Indies, Lucius had this to say about his younger brother, Henry, who had recently graduated from Billerica Academy, and regarding his mother's "wish for his being settled": "I am quite interested for his future Welfare, and sincerely wish that he may procure a good situation, — but I see no likelihood of one here though I should be much pleased at its taking place."[29] Speaking from his current experience, Lucius found the prospect for success in the West Indies marginal, especially considering that the Quasi-War had only recently ended. Michael A. Palmer elaborates: "By September 1800, when a diplomatic accord was finally reached, French seizures, captures, detentions, condemnations, and confiscations of American ships, cargoes, and crews involved 2,309 vessels and would ultimately leave the Federal government to sort out 6,479 claims. Such losses threatened America's newfound commercial prosperity." To these ends, Palmer concludes, "With no diplomatic options immediately available, the administration resigned itself to the necessity of a military response."[30] So when Lucius discouraged the idea of his brother Henry embarking for the West Indies, he had good reasons, at least until shipping was safer and trade improved. While letters helped maintain family connections, they also had their limitations. Perhaps to alleviate the sense of loss over their sustained separation, Sarah requests Samuel's portrait on November 19, 1800: "a small size, oval, and in a neat ebony frame. I do not wish you to incur any great expense, only pray that it may be done by an *artist* in his profession, having seen some intolerable daubs of late in gilt frames." Making this request reminds her, "Methinks I hear you reply that you once asked the same favor of me and was refused. It is very true; but I was so circumstanced that I could not gratify you with propriety, and I assure you I felt great pain in the refusal, although at that time, from motives of prudence, I did not express it to you."[31] Whereas finances did not allow for her portrait in 1791, Sarah was now hoping that Samuel would oblige this request for his.

The strains of maintaining these relationships by letter were at times accompanied by confusion, as when Samuel wrote from Martinique on November 29, 1800, imagining his mother's apparent surprise about his pending journey to England. Setting his letter in a narrative style, he writes in his mother's voice: "What, Sam, just on the point of setting off for England, and we only now to hear of such an intention, — although you had it, and communicated it, four months ago!" Samuel's "dialogue" then continues, "Indeed, Madam, the fault is not mine, if you did not hear of it.— I only desired my secret might not find its way out to this Country yet awhile — and perhaps the person entrusted with it took what he thought the most effectual method to prevent it by keeping it to himself.— A bad excuse, and an impertinent one, dear Sam, — but come, — let us hear, what is the meaning of this voyage?" Although it is not clear if Lucius tried to "prevent" his brother's voyage, Samuel continues his narrative by answering an imagined question from his mother: "How happens it that when you are travelling about in this manner you do not contrive to pay us a visit here?— I suppose we are considered as your nobodies." He then responds to these slightly accusatory, albeit imaginary, questions: "Indeed, my dear Madam, it is not for want of inclination that I do not go to see you.— but Business obliges me to absent myself; — and you know I wrote two Years ago that I could not hope to return to you while the war should continue." His mother as speaker then responds, "Well, Sir, we shall forgive you this time, — but remember that though you men pretend to be the only keeper of secrets,— there are some females who are as good at it as you are for your lives. Approach, and kiss our hands." Now that he has imagined his mother's blessing, Samuel describes his itinerary: "Well, now my peace is made I shall set off without asking leave of any one else — first for Barbados, and then for England." He also assures his mother that he has packed accordingly, with "a good supply of Woolens, and Flannels to meet the Northwesters I shall be greeted with in your latitudes.— I shall take Care to make myself Comfortable as I go on,— both in this aspect and other respects." Without going into details, he notes that he will approach the trip realistically: "I grow too old to be cheated with the hope that the instant I put my foot ashore in England I shall be a happy man.— Once nothing was wanting to make me completely happy but to get from the W Indies to America.— Then, a visit to England Seemed like a visit to a new world.— After that, I was at a loss to know what I wanted."

Now twenty-six years old and a young man of experience, Samuel contrasts his previous expectations, and perhaps those of a ten-year-old, when going to England "seemed like a visit to a new world." He then turns to literature for guidance: "Yesterday, Doctor Johnson told me — Active in Indolence, abroad I roam / In quest of happiness which dwells at home:— / with vain pursuits fatigu'd, at length I find / no place excludes it from an equal mind." This is Samuel's adaptation of the epigraph to Samuel Johnson's *The Rambler*, number 6, Saturday, April 7, 1750, which is itself a paraphrase of a passage from Horace's *Epistles* (1.11.28–30), in which lines one and three use the third- and second-person pronouns: "Active in indolence, abroad we roam . . . / With vain pursuits fatig'd, at length you'll find." Cary thus personalized the quotation to emphasize its relevance to his journey. His letter concludes on a lighthearted note: "Now I am growing learned I shall be apt to puzzle you and myself too, — So if you can make any thing of my letter in its present state you are welcome to it, — for I shall not have time to write another." With a clever blend of genres and tropes—epistolary, narrative, dialog, and allusion—Samuel thus prepared to depart for England.[32]

Sarah responded to Samuel on January 6, 1801, and did indeed send her "blessing": "It is time you should quit the W I. for a new recruit of health and spirits, for altho you may not be deficient in either at present, there is a lassitude one feels in a warm climate, that secretly undermines the best constitution." Still, she is disappointed that Samuel can not visit his family first but understands the limitations imposed by the Quasi-War and remains optimistic: "I confess had your business permitted you, a jaunt this way would have made us all truly happy, some distant period I trust, when the War is at an end, we shall have the felicity we hope for, I look back upon the hours you past with us with delight and say with Shakespeare 'I cannot but remember such things were that were most dear to me.' "[33] She also repeats an earlier request for his "Picture": "let it be executed by an artist in his profession, that it may be an exact likeness, I care not how plain it be, a neat black ebony frame, of an oval form, what size you think proper." She plans to place the portrait "over the chimney piece in the setting parlour," where its "resemblance to the original will constitute its intrinsic value . . . comfort our declining years; until we shall have you once more seated near us." His image in a simple "neat" frame would thus substitute for his presence. In a note from "Wednesday the 7th," Sarah includes a request for "a small terrestrial Globe . . . and accompany it with a Book intitled Geographical Games by Abbé Gaultier with counters," as these items would assist the younger children with their studies. With such discussions, their letters provide historically relevant details about transatlantic consumerism and children's education. Reporting on the family's "domestic affairs," Sarah tells Samuel that "since Low has taken the Farm at halves, we are more satisfied than ever, and are freer from care; his growing family is the only objection." These developments "relieved" Samuel Cary "from the care of the workmen," so that he "has no occasion without he chuses it, to trouble himself with the Farm, excepting only to have an Eye to the produce, as it is selling off." She also notes her husband's difficulty of letting go the daily management of the farm, "altho' he places great confidence in Low."[34] These details illustrate how they continued to economize.

The Mount Pleasant Estate: Reports of a Slight Recovery

The family's recovery took a positive turn as Samuel reported to his father on September 15, 1801, about his recent visit to Grenada. He begins by noting that Samuel Sandbach "has shipped from Mount Pleasant Seventy three hhds. sugar, . . . between 30 or 40 Puncheons of Rum, which have paid off all last Year's Expenses, to the amount, of near £1200.— he has besides still on hand 2 hhds. and 4 Bbls. Sugar which for want of Opportunity to ship." Next, Samuel explains the subsequent transactions: "He will give in payment to T. O. and Co: — The Balance with that house stood on the 9th inst., at £491.7.3 which is all we owe, except Sandbach's Salary and a small balance to the manager.— A Sum of Five hundred Pounds that I had put into the hands of T. O. and Co. in my own name, at the beginning of the Year, remains untouched." Samuel is optimistic overall: "With respect to our prospects for next Year, never perhaps did the Estate with the same quantity of Canes, nor the Island in general promise more." He then provides more details about their expenses: "To the balance due T. O. and Co. on the 9th we shall have some considerable addition to make for negro Cloathing, provisions, Lumber for a Begass-house, Staves, 3 Mules and etc. before this Janry, but as I hope the next rum - Crop will pay off all this, and as we are £500. in pocket, I begged of Sandbach to purchase 4 or 5 new Negroes at Thornton's, for which we are to have 12 Months credit." With the Mount Pleasant estate productive and moving toward profit, Samuel recommends buying slaves from William Thornton, whose family co-owned several plantations on Grenada.[35] Samuel also raises the possibility of selling the estate to Samuel Sandbach: "I sounded him about purchasing Mt. P. but he is satisfied for the present with what he has, and intends going to England next year." Another possible buyer was "a French gentleman . . . Captain Raymond, formerly, in a foreign regiment in the british service." Samuel ends his report with a note about his next travels, "to St. Croix, St. Thomas, St. Kitts, and etc. . . . This will take me I suppose a Month or Six Weeks.— after that I expect to make a trip to Demerary."[36] As these details suggest, Samuel had gained a keen understanding of how the network of merchants and traders interacted and operated.

With the responsibility for the family's financial welfare now shifting more definitively to the Carys' eldest son, Sarah again acknowledged Samuel's importance. In October 1801, she notes that she is pleased he has returned to Fort Royal, Martinique: "Hope you have a new recruit of Health and spirits, the next Voyage I trust will be this way, for the same purpose"; she also thanks him for the presents from England: "The Globe is as elegant and handsome as possible which with the assistance of Abbé Gaultiere will afford delightful amusement to some part of the Family, the new play call'd the Family Budget must be highly instructive to both old and young, will require much self-examination; and no small acquaintance with the sciences." The gifts were yet another reason the family was "all indebted" to Samuel, "for these continual provisions of both Mind and Body, and for those unceasing solicitudes that you continually express for our welfare, you think yourself repaid by the care and tranquility that your dear Father enjoys here in his retirement, yet my love you will have greater rewards still, if not here in another and better life." As Sarah had done many times before, she expresses gratitude to Samuel as the family's provider. And in her wish for a family reunited, she notes earlier in the letter, "Who knows my love but you may chuse a residence here one Day or another."[37]

Later that year, on December 8, 1801, Lucius wrote from Martinique with an overview of his life and an update on his financial progress. The letter begins with a response to news about Chelsea: "I am exceedingly happy at the thoughts of you all being so busy and chearfull at the retreat, electing a new Minister, making a new Road, and so forth." As business is slow, Lucius is "quite idle" and notes that there is "but little amusement of any kind." To fill his time, he is "learning the violin" and hopes to "enliven the Retreat with some good tunes." He is especially cheered that the Quasi-War has finally ended: "You have heard long before this, I daresay of the Peace which has taken place, What think you of it? We expect soon to give up this Island, and the prisoners, say in two Months.— I know not what alteration it will make in my brothers affairs, but I hope it will be for the better." Lucius then speculates on his own financial future: "I shall close all my affairs at the end of the Year to begin afresh in the next, which I shall do with a Capital of about One hundred and seventy Pounds Sterling." Having projected this balance, Lucius notes that this sum is "no trifle considering the little I have had to trade upon, that it was a whole Year after my arrival before I was worth a Sixpence, and that I have not saved a single Shilling of my Salary,— which by the bye has not been increased since my arrival here, and is less than any one else in my Situation gets, and upon the whole but half what I have a right to expect as Bookkeeper." Notwithstanding complaints about his salary, Lucius plans to begin the next year with an impressive capital of "One hundred and seventy Pounds Sterling." He also describes his other activities on the island: "There is one employment which I have here which I believe I have never mentioned to you, it is going in the Country every Sunday to a Market Town, to buy farini (Cassada) for the use of the prisoners here, — I dare say you will think it very odd that I should thus spend the day in trafic which might at least be employed in meditation or reading, but it is a duty inseperable from my business."[38] Given the alternatives he mentions, this action, though a business duty, appears to be an act of charity, though his allegiances are not exactly stated.

Returning to Martinique after a recent visit to Grenada, Lucius sent a promising report to his father on February 14, 1802: "I found Mount Pleasant in a capital way and the finest prospect of a Crop, Mr. Sandbach says, he ever saw and he assures me that we may depend upon making Ninety Hogsheads, though he himself firmly believes there will be a hundred.— They began Crop on the 6th January, had made Eight hogsheads when I left them and at three hogsheads per Acre." Lucius then adds a note about labor: "Mr. S. also thinks that with the assistance of the 4 negroes to be purchased the Crop can be taken off without any hired negroes.— I enclose a Copy of the Journals.— The Works are in very good order." In an interesting conflation of managerial language intended to convey efficiency, the Africans will provide "assistance" even as they are "purchased." After conveying Sandbach's "thanks and best compliments" for his father's recent supply of "a Round Beef and some trees," Lucius informs his father that Sandbach "sails for England in May and intends visiting America soon, as he has a great wish to see it and to spend some time there." And with hopes for his own return to Chelsea, Lucius writes, "I look forward with pleasure to the time I shall see you and anticipate our mutual happiness in again meeting after so long a Separation.— I feel how much I depend upon myself for every thing I hope for and look forward with eager expectation to the independance which is to be the reward of my exertions and which I hope to attain." The sacrifices of separation are thus somewhat justified as they are placed within the context of reward. In closing, he notes the Quasi-War: "We are in daily expectation of receiving accounts of the Treaty and having immediately to give up the Island."[39] Lucius's optimism and sense of duty thus sustained him as he began his fourth year in the West Indies. Like his brother, Lucius deferred his own wishes about returning home.

The family's appreciation for Samuel's help was again clear on February 20, 1802, when Sarah comments on the educational gifts he had sent from London: "My young Folks have at last the opportunity of improvement, and I allow also that they possess inclination, and capacities sufficiently enlarged, to comprehend with tolerable facility what their kind instructress daily lays before them." The children's "instructress" most likely refers to Margaret, who took charge of her younger siblings' education. Sarah then adds, "yet they would shrink back with timidity and diffidence at the thought of being able to teach you." These observations lead Sarah to note, "What Dean Swift says of a woman's learning is enough I think to suppress the greatest vanity: 'after all, her boasted acquirements, will generally speaking be found to possess less of what is call'd learning than a common school Boy,'" adding that "the remark is just, altho not so much so as at the period when he wrote." Sarah then marks differences between women's education in Great Britain and America: "At least in this Country young Ladies stand nearly as good a chance as the other sex," with the caveat that "the only danger in the present mode is, that in gaining mental knowledge they depart from that delicacy of manner so highly essential to female character, and which will always constitute one of its greatest charms." Sarah then notes that her young girls are sheltered from these negative influences: "Mine are secure from that danger; confined to domestic life, at distance from the gay world, they have the finest opportunity imaginable for the cultivation of their minds, fixing religious principles, and fostering those virtues, that will enable them to look forward to that life, where to be applauded should be the highest ambition of every reasonable Being."[40] Whereas Sarah is ultimately proud of Margaret's role as "instructress," she also addresses potential limitations that women face in pursuing their academic interests.

The quotation Sarah attributed to Dean (aka Jonathan) Swift is actually from Hannah More, who is paraphrasing Swift's essay "A Letter to a Very Young Lady, On Her Marriage" (1727). In chapter 7 of More's *Strictures on the Modern System of Female Education,* volume one (1799), entitled "On female study, and initiation into knowledge," she couches her paraphrase in these remarks: "But let her who is disposed to be elated with her literary acquisitions, check her vanity by calling to mind the just remark of Swift, 'that after all her boasted acquirements, a woman will, generally speaking, be found to possess less of what is called learning than a common school-boy.' " Here is the section from Swift's essay that most likely inspired the paraphrase: "I know very well, that those who are commonly called learned Women, have lost all Manner of Credit by their impertinent Talkativeness, and Conceit of themselves: But there is an easy Remedy for this; if you once consider, that after all the Pains you may be at, you never can arrive, in Point of Learning, to the Perfection of a School-Boy."[41] Several advertisements for Hannah More's essay and books appeared in Boston-area newspapers between 1798 and 1802. Considering that Sarah does not reference More, she may have found the quotation in an anthology. In any case, Sarah's quotation was inspired by her discussion of Margaret's role as educator to the younger Cary children, with the implication that Sarah's daughter is both learned and modest.

On March 31, 1802, Sarah again addresses a desire for family unity in a letter to Samuel, who was "going or gone to Visit England." And although she wishes him well in his newest business ventures, she has regrets: "I readily confess that the wish nearest my Heart is to have you here, but if your emoluments are likely to encrease by keeping away some time longer I ought and do submit; for altho I hope I have learnt to estimate riches as they deserve (that is as they supply us with the conveniences and not the Luxuries of life) I yet well know the worth of a competence." As the act of seeking fortune continued to scatter the family, Sarah would "submit" to their separation "some time longer."[42]

Letters continued to sustain Sarah's relationship with her eldest. She writes to Samuel on October 17, 1802, in a particularly reflective moment, marking his birthday: "This Day 29 years ago gave me a Son and made me the happiest of Women; if I except the absence of your Father at that time, which was the only barrier." She then speaks directly about their brief time together: "I cherished you as an angel sent from Heaven, and 3 months nursed you at my own breast, and God knows with what reluctance I left you to the care of my Mother, the best of women, but so it was ordained. The first rudiments of your Education were received from her." Turning to the difficulty of that decision, Sarah reveals, "The trial was severe, my affections were divided between a beloved Husband, and a lovely Infant who deservedly possessed my tenderest regard; I tore myself from you, and for a time was as I thought completely wretched; you was insensible of your loss, and the Idea of seeing your Father brightened the prospect and I resolved to be as happy as circumstances would allow; I arrived safe in Grenada." What had been implied before about the assumed temporary nature of this separation is now explained: "The War breaking out, prevented so frequent a correspondence with America as we wished which occasioned my often wishing that I had (altho' contrary to your Father's opinion) taken my dear Boy with me, and I know that he often wished so too; in mean time you improved apace, and became the favorite of your Friends." She then notes their brief reunion: "At Ten years old we concluded to have you out to Grenada, and send you to England to compleat your <u>education.</u>" Moreover, Sarah now views their separation as preordained: "Thus you see my dear Sam that from Step to Step it <u>has been ordered</u> that you the sweet little Fellow I resigned to my Mother should become at last the protector of your Family." These sacrifices were again evident in 1791: "My trial of quitting you and leaving you in Grenada <u>under Postlethwaite</u> was greater than any I had before experienced, yet it was the only means of making you competent to performing the actions that have made you estimable above what the affection and love we bore you would have made you to your family, do you comprehend me, my love?" Bringing these events into the present, Sarah emphasizes the importance of Samuel's contributions: "O my God I bless thee for giving me a son who not only never occasioned me a moment's regret or pain, but who has supported and provided for his family, when to human appearance they would have been deprived of every other resource, and who has from his infancy, been a source of delight and honor to his Father and Mother." In retrospect, it appears to Sarah that the difficult events have strengthened Samuel and prepared him for adulthood. Somewhat self-consciously, Sarah notes the tenor of these recollections: "Your Birth Day has led me into the train of reflection in the foregoing. I know not what reflections it will occasion to my dear Sam nothing unpleasing I hope."

Finally, on the topic of marriage, Sarah revises her reaction from a decade earlier, when she wrote on September 13, 1792, "You startled me indeed, when I come to that part of your Letter where you mention Matrimony, that wou'd be madness in the extreme. I am glad, however, to find that our sentiments accord there, 25 is a good age, provided there is a sufficient fund to maintain a Family." Now, in 1802, her approach has softened: "It would be hard indeed if you should think yourself obliged, for the sake of your Family, to forego the pleasure of uniting yourself to a Lady you love, but if that Lady should be rich Sam, riches you know are a good ingredient in Marriage, and certainly no barrier to love; well, be it as it may if you are satisfied I shall be so." On this last point, Sarah comments further: "How sincerely do I hope for the success you wish for in your affairs, and a permanent establishment, Could it be in America, or even in England, or any part of Europe I should be happy, and shall always regret that my Family seem to be necessitated to live in the West Indies, but every thing is for the best." Sarah thus encourages Samuel while also accepting what seems to be their inevitable state of separation. She concludes her eight-page letter with a report that Mr. Low's family is leaving, and that, as a result, "Your Father has engaged another Family to come into the House and take the Farm at the halves."[43] Sarah had much to be grateful for, and yet she still had unresolved issues about the necessity of her sons remaining so far away from home.

Strains of Separation and the Incessant
Movement in Pursuit of Fortune

In Margaret Cary's narrative of these years, she provides information where there are gaps in the family correspondence, as in her November 1, 1853, letter to her nephew Edward M. Cary, in which she notes that Samuel "found a situation for Lucius in Demerara, where he remained till he came of age, in 1803, when he made a visit to Chelsea." It was a joyful event: "We were all, as you may suppose, delighted to see him. He came in fine spirits, ready to enjoy any pleasure, domestic or social." Lucius "stayed but a few months" before going to Bath to see some merchants, as he "was impatient to be in business." Margaret also describes her brother's disposition: "He was very quick in his feelings, his natural temperament having been increased by a residence in a hot climate and among slaves."[44] However Lucius expressed his feelings, the reference to living "in a hot climate and among slaves" as a contributing factor, appears to remove his responsibility for his "temperament" on some level. Lucius returned to Demerara in 1804, and for the next six years he engaged in business. There is a three-year gap in the extant Sarah-Lucius correspondence, until June 2, 1807, when Lucius writes to his mother from "Demerary," beginning with an apology for his "long Silence, but Letter writing has become by no means a pleasing task to me, as I believe is always the case where one has no pleasing Communication to make." He provides no details about the unpleasant communications. Lucius then reports about letters from his sisters Sarah and Nancy, which confirm his hopes "of Charles succeeding in Charleston." In writing to his mother, Lucius responds to a copy of the letter from Charles that Margaret had sent: "I am glad to find that there is a possibility of his being enabled some time hence to take unto himself a Wife, which I know is a favorite plan of his." His younger brother Henry is also doing well: "At the same time I got the news that Mr. Henry Cary 'transacts Commission Business' and was almost as much pleased to hear of his large Profits as if they been my own." Lucius further expresses a desire for the family to be united, as he tells his mother, "Depend upon it nothing but necessity would ever keep me away from a Fireside like yours."[45] Like his older brother, Lucius felt both the draw to the islands and the desire for home.

As Lucius noted, Henry Cary had settled in New York, where he worked as a clerk from 1808 to 1812 for Michael Hogan, a prominent merchant. During this time, as Joseph Alfred Scoville explains, Henry lived in Hogan's house on "No. 52 Greenwich street, as was the custom with clerks those days. He resided with Mr. Hogan, even after he went into business on his own account, in 1812, at 18 Mill street." In *The Old Merchants of New York City* (1870), Scoville elaborates on Henry's clerkship days: "There he acquired that fastidious taste, and the love of good living that he was known to possess, for many years. . . . Here it was that Henry Cary first saw that a merchant could be a scholar as well as trader, and that the two pursuits were not incompatible with each other."[46] This latter comment refers to Henry's literary efforts: "Henry Cary was a writer well known to the readers of the *Knickerbocker Magazine*, when its editor was Lewis G. Clark. Mr. Cary's articles, both poetry and prose, were signed John Waters." Scoville also reports, "He did not want pay for his voluminous performances: that exactly suited the treasury of the *Knickerbocker* which was never known to be flush." By June 1812, Henry was advertising from 38 Mill Street in New York, for rice and later a variety of goods, including jewelry, land, logwood, Madeira wine, and cotton.

After a year's gap in correspondence, Sarah writes to Lucius on September 2, 1807, marking his twenty-fifth birthday: "The day after tomorrow brings you to 25, so our years roll on; were you with us, it should be a sort of jubilee, we would make merry, as it is, it will be a kind of solitary remembrance, a glass of wine perhaps, to the Health of our dear son and brother, sincere and affectionate wishes for his welfare, accompanied with the unavailing sigh of every individual of the family, at the distance that separates one so deservedly dear." Given their separation, Sarah offers this imaginary celebration at Chelsea. She then provides a summary of his brothers' activities as they pursue their various careers: Charles is employed "in a ship" headed for Matanzas, Cuba, and "receives sixty dollars per month," while Thomas has "returned Home from the Academy and has pass'd an examination at college, which he is to enter in one month." Sarah then acknowledges Lucius's role in affording Thomas the opportunity: "The Bill you remitted will be appropriated to his use, and he is very grateful for it, we shall use all the economy possible." Noting their prudent application of Lucius's funds and that his "Father is reduced to a slender income," Sarah then expresses appreciation for the family as a whole: "But while we are blest with Sons like yourself my dear Lucius, Sam, Henry, and the rest as far as it is in their power; we shall not want, and as you are disposed to assist one another, we will endeavor not to be anxious about you; We have been blest with a large Family, and that God who gave them to us, will provide for them, as He has for us." She then adds, "Your Father is in fine health and so am I, we ride 2 hours every morning and pass the rest of the day in reading, walking and etc."[47] These disclosures about the family's dependence underscored the sacrifices their sons had made regarding their own personal hopes and dreams. In a letter to Lucius on December 16, 1807, Sarah emphasizes the importance of maintaining their correspondence: "Next to the pleasure of receiving Letters from those we love, is that which arises from knowing we have not ourselves been negligent in keeping up the correspondence. . . . I take the tender interest of a friend in <u>your concerns,</u> and participate with you in every thing, in short my happiness is closely allied to yours, and I look forward to the time when you and I shall pass many happy hours together."[48] In noting the letter as a source of "pleasure" and "enjoyment," Sarah also imagines a time when letter writing will no longer be the sole source of their communication.

From 1808 to 1810, Lucius continued to conduct trade from Demerara, as indicated in several notices in the *Essequebo & Demerary Royal Gazette*; for example, in January 1808: "Now landing from schooner Success, ex Portsmouth, N. A. — Fish, beef in barrels and half barrels, clap boards, mackrel, &c. 2d Jan. 1808. Lucius Cary & Co." By April, he had formed a new firm: "Hugh Hyndman having joined the Concern of Lucius Cary & Co. the Business will in future be conducted under the Firm of Hyndman & Cary. Demerary, 9th April 1808." This affiliation was again noted in May: "FOR LIVERPOOL. The Ship Mary, Captain Afflick, will sail positively with the first Convoy. For Freight please apply to the Master on board, or to Hyndman & Cary. Cumingsburg, 28th May, 1808."[49] Lucius continued trading in Demerara for the next two years.

Samuel Cary's Memorandum Book and Reflections on the West Indies

Similar to his brothers, Samuel had certainly deferred his private ambitions as he constantly traveled in search of trade and mercantile opportunities to support his family. In doing so, he had remained single and not established a home of his own. In letters to his family, Samuel recounted these activities as a dutiful eldest son. And when he did express differences about business practices and other matters, he generally submitted to his parents' wishes and authority. In his more private writings, however, Samuel addressed concerns about his situation in the West Indies as he tried to reconcile his actions with his beliefs and principles. These struggles are evident in a two-by-four-inch book with the title on the first page, "Extracts from the memorandum book of my brother, S C.," which is described in the finding aid at the Massachusetts Historical Society as written "in the hand of Ann M. Cary, 1800–1801, 1803–1810." The description also explains that the "extracts consist of miscellaneous reflections and diary entries of Ann's brother" and describe "his thoughts on human nature, history, literature, and religion; his life as a farmer, probably on the family's plantation in Grenada, British West Indies; and his treatment of slaves."[50] The extracts are assumed to be direct transcriptions and appear more similar to entries in a journal or commonplace book than those in a formal memorandum or ledger, but they do reveal Samuel's processes of contemplation and his attempts to find order in his life. With commentary as well as direct quotations and paraphrases, these extracts help to explain why Samuel was so devoted to his family and yet still conflicted about his situation. Unlike a diary, which is usually sustained periodically with daily or weekly entries and may not necessarily include commentary on the events recorded, and yet similar to a commonplace book, which compiles and records passages for study and refection, filed under various classifications and headings, Samuel Cary's memorandum book appears to be intended for both contemplation and future reference.[51] Moreover, as James A. Bear Jr. and Lucia C. Stanton note, Thomas Jefferson's memorandum books cover a breadth of material from "financial accounts" to "memoranda from his law practice" and "weather records, wine lists, or other miscellaneous material." Jefferson's extensive accounts also provide "an incomparable documentary record of the life of one man and of his world. . . . The trail of purchased provisions and commodities sheds light on almost every aspect of Jefferson's world, from the state of technology and the arts in the new republic to the realities of plantation life and the southern agricultural economy."[52] Boston newspapers for the years 1800–1810 include more than a hundred advertisements for memorandum books, available with blank or lined pages. Starting a new year with a memorandum book was popular and often necessary, as it usually included a calendar and an almanac. Jefferson's use of the memorandum book and its sustained popularity as a record-keeping device thus allowed for some attempt at order. In Samuel Cary's case, the entries provide an interesting counterpart to his letters because the entries are both contemplative and revelatory about his life in the West Indies. As such, they expand the memorandum book's function beyond figures and observations.

During the decade covered by Cary's memorandum book extracts, 1800–1810, Samuel was living primarily at Martinique and traveling throughout the West Indies, with occasional trips to England. Lucius documented his brother's travels in his letters, noting that Samuel went to Barbados at the end of July 1799, to Surinam in late August, again to Barbados in October, to Grenada in December, and back to Martinique in early 1800. For good reason, then, Lucius tells his mother on December 3, 1800, "My Brother has been quite unsettled these several months, and is not yet quite fixed at Saint Pierre." On January 6, 1801, Sarah directed her letter to Samuel in London, and in July 1801, to Martinique. On September 6, Lucius notes, "My Brother is at present in Grenada which place he sailed for a few days ago and is expected back by the end of the month." On February 14, 1802, Lucius tells his father, "I have written on to Demerara to my Brother." By March 31, 1802, Sarah was directing letters to Samuel in London and again in October. Samuel continued to travel extensively, as dates for the entries indicate: St. Croix, October 17, 1803; Caracas, December 10, 1808; Barbados, July 23, 1809; Fort Royal, February 26, 1810; and St. Pierre, July 6, 1810. So not only do the extracts document Samuel's whereabouts, but they also underscore how intensively he was attempting to establish and secure financial prospects.

Samuel's commentary on both classical and contemporary writers, including Joseph Addison, Hugh Blair, Miguel de Cervantes, Marcus Tullius Cicero, John Milton, Alexander Pope, William Shakespeare, Jonathan Swift, and Voltaire, reveal his wide reading interests, from essays, poetry, and drama to sermons, oratory, and philosophy. Along these lines, the first extract reads, "Our own genuine thoughts, tho' trivial, are of more value to us than the most brilliant that we read." This reference to the value of one's "own genuine thoughts" appears to serve as a guide, for an entry a few pages later states, "In reading, I think it is of advantage to select that kind which is best adapted to the actual state of the mind . . . All good authors should not, perhaps, be read at all times." Directly below this note is an entry on "Reflections attending a repetition of the Lord's prayer," followed by a critique of Milton. Samuel later poses this question, with no date ascribed to the entry: "Did Abraham through devotion, offer to sacrifice his only son, his strongest attachment to life, and can I not from the same motive, consent to live apart from my family for a few years?" By drawing this parallel to Abraham's sacrifice, Samuel reflected on his own sense of duty and sacrifice for his family. By reading various sources, Samuel thus engaged in a philosophical, scriptural, and literary dialogue with his readings.

In addition to personal reflection, Samuel discusses history, as in the entry on "Carib Country — St. Vincent," which begins, "This is the spot where lately the inhabitants lived after simple nature.— Without seeking to amass riches, the carib's object was to excel in fishing; shooting and managing a canoe in the high surf — The women cultivated the ground — The carib was free." He follows this with a question, "But does happiness consist in this mode of life?," and then an anecdote: "A gentleman told me, that amongst a parcel of caribs who surrendered themselves prisoners to him, was a woman with a child in each arm and one on her back.— As the party had to cross a river, the gentleman desired a carib man to assist her. The carib refused, and on being upbraided, he made answer, that it was the custom with them for the women to do all the labor." Samuel then reflects on this narrative: "Without the enjoyment of refined female society, with the faculties of the mind little cultivated, and few ideas, — by how much do the enjoyments of the savage exceed those of a wild beast?"[53] As Samuel is himself apparently without the company of "refined female society," this anecdote appears to illustrate how gentlemanly ways may suffer from such separations, thus serving as a critique of gender roles, if not a cautionary note on some level. Regarding these passages on the Carib history at St. Vincent, Christopher Taylor provides important background: "The Black Caribs fought the British army to a standstill in a grueling six-month war in the early 1770s, rose again at the end of the decade to help the French oust the British." Taylor then explains, "Finally, in March 1797 the remnants of the Black Carib nation—barely two thousand men, women, and children—were transported in British ships 1,700 miles away to the northwest, where they were deposited on the Spanish-controlled island of Roatán off the coast of Honduras."[54] The black Carib struggles have parallels to the Fédon rebellion in that imperial powers attempted to dominate indigenous and free black populations. Samuel does not address these more immediate issues nor the exile of the Caribs but continues instead to consider the relationship between happiness and riches. This theme is addressed in an entry directly below: "To seek to secure ourselves from want is incumbent upon us; to follow business as a useful profession is honourable; but pressed of means of support, to spend our lives in struggles to avoid poverty, is slavery." Here the "honourable" merchant or trader who lacks financial support is apparently enslaved by the pursuit of wealth.

This thread continues in the next entry, which poses the question, "Can his pleasures be valuable who never exercises the feelings of the heart?" Pleasures obtained without feeling are thus subject to reconsideration. If the extracts are indeed presented in chronological order, the next entry continues with a similar tone of self-examination: "Charity covers a multitude of sins in our account with Heaven; a good table and open house does the same in the eye of man." Beginning with a paraphrase of 1 Peter 4:8 (KJ21), "And above all things have fervent charity among yourselves: for charity shall cover the multitude of sins," Samuel has added his own domesticated image of generosity placed in terms of finances ("account") and commodities ("a good table and open house").[55] Extending charity and benevolence to the home suggests a way to reconcile the source of wealth with religious beliefs, which if read in a confessional context may also be an attempt to assuage guilt, if not directly because of participation with slavery, then perhaps as a general reference to the decadence associated with the West Indies at the time. In an entry a few pages later, Samuel notes, "Pope in a letter to Swift, says, 'It is the best way to live extempore.' "[56] Here, Samuel references a passage from Alexander Pope to Jonathan Swift, June 1730: "I have formerly made some strong efforts to get and to deserve a friend: perhaps it were wiser never to attempt it, but live extempore, and look upon the world only as a place to pass through, just pay your hosts their due, disperse a little charity, and hurry on."[57] This entry may thus suggest an attraction to living spontaneously in the present. If so, Pope's recommendation may lessen a need for self-examination, if not reflection on the past. As extracts and as undated entries, these individual notes may or may not have been intended as a set of related thoughts, but appearing in the memorandum book indicates some level of connection between reflections and actions.

In another entry, dated "Decr 15th 1800," although the number "8" is blotched, appears at the end of the book after an entry for "St. P. 6th July 1810," followed by five lines in the shape of a reversed pyramid. This entry coincides with Samuel's letter to his mother on November 29, 1800, in which he describes his departure from Martinique to Barbados on his way to England. The heading reads "Voyage to the Pelew islands," and the entry begins, "The value of the human heart, not debased by the vices of civil life, and the natural behaviour resulting from its genuine emotions, are very well depicted. How much the knowledge of any european, though not skilled in any manual art whatever, might contribute to the case and comfort of such a race." In what appears to be a reference to George Keate's *An Account of the Pelew Islands Situated in the Western Part of the Pacific Ocean. Composed from Journals and Communications of Captain Henry Wilson, and Some of His Officers, Who, in August 1783, Were Shipwrecked, in the Antelope, a Packet Belonging to the Honourable East India Company* (1788), Samuel considers the effects of "civil life" on "natural behavior" and wonders how a European might "contribute" to "such a race." Though the comment is not followed by a question mark, this entry seems to question whether these contacts are mutually beneficial or are indicative of inevitable change resulting from an encounter between "natural behavior" and European "knowledge." From another angle, Samuel could be rehearsing a utopian vision of how these contacts might manifest. Moreover, as Geoffrey Clark points out, "The widespread influence of Keate's *Pelew Islands* can be traced in the number of editions, translations and abridged versions produced in the late-18th and early-19th century." One of these publications was the *Gentleman's Magazine*, as Clark notes, to which Samuel most likely had access. Clark also finds that "Keate's over-refined idealisation of Palauan-English relations in *Pelew Islands* appears to have softened or ignored instances of cross-cultural crisis that conflicted with his philosophical belief that order, propriety and good conduct were essential features of a genuine civilization."[58] This element of idealism parallels that of Samuel's ongoing discussion of native peoples, in which he ponders the "simple" life in contrast to the potential downfalls of modern ways.

The entries from the years 1803 to 1810 include especially self-reflective passages. "St. Croix— October 17th 1803," begins, "My birthday — 30 years of age. — How soon are years spent! In a few more I shall perhaps have a family, grow old, and pass away. — I know not how soon the Almighty may demand me — It is my business to be ready when called for." In search of further perspective, Samuel considers the value of material goals: "At the prospect of worldly happiness my solid principles have melted and been dissipated, like new formed ice before the meridian sun. We ought to be the artificers of our own happiness." Samuel thus asks for guidance as he contemplates how the pursuit of "worldly happiness" has caused his "principles" to melt and dissipate, which leads to a confessional tone: "Forgiveness is a painful duty — it has been called the utmost effort of human virtue — how do we increase the difficulty of practising it by leaving so much of our peace at the mercy of the world. — I acknowledge, O God, the favor thou hast done me by giving success to several of my undertakings." In noting the difficulty of "forgiveness" and expressing gratitude for his successful "undertakings," Samuel does not explain exactly how practicing the "duty" and "virtue" of forgiveness has been obstructed. Nevertheless, he concludes, "If my principles be just, deign to strengthen me in them, —if erroneous, let me be convinced of their falsity, and acquire as strong an attachment to true ones." Reading these passages in the context of either mercantile pursuits or involvement with slavery suggests a desire for clarity, if not forgiveness.

Samuel then ponders another set of choices, regarding marriage, in an entry from late 1803 to 1804: "Should a man marry a woman of a different religion from his own? — Why not? are either of them of the religion they profess, generally speaking, from conviction, or because they have been bred to it?" Noting differences between practicing a religion that one is born into and practicing one that has been adopted through conviction leads him to consider a higher principle yet: "The Almighty permits them both to live, perhaps to serve him, to have apparently an equal chance for future happiness." He then addresses social differences that could prevent this potential match: "If they divest themselves of the prejudices of education, and compare their own genuine thoughts upon the subject, probably they will agree in essentials." Samuel then places these two people, united in common principles, into the larger perspective: "The Almighty has not particularly revealed his truth to either of them. — He has not in those revelations which we believe to proceed from him, forbidden their union, nor do the apostles of Jesus

Christ any where pretend so to construe his will." As Samuel contemplates this marriage scenario, he poses questions about authority, both divine and scriptural, and in a return to an earlier reference about "genuine thoughts," appears to suggest that such a union is a viable choice. Samuel wrote these passages roughly a year after his mother's October 1802 letter, in which she revised her initial resistance to Samuel's marrying.

The next entry, "Fanny Bark_r_ St. Croix," again addresses matters of the heart. Although Fanny is not further identified here or in his letters, Samuel begins with an assessment of her temperament: "She has the warmth of temper, but if to that be owing, as probably it is, that the regard she has for her friends be so lively, it is impossible to regret it." This quality is balanced by her "extraordinary unaffectedness of manners." In addition, she "delights, ravishes all hearts. — Her understanding is plain and good.— She is mistress of all the duties of housewifery, practices them with chearfulness, and takes pleasure in continual employment. Her qualities are not brilliant, she has but few of the accomplishments in fashion." Still, Fanny is discerning: "She will give little application to what does not interest her." Regarding literature, subjects that "suit her fancy are principally poetical. — She has not much reading otherwise, but considerable taste, a just way of thinking, and expresses herself well;— with all trusting to her feelings, she judges right in ordinary concerns." This portrait also notes "the bewitching modesty, the delicacy of soul, which nature has adorned her with," before concluding with a sense of admiration and a note of caution: "Happy the man who shall gain thy heart, sweet girl; — It will be all his own — And may Heaven in its kindness guard thee from bestowing it unfortunately!" These passages are thus interesting for their idealization of a contemporary woman and for the mystery of Fanny Bark's identity.

In an entry from 1804 to 1805, Samuel turns to the more sobering topic of slavery: "August 13th Paris died — one of the poorest negroes on the estate — now an angel of light." After Paris is released from slavery to become "an angel of light," Samuel reflects on his own state: "My heart does not reproach me with being a severe or careless master to him; But when I consider the nearness of my present state to eternity; my heart is struck with the thought, and my own neglect of it." Although Paris's death does not cause Samuel to "reproach" his behavior as master, it does lead him to consider his "own neglect" of eternity. In August 1805, Samuel poses the question, "What spirit is left to him who is exhausted in body or mind?" This entry is followed by an unattributed quotation—"If I am to die tomorrow, that is what I have to do tomorrow"—and Samuel's comments: "Logan's speech bears, I think, an equal degree of magnanimity. — 'Logan will not turn on his heel to save his life.'" This second quotation is from the speech's conclusion: "For my country, I rejoice at the beams of peace. But do not harbour a thought that mine is the joy of fear. Logan never felt fear. He will not turn on his heel to save his life. Who is there to mourn for Logan? Not one." Chief Logan's family had been murdered at the end of Lord Dunmore's War in 1774. He did not attend the peace negotiations but instead sent a speech, which was widely printed in newspapers. Taken together, these quotations address questions of mortality and the purpose of life. Moreover, Thomas Jefferson prefaces a transcript of Logan's speech in *Notes on the State of Virginia* (1782) with these comments: "I may challenge the whole orations of Demosthenes and Cicero, and of any more eminent orator, if Europe has furnished more eminent, to produce a single passage, superior to the speech of Logan, a Mingo chief, to Lord Dunmore, when governor of this state."[59] For Samuel, the combining of quotations with commentary again reflects his contemplative mode.

Samuel also celebrates beauty in nature, as in his "6th April 06" entry, in which he catalogs elements that have given him pleasure: nature, literature, society, and people. By contrast, the next entry poses questions about his profession: "If it please Heaven that I should not succeed as a planter — so be it. Be it my care to perform my duty to those, whose lives and happiness are, in a great measure, entrusted to me. Let my happiness result rather from the welfare of my negroes, than reflection on my possessions — There is joy in the sympathy of a contented countenance, more than in wealth." Here, Samuel acknowledges that his success is tied to his sense of duty to his family, "whose lives and happiness" are "entrusted" to him, and that he prefers his "happiness" be derived "from the welfare of [his] negroes" rather than from his "possessions" or "wealth." Thus, more explicitly than in his letters, Samuel expresses concern for the African slaves.

Notably, this entry appears twice, which may be his sister Ann's repetition, but if not, it might indicate Samuel's process of evaluating several issues together: career, duty, and slavery. Two weeks after the second duplication is an entry on his birthday, "Oct 17th '07," which begins, "My birthday 34 years. The first thought that occurred to me this day was, that in praying that Heaven's will might be done, the prayer should refer to our own actual circumstances, — otherwise that it has little meaning. I turned back to the thoughts which once formerly occurred to me, on a repetition of the Lord's prayer, and felt satisfied with my thoughts on this part of it." Having set a frame for his entry, Samuel turns to his role as a slave master:

> I had to shew to the negroes to day, that it is my intention to be master over the proudest of them. I had some punishments to inflict — I felt an eager desire to have my conduct, as it has partly been before, under the government of princi-ple alone, and to take the counsel of my genius, though it be tardy, previous to any step, — to bring my person to be the mere servant to my mind. It afterwards occured to me, and the thought gave me pleasure as flattering me, that I might be beginning a better course of life, that it was my birth day.

From reflections on the "Lord's prayer" to a sobering acknowledgment of inflicting punishment, Samuel exposes the fundamental cruelty of slavery. In doing so, he evaluates how his conduct is to be governed—by "principle," "ge-nius," and "mind." He then considers the significance of such contemplations on his birthday: "Yet is there any foundation in reason for that thought giving me pleasure? Is a man's birthday any more to him in reason than any other day?" Although Samuel notes, "It is easy to sneer in answer to such a ques-tion, but sneers are no arguments," he concludes, "It is certainly the custom with us for a man to distinguish the day, by an entertainment or otherwise — and I think I have read of eminent men, who have considered it, and to whom it has proved prosperous or ominous." Uncertain about the weight to ascribe to these overall reflections, he provides further explanation: "To say the truth, I write this as an apologetick introduction to what I am going to write." Even though Samuel began the day "more in spirits than usual," he "afterwards felt a proportionate depression of them — 'It is my birth day,' thought I, — 'it is to me perhaps the ides of March.'— Well I thank my God, if there be any call upon my fortitude this day, I believe myself with his assis-tance equal to it." It thus appears that whatever harm he had to inflict would somehow be sanctioned.

As the entry continues, however, the imagery and tone reveal a darker state of mind: "I write this by candle light — all is silent — Such is the impression that this occupation makes on my mind, that I turned round to the door just now, in the state of mind almost of Brutus, when he saw his genius. Pshaw! these thoughts are the result of indolence of mind and want of society. I had one thing more I wished to commemorate for future reflection." Samuel ap-pears to reference a scene from Shakespeare's *Julius Caesar*, in which Brutus addresses a ghost: "It comes upon me. — Art thou any thing? / Art thou some god, some angel, or some devil, / That mak'st my blood cold and my hair to stare? / Speak to me what thou art" (4.3.321–24). Considering this allusion to a villainous character, this entry as a whole suggests conflicting forces of influence: divine, angelic, and satanic. Samuel's reference to the "ides of March" along with this passage from Shakespeare at the very least suggest that he is questioning his place in life on his birthday, if not his perception.

On February 8, 1808, Samuel again searches for guidance in an entry titled "A Planter's life compared with a merchant's, or any other," which addresses a choice of professions: "The merchant thinks his profession requires more mind than the planters, that after it is well ascertained what an estate can produce, there is no great talent required to follow the beaten track. I believe, it will be granted, that the thought as far as it goes, is just." Having described how merchants are perceived, he elaborates: "Is the merchant therefore more elevated on the scale than the planter? Will the merchant allow that he thinks himself acting up to his duty, if he provides for a father, a sister, a mother, a whole family? Will he allow that there be few of his profession who exceed this extent of duty?" As Samuel is part of both the planter and the mercantile class, he considers how a sense of duty may moderate self-interest and by extension assertions of superiority. On these points, Samuel elaborates, "If then those who happen to be not of our own colour may be regarded as our fellow creatures, the planter who employs himself industriously, in regulating the concerns, and providing for the welfare of his slaves, does an act as great at least, as the merchant although he be not so much talked of, and perhaps his profession affords as ample employment for the occupations which elevate our nature as the merchants." Touting the virtues of the planter as a model of industry, Samuel appears to elevate the role of the planter and, as such, presents an interesting parallel to his father's own process of positioning himself as a humane plantation manager.

In the next entry, which may be from 1808, Samuel is even more forthcoming about slavery, as he reflects on the death of one of his slaves: "Feb 14th. — Margaret died last evening. Her pains, the passions of her mind, which probably was the occasion of them, are over." Similar to Paris's death noted earlier, Margaret's passing is also portrayed as a release from pain and torment. The entry thus continues: "She is admitted, no doubt, at once to the beauties of a new world, her mind relieved from torment, her acquaintance made with new beings, her children restored to her." He then interjects with this comparison: "Just, appears to me the idea of Linnaeus that one reason of our not being allowed to see the other world is, lest the patience necessary for carrying us through the present one, should fail us." Samuel then draws this conclusion: "And what is the mighty misfortune of being a negro slave in this short life, if one is thereby made more willing to leave it; and if slavery here, is no cause of discrimination in the other?" His acknowledgment of the "mighty misfortune" of being a slave and that this state has no bearing on being admitted to "the other world" ultimately admits to the injustice of slavery.

Samuel returns to these topics on "March 11th 08" in an entry that begins, "I am strongly tempted to note an accident which occurred to me this morning. — I was reflecting that however agreeable to religion it might be, to treat the negroes well, it is improper to have any familiarity with them, which may make them at all companions." Without specifying what he means by "familiarity," Samuel proposes a corrective: "The best guard against that, would be the having more society than I have, — the having a family." He then imagines, "as one amusement for such a family my father's idea of reading daily at breakfast a paper of the Spectator, came into my mind as both pleasant and instructive. I will try it, thought I, as I drew my chair to my solitary breakfast table. The first opening of the book not pleasing me, I turned to another part. The following passage first struck my eye." Here, Samuel includes a quotation from Joseph Addison's the *Spectator*, Monday, March 12, 1711, which reads in part: "It was said of Socrates that he brought philosophy down from Heaven to inhabit among men; and I shall be ambitious to have it said of me, that I have brought philosophy out of closets and libraries, schools, and colleges to dwell in clubs and assemblies, at tea tables and in coffee houses." Addison then advises "all well regulated families, that set apart an hour in every morning, for tea and bread and butter . . . to order this paper to be punctually served up, and to be looked upon as a part of the tea equipage."[60] An entry that begins with Samuel's concerns about having improper "familiarity" with his slaves leads him to consider family, his father, Addison, and Socrates as he searches for context in what appears to be a disorienting "accident."

Samuel's reflections on his isolation appear again on "April 16th 08," in an entry titled "Journal": "Rose early to go to town — in the boat — such uncleanly manners, such fullness of one's self, such vacancy of mind, will a solitary life surrounded with dependants only, not elevated by dignified female society bring even a man of information to." This last phrase refers to "a scholar" or "man of knowledge" and thus underscores a despair heightened by fears of poverty: "What a misfortune is old age, if to such feebleness be added poverty, which deprives a man of external respect." These concerns are then connected more directly to his own family: "My father! O God! enable me to secure him some money to save his independance and respectability.— I ask not wealth, — but save me, I beseech thee, from guilty thoughts in my efforts in this world." Fears of his father falling into poverty intensify his sense of duty, and though the source of his guilt is not stated, the previous entries generally reference his life in the West Indies and by extension slavery. In this same entry, he changes the topic to mathematics: "A little of Euclid, and reflected that tho' I may perhaps be toiling in vain, as to the purpose of my present undertaking, I am at least acquiring a habit of employment and hardness." His present "undertaking" may be related to the one described in an entry from February 24: "I am engaged in a most arduous undertaking, — and if I can procure no addition to the income of the estate, I fear a doubtful one; as to its eventual success. — If I must fail however, let me at least fail with decency. Let nothing deprive me of equanimity.— Let me always act by the principles which I have sanctioned by experience, — let my independence be dearer to me than success, — for success without that will lose its charms." The specifics about the "undertaking" are not stated, but the effects two months later suggest that it would not be as successful as he had hoped. Samuel continues his self-examination as the April 16 entry continues: "3 o'clock — I have recovered my thoughts of this morning. — Were I to break a limb now I could bear it — Were I to be required to die to day, I should not shrink. Though I am not now acquiring wealth, is not this thought worth more than wealth?" With a note of acceptance about his fate, Samuel's acknowledgment provides some relief as he searches for perspective. He thus continues, "Some part of my conduct today requires reflection — I ought neither to speak, to smile, to move where I take no interest." The next section of this entry might be referring directly to his father's assistance in establishing Samuel in business, although the referent of "he" is not explicitly identified: "For — what pains he gave himself to with giving me an invitation that I would not have accepted of. — Is it not easier for me to recover my former habits of self command now than it will be hereafter, if I should attain to a more satisfactory mode of life than I lead, to overcome those which I cannot avoid forming now?" Samuel's anxiety about success is thus compounded by a loss of "self command," which appears to have been further influenced by the "solitary life" he describes at the beginning of this entry.

The next day, Samuel continues to reflect on his current situation and, subsequently, on his state of mind. The entry dated "April 17ᵗʰ— Sunday" thus begins with a question: "Must I not candidly own, that constant employment with anxiety about my engagements is the most fortunate way probably to rectify a mind like mine?" The attention paid to his "anxiety" will hopefully bring reform, or at least some degree of repair. He then includes notes about Scottish minister Hugh Blair's "sermon on the Divine presence," and later, on April 26, on Blair's "Extremes in religions and moral conduct," which leads to these assessments: "I think, to my having gone to an extreme, I owe the gloom that is over my mind. I suspect that I have endeavored to shine but on one side, — that I have neglected some things from being taken up with the idea of success in my engagements to my father." In trying to provide for his family and ensure his father's financial security, Samuel thus notes a "gloom," both mentally and emotionally, prompting him again to seek context in this April 26 entry: "I think, on reflection, the disposition of mind I ought to have under all events, is that I had in — 02, trusting my happiness to no mortal, and fearing little for the future; — governing myself, allowing myself to be never idle, but showing at all times the most suitable occupation. Perhaps, I should in addition rely upon Providence for the time to come; preserve decorum in my way of life." His salvation thus takes the form of discipline and faith, two areas that Sarah had consistently encouraged him to cultivate as well. On October 29, he again weighs in on the topic of success: "In making a fortune one must have patience — It is not to be done all at once, but by degrees." And in marking the changing nature of trade, he adds, "It is uncertain how long I may continue at Fort Royal. Therefore I ought not to get deeply engaged there in business. — In like manner it is uncertain how long I may continue in this world,— therefore it is not prudent to get deeply engaged here." These two acknowledgments of limitations of place and time echo his April entries, in which he contemplates his role in the world at large and in his family.

Samuel would continue to travel, as indicated by entries from "Caracus 10 Dec 08 — Church of St. Pauls" and "Barbadoes July 23rd 09." When writing his entry "Fort Royal 26th Feby 1810," Samuel is again at Martinique, where he notes, "For my part I cannot think that there will be any very great change at death. — Nature does most things with regard to mankind by gradation." This reflection on mortality is followed by entries about dueling and then a note from St. Pierre, on July 6, 1810, regarding "Voltaire's death of Caesar," a play that "departs from historical truth — which I think is not allowable." As these entries show, Samuel considered a range of topics and reflected seriously on his life, often struggling with the goal of achieving success to the detriment of his own personal happiness. Despite Samuel's tremendous efforts to support his family, the long-hoped-for intention that Mount Pleasant would generate family income was not to be. He was, however, instrumental in brokering the sale in 1810. In doing so, James W. Roberts reports, Samuel "took control of his father's Caribbean affairs once and for all. After benefitting by the British contracts at the turn of the century, Sam had helped service his father's debts in Glasgow, and assisted with expenses in Massachusetts. Now he arranged with John Campbell Sr. & Co. to finally dispose of Mount Pleasant plantation." Considering the long-term fallout from Fédon's rebellion and the struggling West Indies economy in general, Roberts also observes, "It was disappointing, but not unexpected, therefore, when Cary Jr. explained that the plantation's sale did little more than cancel remaining debts with the Campbells: there was no grand plantation legacy."[61] For Samuel and his parents, Grenada had proved far more difficult than imagined.

Dreams of the Son Unrealized: The Passing of Samuel Cary Jr.

On November 1, 1810, just twelve days shy of his hoped-for return to Chelsea for a much-needed recovery of his health, Samuel Cary Jr. died at sea at the age of thirty-seven.[62] In Sarah's letter to Lucius on November 18, she relays a sad report along with her grief: "No language can convey to you the surprise and shock I have undergone in the late melancholy news of the death of our dear Sam; Robert had written that He was unwell and talk'd of going off the Island for his recovery, yet this did not prepare me, I supposed that a little change would answer every purpose and he would by that means soon recruit, still less did I contemplate an intention of coming to America." Long familiar with the fevers and illnesses associated with the islands, Sarah was still not prepared for this tragedy. She then explains how the news was conveyed: "Think what was my Agony when your Father (in the tenderest manner too) inform'd me he had just read in the Newspaper that our dear Samuel had died on board a schooner (Bartlet) bound from Martinique to Marblehead." She was, as she tells Lucius, "wholly unprepared for the event." Sarah and Samuel began to collect their strength and, as she continues, "As soon as the tide of grief had a little abated we began to think what was to be done." Captain Bartlet, in turn, provided an account to Charles of Samuel's final days, noting that, as Sarah explains, he "had been calm and tranquil the whole of the voyage and died a peaceful quiet death for the most part silent but always willing to reply to any questions ask'd of him." Samuel had apparently gone "on board so extremely low that those who accompanied Him told the Capt. they did not expect he would reach the Shore. He was finally unable to ask for what he wanted, and wrote down with a pencil his directions for the medicine and little things he wished for in the night and once said even <u>chearfully</u> 'When I get by my brother in Law's fire side I shall soon be well' and ask'd if the vessel kept her courses." Samuel's final, hopeful words may have been comforting. Yet knowing that Samuel had been so close to his destination was an added source of sorrow, as Sarah explains: "Capt. Bartlet had 34 days passage from St. Pierre, and our dear sufferer died 22 Days after they sail'd, on the 1ˢᵗ Day of November." The family's collective grief was particularly hard felt by Samuel Cary Sr., as Sarah conveys: "This has been a dreadful blow to your Father I know not which predominates more in his mind, gratitude to the Almighty for having given him so excellent a Son and sharing him so long, or the pain and grief of parting with him, for my part I desire and wish to submit to those decrees that I know are inevitable, yet find I want that consolation that I endeavor to bestow on him." Sarah then addresses Lucius directly: "What is this life my dear Lucius and all besides, is it not vanity? and folly in the extreme to forget that we are fast hastening on to another." In closing, she again tries to console him: "I have still much to say to you but my Letter can not add any pleasure to you, and I would not for worlds give you any additional pain to what you will already feel, long before you reach this page, farewell my beloved Lucius, take care of your health, and if occasionally you will write to Robert and give him some advice, you will do him an essential service. I long to hear from you again, and am your most affectionate Mother."[63] In this last note, Sarah thus continued the line of brotherly mentorship in the family, as she encouraged Lucius in his own role as an elder brother.

This sad event thus brought many hopes in the family to a halt, including plans for Samuel's own retirement at Chelsea and a general optimism about the family's future. As the next chapter addresses, Lucius and his brothers would now supplement the family's income. The loss of Samuel, however, dramatically changed the family's narrative. For Lucius in particular, his aspirations would now be challenged and tested as he continued to make sacrifices for the greater good of the family.

CHAPTER SIX

Sustaining a Family

Grenada and Chelsea, 1810–1826

As the Cary family continued to mourn the loss of their brother and son Samuel, his siblings would take up the charge of providing financial support. Lucius continued to establish trade throughout the West Indies and the Caribbean, including at Grenada, Martinique, Demerara, Bermuda, and Jamaica. Charles, Henry, Edward, Thomas, George, Robert, and William established businesses in New York, Philadelphia, and Boston. Margaret, Harriet, and Ann remained at Chelsea to assist their mother with the household. Sarah had married the Reverend Joseph Tuckerman, a Unitarian clergyman, in 1808. Their father, Samuel Cary, devoted himself to the Chelsea farm. Throughout, Sarah Cary continued to guide her family with strength and resolve, even as they faced the persistent tensions between seeking fortune and maintaining family connections.

In late 1810, Lucius left Demerara, as recorded in the *Essequebo & Demerary Royal Gazette*: "Saturday, October 13th, 1810. Secretary's Office. This is to inform the Public, that the following Persons intend quitting this Colony: . . . Lucius Cary, in 14 days, from the 1st Octb." In "November, 1810," Lucius writes from "Barbadoes" to his sister Ann, whose nickname is Nancy: "My Dear Nancy, — You will be surprised to see my letter dated from this place. Indeed I am myself a little surprised to find that I am not in Demerara, for, being so long accustomed to that place, I am absolutely lost whenever I see or hear of any object unconnected with it." Lucius is thus sending this letter before he hears of his brother Samuel's death. He stays in Barbados until at least May 1811, as indicated in a second, undated letter, which also states: "Not long ago I received your two favors of February and March, accompanied by several others from my mother, Margaret, and Henry."[1] There is no mention of Samuel's death, which suggests that Lucius had not yet received Sarah's letter dated November 18, 1810. Shortly before departing for London in 1812, Lucius writes to his mother, beginning with this overview: "After Seven Years close application to Business, I am now about to enjoy I hope for a little time the fruits of my Industry.— My Letter to my Father will inform you that I am just about to begin my Voyage and that the Lapse of a few months will bring me into the midst of my dear Friends at the Retreat." Having established his itinerary, Lucius reveals, "The monotonous Habit of life I have led since I left you causes me to feel a number of different sensations at the thought of a change though it will be but temporary, however I have a right to expect more good than ill from it — and according to Doctor Pangloss 'Tout est pour le mieux.'" Lucius's description of his "monotonous Habit of life" not only echoes his brother Samuel's assessments, but his reference to lines from Voltaire's *Candide* (1759), "all is for the best in the best of all possible worlds," also hint at his father's initial enthusiasm when he had embarked for St. Kitts. Regarding a return to Chelsea, Lucius notes, "I rejoice at the Idea of again seeing you, and frequently ask myself if any change of Circumstances or Events can Compensate me for the long separation, — but it must be my object to enjoy the future and not look back to the past." He then solicits gifts, or "Commissions," as he puts it: "I expect to hear frequently from all the Family and to get a memorandum from each of the little articles I must bring with me. — As I shall have plenty of Leisure and some Cash I shall be able to attend to all Commissions and if any body omits to employ me, I shall think I have some right to be hugged when I see her or him."[2] Lucius thus bid an optimistic farewell.

True to his expectations, Lucius found his new location satisfactory. He reports to Sarah on May 20, 1812, "Well my dear Mother, here am I in London — transported from the Land of mud, anxiety and trouble to a fashionable first Floor in the gay Metropolis." As if sensing his mother's reaction to this salutation, he then paraphrases lines from Richard Cumberland's *The West Indian: A Comedy* (1771): "'My happy Stars have given me some Money and the conspiring-winds have blown me hither to spend it.' — No not to spend it, say you, to use it — not to abuse it." In Cumberland's play, these lines are delivered by two separate characters, starting with Belcour: "My happy stars have given me a good estate, and the conspiring-winds have blown me hither to spend it." Then Stockwell replies: "To use it, not to waste it, I should hope; to treat it, Mr. Belcour, not as a vassal, over whom you have a wanton and a despotic power; but as a subject which you are bound to govern with a temperate and restrained authority" (1.5). By dramatizing differing views of economy, Lucius attempts to make light of the contrast, while also anticipating his mother's response: "Well well may we never differ more in opinion than we do upon this Subject!" Having received Sarah's letters from December 1811 and March 1812, in which she apparently emphasized the importance of "propriety and virtue," Lucius responds, "Believe me, what you say has my best attention," and then notes, "I have an innate pride sufficient to preserve me from any conduct which can cause my Friends to blush for me." Shifting to a summary of his activities since his arrival in London, Lucius reports that he has been visiting with the Marryats, former neighbors from Grenada: "I was received in the most cordial manner and promise myself great happiness and pleasure from their Acquaintance. — I was afraid that the lapse of time or some other cause would have lessened their Friendship, but it appears to have increased it." Lucius's time thus far has been "quite employed in calling on them and filling up my List of Invitations for the ensuing Fortnight, after which, I shall take a trip to some of the mineral Springs." In closing, he relays an anecdote that Marryat told him about an investment that went awry: "The Estate he bought from the Count de Crillon turns out to be a deception and that the Count is a vagabond of the name of Simon who fled from this Country."[3] According to Henry Adams's account, the Count Edward de Crillon was a con man also accused of being "an agent of the Emperor's secret police," as in Napoleon's.[4] It is unclear why Lucius included this note, other than as a dramatic incident.

Lucius then embarked on a three-week excursion to the mineral baths in Cheltenham, for "two reasons," he tells Ann on June 5, 1812. "One is because it is a fashionable, agreeable place; and the other from having been ordered by the physicians to drink a course of the waters, which are peculiarly beneficial to a constitution discomposed or debilitated by a warm climate." On "June 13th," he notes, "I shall go on with my letter," and reports, "My acquaintances here all remark the benefits I have derived from the waters, and I feel capitally. Tomorrow I change my pump, and drink *steel* in place of *iron*. The country air and temperate habits of the place are, however, great causes of the improvement of one's health." The next week, he would travel to Bath with "Two brother West Indians" in their "barouche." Generally speaking, Lucius tells Ann, "People are often satisfied if they are included in the mass of respectable society; but there is in every place a select, a superior society, who, while they mingle with others, still preserve a distinction. Now it is my desire to be one of these, and to be so, not from introduction or recommendation, but because it naturally belongs to me to be so." Although Lucius found such company attractive, this ostentation was of a kind his mother had often cautioned him against. He concludes his letter by telling his sister, "Give my best love to all the family." And perhaps anticipating Sarah's thoughts about his riding around England in a barouche, he adds, "Kind regards to my mother, and tell her that I have not missed church since I landed in the country."[5] England had thus brought Lucius a welcome change "after Seven Years close application to Business."

A Somber Development: The Passing of the Family Patriarch

On August 1, 1812, Samuel Cary Sr. died. There were at least six notices in papers from Boston to New York marking his passing, as on August 5 in Boston's *Columbia Centinel*: "In Chelsea, on Saturday last, Samuel Cary; Esq. AEt, 69." Regarding the thirty-nine-year marriage between her grandparents, Caroline Curtis reflects, "It had been a marriage of love from first to last. He was a man of imperious nature, at times giving way to high temper, but with all that, deeply religious. . . . I know, from what I have heard, that he did not always succeed in controlling himself; but his wife's love showed itself as strongly in helping him to be his nobler self and in giving him constant companionship." Curtis also notes Sarah's devotion to her family: "My grand-mother seems to have been a woman with great influence about her. With all these sons, scattered in different places, her correspondence was constant and most open, and to her husband her devotion was absolute."[6] Sarah would now manage the Chelsea estate, as suggested on October 23, 1812, in the Boston *New-England Palladium*, with a "Notice" from the "Executors of the last Will and Testament of Samuel Cary, late of *Chelsea* in the County of *Suffolk*, Esquire, deceased," asking that "all persons having demands upon the estate" should contact Sarah, and those who are "indebted to the said Estate, are called to make payment." The notice was signed, "Sarah Cary, *Executrix*."

Unfortunately for Lucius, his father had died by the time Lucius returned to Chelsea from London. Margaret Cary provides a narrative of her brother's return: "When he reached the tollhouse on the Chelsea side of the bridge, he inquired after the family and learned the death of our dear father. The shock was very great and our meeting very mournful for a while. I see him now, in my memory, walking the little parlor in an agony." As Margaret explains, Lucius felt this loss most acutely, especially as he now had to go forward without his father and his older brother as guides: "He loved his father dearly; he came full of affection; he expected a cordial sympathy in his prospects, and to meet the approbation of one whom he highly reverenced, and who could enter into all his plans; and then to think that by coming here first he might have seen and enjoyed him."[7] Writing from New York, in an undated letter to his mother following his father's death, Lucius begins with praise for Sarah: "How happy you make me, my dear mother, by the expressions of resignation and comfort which your letters contain! The contemplation of the virtues of the dear friend we have lost is indeed a theme replete with sources of affection and consolation." He then adds this remembrance of his father: "In attachment and devotion to the welfare of his beloved family he was excelled by none. . . . The calm tranquillity of his death proceeded from the consciousness of a well-spent life, and is a trait which gives tenfold force to the maxims of virtue which he inculcated." After acknowledging their mutual grief, Lucius extends his comfort: "Let us look to the future, therefore, and consider how rich we all still are in the possession of our remaining friends. Please give my best love to all with you. You really, my dear mother, are fortunate in having your dear girls on one side and your fine young men on the other."[8] As these recollections convey, Samuel Cary's long life was well remembered. And, in another context, Samuel Cary experienced both the heights of West Indian planter wealth and the subsequent decline.

The Pursuit of Fortune Continues:
Lucius Cary's Travels and Sustaining the Family

For the next several years, Lucius would travel throughout the West Indies. In a letter to his mother from Demerara, on February 1, 1814, his role as a supporter of the family is clear: "I attend to what you say of George, and have written to beg Henry to provide my proportion of the necessary sum for his College Expenses which I will readily pay." He also includes a note about his brother Samuel: "In my way up here last year, I stopped at Martinique, and there fell in with an old Negro belonging to Sam, — he was subject to epileptic fits and was living with some people in Fort Royal on charity, every one refusing to allow any thing for him." Lucius then describes his decision regarding this man: "I brought him away with me however, and have since brought him bound and disposed of him so that there will be a hundred Dollars more for the little fund my dear brother left." The phrase "to be bound out and disposed of" would have usually been used in reference to indentures of apprenticeship. Here, however, the phrase "brought him bound" followed by the reference to money suggests that this man was sold. He then adds, "I have also recovered a small sum of about half that amount coming to him from a House in Grenada." Lucius's concern for his brother's financial legacy thus also reveals the painful vulnerability of his former slave. He then makes several additions to his letter, with a note about his brothers: "11ᵗʰ Feby: I am very glad to hear that Charles is doing so well— and that the Boys have got into College." Then, two months later, while still waiting for a ship to collect his letters, he adds, "April 20th.— I am coming on very well and shall see you before Xmas, 'coûte que coûte,' that is 'cost what it may; at all costs.' "⁹

There appears to have been a delay, for on January 10, 1815, Lucius writes to Sarah from Bermuda: "It was on the ever memorable fifth of November that having brought all my affairs to a close and bid good-bye to about a dozen old Friends whose lives and a congeniality of Habits and minds had endeared to me, that I put myself aboard the Fleet and with a fair wind made sail, I hope for the last time, from Demeraray." With yet another resolution to go forward, Lucius explains, "A few days brought us to Grenada," where an un-expected delay of a "fortnight" allowed him "to make a Tour of the Island, make several new acquaintances and renew a number of old ones." After a visit to St. George's, he went to Grenville Bay, about which he tells his mother: "You may be sure I did not miss the opportunity of reviewing the spot where I was born and spent my boyish Days." He then visited the Horsfords: "They were highly pleased to see me.— We went back in comparing notes, to the Year '70— traveled over the whole History of the connection between our two families from its commencement to the present time." Next, he traveled to Mount Pleasant, where he "called on the present proprietor" and "was glad to find every thing went on well." He then reports, "I saw several of the old Negroes — on the other side of the Island, the only old Friends I met were Joe who went with you to America in '84— and Glasgow,— both well and glad to see me." In noting that Joe had accompanied them to Chelsea in 1784, Lucius provides information not otherwise included in the extant Cary cor-respondence. His reference to Joe and Glasgow as "old Friends" may reflect his childhood memories that elide servants and slaves. Altogether, Lucius appears to have enjoyed his visit: "I spent my time on the Island very well and after feasting to my Heart's Content on Turtle Fins and old Wine embarked in the Fleet for St. Thomas, which is the General Rendezvous."¹⁰

A few months later, on March 1, 1815, Lucius writes to Sarah from "Saint Johns, New Brunswick," where he plans to travel the "four Hundred Miles which divide us," by road or by water. He comments on discovering that the War of 1812 had ended in February: "On arriving, I have received the unex-pected but most welcome and satisfying news of peace." Lucius was optimis-tic and considered it "a good omen." He finally arrived at Chelsea on March

23, 1815, "between one and two o'clock," as Sarah reports to Henry, including this description of Lucius: "A fur cap and large greatcoat had so completely transformed my dear Lucius that I did not immediately recognize him. As soon as I did, you will easily believe that I sprang from my chair and the emotions that followed among us."[11] In April, Lucius accompanied his sister Margaret from Chelsea to Brunswick via Hartford and New Haven by stage, then by steamboats to New York and on to Brunswick. Margaret would travel on by stage to Trenton and by steamer down the Delaware River to Philadelphia, where she would stay until the end of May. This journey was notable for its innovative combination of stage and steam travel, which had only recently become available. "By the end of the War of 1812," George R. Taylor explains, Robert R. Livingston and Robert Fulton had "established steamboat service from New York to New Brunswick on the Raritan. With the end of the British blockade in 1815, they inaugurated steamboat navigation on Long Island Sound by sending the *Fulton* to New Haven."[12] Margaret would then travel from Philadelphia to stay with the Stout family in Belleville, New Jersey, a township just west of the Passaic River.

When Lucius returned to New York, he and brother Henry formed a partnership, as noted in the *Evening Post* on May 1, 1815: "Their future business will be conducted under the firm of L. and H. CARY." They would sell a variety of goods, including cotton, coffee, rice, molasses, tobacco, and wine. This partnership would last three years until it was dissolved on May 4, 1818, as reported in the New York *Mercantile Advertiser*: "The firm of L. and H. CARY, expires by its own limitation this day, and is accordingly dissolved. . . . The business of the above concern will henceforth be conducted by *Henry Cary* and *William F. Cary,* under the firm of Henry Cary and Co." As these various partnerships formed and dissolved, the Cary brothers would eventually find success, as contemporary Joseph Scoville explains: "The business done by the Carys has been immense for many years. It is a purely commission business, and they are agents for many of the leading East India merchants in Boston. Consequently they sell largely and principally East India goods, and have consequently of East India men."[13] Under Henry Cary's leadership, the business expanded its markets. Advertisements from 1818 to 1820, for example, show that Henry Cary and Co. sold an even greater variety of goods, including "rum and molasses, brandy, rice, North West Martin Skins, Iron, cut glass, sugar, vermillion, Buffalo robes, Squirrel linings, Parchment Beaver, Muskrat skins, furs, tea, muslins, China goods, and Nankeens [yellow Chinese cloth]." In doing so, they generated new sources of revenue for the family at Chelsea, which alleviated some pressure on Lucius as a main source of financial support. And after years at sea, his older brother Charles settled at Chelsea, where he became the town treasurer.

In summer 1818, Lucius accompanied his sister Ann on a trip to Niagara Falls, during which he secured their various means of transportation by carriage, stage, and steamboat. In Ann's letter to her sister Harriet from aboard the "Steamboat Franconia, Lake Ontario, July 16, 1818," she describes their first view of the falls: "We found a path where boards were laid, followed it till we came to the spot, — the bushes quite wet, the spray falling over us. Here it was grand, — the water dashing down the rapids and falling over the precipice immediately beside us." The next day, Ann writes from Kingston about the beauty of the scene, tempered only by Lucius's departure: "The boat is gliding through the lake, the sun shines on the distant shore, and the moon will soon rise in all her splendor. All is beautiful round me, and my feelings would be in unison with the scene if it were not for parting with my dear Lucius." From Kingston, Lucius would travel to Montreal before heading to New York and then on to Bermuda, while Ann would stay in Kingston until her brother George arrived to accompany her home to Chelsea.[14]

Lucius arrived in Bermuda in August 1818. In his first letter to his mother, on August 28, 1818, he writes, "I am happy to inform you that I arrived here yesterday after a passage of ten days, rather long owing to the light winds which prevail at this time of the Year and to the little Sloop not having the keels of Atalanta," a contrast then to the swift runner from Greek mythology. Hoping to send his letter in a "Vessel sailing tomorrow for Providence," Lucius adds a few notes about Bermuda: "I have not time to say more than that it is excessively warm, and the reflection from the white stone very trying to the Eyes.— But I land with much the same feeling with which I entered the Poets Corner at Westminster Abbey some Years ago — determined to be pleased." Lucius then began setting up his household, sending his mother a follow-up report on October 15: "I have been principally occupied in furnishing my house and getting settled as it is called," an undertaking that prompts a request: "I believe I must have the prints which hang up in your West parlor, and I believe you will spare them without much reluctance.— Those things generally lose interest with their novelty, and I will try to replace them with some others." He then comments that the layout of Bermuda has contributed to his daily routine: "I am obliged to take a good deal of exercise, which is just the thing for me.— The business of the Island is done in two distinct towns, and I am obliged to be continually on the trot between them." This is likely a reference to Hamilton and St. George's, a distance of thirty-two miles on today's roads. In closing, Lucius notes, "Perhaps you are not aware that Bermuda was the scene of Shakespeare's play of The Tempest."[15]

In response, Sarah writes on November 13, 1818, in what appears to be an enjoyable narrative style in the Cary family letters of rendering an imaginative scenario, in this case of herself in Lucius's new home: "I am often with you in Idea, furnishing your House, arranging your domestic affairs, in the parlour and in the kitchen, if you would condescend to go there, as sometimes all Housekeepers must you know, and then set down by your side, and talk over our concerns together, the past, the present, and lay plans for the future." Having presented this fanciful conversation, which creates a space for their relationship to exist despite their separation, she then comments on his current situation more directly: "To my view you are happy, tranquil and by the dissolution of the partnership, relieved from many things, not intirely pleasing, to a man of your habits and taste, am I not right? If it is delusion, it is of that sort that serves to make me more contented, at the thought of our separation." Without more details about why Henry and Lucius's partnership dissolved, Sarah infers that Lucius prefers working directly from the islands rather than having to be responsible for both selling and supplying the goods. In keeping with her usual style of moving between several topics in one letter, Sarah adds a note on "Sunday 15th, 5 in the afternoon," which includes an account of her trip with her daughter Ann to see "Sister Cary," Mary Gray Otis: "We had a very pleasant journey, altho it happened to be a very cold day. The harvesting is now at an end and the beauty of the country nearly at an end, for the season. The elegant colours exhibited in the Woods, and abundance of evergreens, however, compensated in a great measure for the loss of verdant fields. We sat off at eight o'clock, took a chicken at two, at Ipswich, and arrived at Newbury Port at 4 o'clock." According to Sarah, the reunion was "kind and cordial, and revived in us all the good feelings we felt for each other after a separation of ten years."

Moving on, Sarah notes that Henry has requested a "picture" by Gilbert Stuart, for which she explains, "I am to get to Stuart tomorrow." This request then prompts her presumably to reflect on the John Singleton Copley portraits that commemorated her marriage to Samuel: "When I look upon your Father's profile and think how much pleasure it gives me to think I have it, I cannot refuse to gratify his wishes, and think that when I am gone, my family may value a resemblance of their Mother as much. Otherwise I should say, that the likeness of the young and handsome only, should be preserved on canvas." She then makes her own request of Lucius: "Apropos can you not gratify me by sending your picture, if you have any one, artist enough to take you, in Bermuda." In a note from "9 in the eve," Sarah comments on her daughter Sarah's happy marriage: "Sarah and Mr. T[uckerman] are just gone from here and begged me to say every thing expressive of their kind regards, and best wishes, I never saw Sarah look better."[16] Then, in Henry Cary's letter from New York on May 19, 1819, to his mother, he begins by apologizing for the delay in thanking "her for the favor of her portrait" and describes the "over-flowings of pleasure which it produced." Initially, however, he was "disappointed": "The expression of countenance is different from that in which you were accustomed to rise up before me, and I could not help at first exclaiming to myself: 'Why, this is not my mother!' But after it was hung up, I found your character and attitude so perfectly delineated that I felt the influence of your presence, and that Stuart had done all that his art admits of."[17] In this regard, the ongoing conversation about pictures elicits yet another response.

After a four-year gap in their extant correspondence, Lucius writes to his mother on April 20, 1824, from his new location in Kingston, Jamaica. In doing so, he acknowledges the receipt of her letter from February 25, which "coming by a fast sailing vessel, reached me in three weeks after the date of it — a pleasing and uncommon circumstance which seemed to bring us nearer together when I received it." He then notes he is "happy to know" that she "had obtained a new source of pleasure from having a Daughter settled in town" and refers to his mother's wish that all her children could be closer to home: "I hope all your other wishes will be successively gratified, my dear Mother.— It is inconsistent with our nature to be without them." Then, returning to an oft repeated desire for reunion, "I should be happy if I could accomplish one of them by adding my presence to your little Circle.— I do begin to feel an uncommon Yearning that way and perhaps may not always find it so necessary to control that feeling as I do at present." In a postscript, he comments on the pending abolition of slavery: "You perhaps hear of the measures which are taking to ameliorate the situation of the West Indian Negroes.— The disuse of the whip and the promotion of matrimony, saving banks and etc.— are paving the way to a final emancipation."[18] Edward L. Cox elaborates, "After the Abolition of the Slave Trade Act of 1807 denied planters access to traditional sources of African labor, they took additional steps toward amelioration"; additionally, "In the wake of revolutionary upheavals at home and aboard, legislators grudgingly considered it in their interest to ameliorate the condition of their slaves lest they be driven to open revolt." David Beck Ryden places these developments in a larger context: "The climbing sugar prices during the 1790s undid the Ramsay-Clarkson economic argument until the early 1800s, when a catastrophic and prolonged collapse in the sugar market reintroduced the concept that abolition was a macro-economically prudent measure." As a result, Ryden explains, "The painful economic downturn in sugar markets proved to be fortuitous for the cause of abolition."[19] Slavery in the British Caribbean would finally end in 1838.

The Family Reunited, albeit Briefly

In 1825, Lucius returned to Chelsea for a visit with his mother and family before traveling to England, where he had plans to retire. In Margaret's November 1, 1853, letter to her nephew Edward, she explains that after living in Bermuda and Jamaica, Lucius had "made a fortune sufficient to justify him, as he supposed, to live in England on his income. He chartered a schooner, and came to Boston in the summer of 1825; time enough to pass a few weeks with his dear mother. . . . He was full of affection, had drawn plans for the improvement of the house, and arranged a plan for each of his sisters to receive fifty dollars every Christmas."[20] Lucius later writes to his mother on July 13, 1825, aboard the "Hunter, at Sea": "My visit has gratified me extremely and I go away a new Man . . . about the 10 September you may expect to hear from me.— Good bye, my dear Mother!" On August 5, he writes from Kingston, Jamaica, "I have the pleasure to inform you of my arrival here on the first Instant, the day I had planned for," and then explains why he is writing two months earlier than the projected September date: "Meeting with head winds, I did not stop either at Turks Island or Cuba, but came direct." Reflecting on his recent visit, he confesses, "I left Boston with feelings to which I have been of late a stranger, and my visit was just long enough to allow me to extricate myself.— Now, having renewed my personal acquaintance with you all . . . I can go on in a more connected intercourse with you than heretofore." Having noted this restorative effect, Lucius also acknowledges the importance of letters in maintaining these connections, as they provide important opportunities for reflection and perspective: "We shall now be divested of that unquiet feeling which is so apt to be generated by the long separation of friends.— I leave you surrounded by so many sons and daughters, so encircled with ties, that you really need the enjoyment of a distant Correspondent, a pleasure peculiar in itself and therefore adding to your general happiness.— You see I can find new arguments for my absence without adverting to those which already exist." Perhaps, as he prepared for England, there was a degree of justifying his distance from home yet again. A week later, on August 12, Lucius sends kind wishes from Kingston: "Now, I hope this will find you all well and the warm weather replaced by the cool breezes of autumn." And on August 29, after writing about his voyage, health, and brothers and sisters, Lucius acknowledges his mother's important influence in his life: "Every thing depends, as you have often told me, upon the manner in which things are done." To this end, he continues, "I should have mentioned to you, in the first instance, the little arrangement I intended making for my sisters,— should I not?"—a reference perhaps to Margaret's comment above about the "plan for each of his sisters to receive fifty dollars every Christmas." He then concludes, "Adieu my dear Mother I am always Your affectionate L. C."[21]

These letters to his mother would turn out to be his last. Shortly after Lucius's visit in June, Sarah Cary died at home, on August 26, 1825, at the age of seventy-two. Several funeral notices appeared in newspapers, as in the *Salem Gazette,* August 30, 1825: "Died. . . . At her residence in Chelsea, in the 26th inst. Mrs. Sarah Cary, widow of the late Samuel Cary, Esq. aged 72." On September 28, Ann writes to Lucius with an account of their mother's final days: "Never was a more beautiful termination to a life devoted to duty and the constant exercise of the best affections. 'I am ready to go,' she said to Mr. Tuckerman a few days before her death; 'but if further trial is necessary for me, I am willing to stay.' In this state she continued, except that her desire to depart grew more ardent. The wish to live for her children, which she strongly expressed at first, seemed to fade, not that they became less dear, but the desire of being with God in heaven took possession of her heart." In Ann's description of her mother's final wishes, Sarah remains devoted to her children while also expressing her faith in providence. By way of comforting her brother, Ann recalls their mother's pleasure in seeing him again and in receiving his letter upon leaving Chelsea: "With what satisfaction, my dear brother, must you think of your visit, and how plainly see the hand of Providence in guiding you hither! It was to her a source of unalloyed pleasure. Even your sailing at the time you had appointed was to her a cause for gratitude, as it could leave you nothing to regret. 'Dear, dear Lucius,' she would often say; 'that I should have seen him so lately! And that little note by the pilot, too!' Indeed, your recollections must be very sweet." Ann also thanks her brother for helping defer the funeral costs: "You may believe, dear Lucius, we thought with gratitude of you when we could each go to our own purses and pay the necessary bills for our mourning dresses, which were very expensive, as the time was short and we could not attend to them ourselves."[22] Again, Lucius's support is acknowledged and appreciated.

On October 8, 1825, from Kingston, Jamaica, Lucius responds to his brother Thomas's letter of September 3, after hearing about his mother's death a few days earlier from his brother William: "The news they gave me of my mother's death was most painful; but now that I can see with how many consoling circumstances that event was attended, I can bear the loss, particularly when I consider how supreme her happiness must now be." He then turns to legal matters regarding settling the estate: "The arrangements you mention of leasing the farm, and of appropriating some of our legacies and revenue from it to the improvements which are necessary, I agree to most cordially; and inclose a letter to Charles, with authority for that purpose, which please seal and send him." He also makes a suggestion: "One thing I think should be immediately attended to, and that is to inclose the family tomb with a handsome and durable iron railing, as well as to have the aperture built up in the usual mode. In building a new barn, also, and any buildings, fences, etc., some care should be taken as to the position and shape."[23] In coping with his loss, Lucius focused on honoring the family tomb and was mindful that the shrine be protected as the farm expanded.

Ann's earlier acknowledgment of her brother would prove especially important, for only a year later, on August 26, 1826, Lucius died suddenly in England at the age of forty-three, as later announced in the *Boston Commercial Gazette*, October 2, 1826: "Deaths. At Clifton, England, Lucius Cary, Esq. aged 43, son of late Samuel Cary, Esq. of Chelsea." In Henry Cary's letter to his brother Thomas from New York on September 28, 1826, he encloses an account of Lucius's last days from Joseph Bette, in Clifton, England, August 27, 1826, addressed to the firm of Messrs. J. Marryat and Son, which Henry prefaces, "Dear Tom, — The inclosed has just reached me. I send it forward immediately, in order that you may prepare the family for its melancholy contents." Bette explains that Lucius had arrived on August 19 from Cheltenham: "He spent the Sunday with me, and the next morning we went to Bristol together." They parted ways, as Bette had "some business to attend to," and agreed to meet later that day to dine. Lucius left a note, however, that he had "taken very ill in Bristol, and had gone home and got medical advice." He was diagnosed as being "in a very bad way" and remained in that state for the entire week in Clifton, even though Lucius insisted that he return to Cheltenham. Bette then provides an overview of the final days: "While at dinner, I received a message from the mistress of the boarding-house he was staying at that he was much worse, and requesting my immediate attendance. When I went I found him speechless and insensible, and in this state he remained till his death." Joseph Bette then took "temporary possession of his effects" and made arrangements for Lucius's belongings and for the undertaker. Bette's letter continues, "From a conversation I had with my late friend, I understood he had a moderate competence, and I rather understood he had funds in your hands." Regarding the funeral arrangements, he notes, "I shall be obliged to you, at any rate, to let me have an answer by Monday's post, mentioning if you are coming, and, if you are not, whether I am authorized to draw on you for the expense, and what you wish to have done with his clothes, etc." Lucius was subsequently memorialized, as noted in *Caribbeana*, at "Clifton Church, Bristol," in the "North-east portion of the churchyard and near the east boundary wall:— In Memory [sic]/*LUCIUS CARY ESQ[R]*/late of Kingston Jamaica/and Formerly of St George's/Bermuda, Obit 26th August/1826 Ætat 43. 1826. August 26. At Clifton, Lucius Cary, esq. of Jamaica."[24]

Margaret provides her own narrative of Lucius's passing in a letter on November 1, 1843, to her nephew Edward. She begins by explaining, "In 1826 he went to England, but his constitution was worn out in the West Indies. He went to Bristol for his health, and there, after a few days' confinement to his bed, he died." Regarding his estate, Margaret notes, "He had made his will before he had left the West Indies, and supposed his property worth $30,000. To each of his sisters he had left $3,000. But in the West Indies it is wonderful how little riches are to be depended on." Margaret then adds, "Our dear brother William, though he was just engaged to be married to Miss Nancy Perkins, kindly undertook to go to Jamaica and secure what he could of the property. This only amounted to something near the legacy to his sisters, — over, but I forget how much, $2,000 apiece, but which has made us all comfortable, in addition to the $2,000 left by our dear father to each before the general division of his property." Margaret also reflects on Lucius's attitudes about wealth: "He liked to weigh the question whether there was most enjoyment in making a fortune or in spending it, and I believe he generally decided in favor of the former. That he did enjoy, and it was in mercy that he was preserved from feeling the disappointment of his plan of life." Margaret concludes with a remembrance: "He was an excellent son, a kind brother, a faithful friend, generous and noble in all his dealings. His Bible was his companion, and the gift of a friend. Having fulfilled his duties here, we may trust him to the sure mercies of our Heavenly Father. This is but the commencement of life, but how unlimited its extension! But, short as it is, the direction the spirit takes here will carry it through all eternity. Adieu."[25] As Margaret Cary relayed this emotional narrative, she again provided important context as the family's faithful historian.

〜

This chapter brings this study to a close, showing how the Cary family had attempted, yet again, to regain stability, and how in doing so, they drew on one other and faced their difficulties with resilience—as Sarah had taught them to do so many times before. Their story is thus in many ways one of tensions between ambitions and fortunes, as the West Indies attracted several generations and caused them to confront hazards—moral and physical. The Carys' reasons for becoming involved in the sugar trade, which was dependent on slave labor, are variously explained. And as evident in the family's business ledgers, account books, journals, and letters, as well as in the extensive transatlantic shipping lists and numerous newspaper accounts, this period, from 1764 to 1826, marked an intensive, interconnected, and, at times, frenetic exchange of information and transactions in early America. Still, this intensity does not mute the sorrow of slavery, nor ease the frustration of chasing after fortune with little reward. For the Sarah and Samuel Cary family, the period was a time of tremendous hope as well as frequent separations, as they tried to unite family while also seeking fortune. In doing so, they attempted to reconcile the vastly different worlds of Boston and Grenada. As householders, merchants, planters, and traders supporting an extended family, they continually tried to see their way through. And at the center of this family narrative, Sarah Gray Cary provides a steadying voice and presence as she guides and counsels. For Sarah, this center was one of duty and reverence, even as her own dreams of a family united remained elusive.

Abbreviations

CFDC	Cary Family Diaries and Commonplace Books, 1798–1817, Massachusetts Historical Society, Boston
CF Papers III	Cary Family Papers III, Massachusetts Historical Society, Boston
CL	Curtis, ed., *The Cary Letters*
CO	Colonial Office Records, National Archives, Kew, UK
DHC	Chamberlain, *A Documentary History of Chelsea*, vol. 1.
"Directions"	"Some Directions for the management of a Sugar Plantation," Samuel Cary Papers, Massachusetts Historical Society, Boston
DRTC	The Diaries of the Rev. Thomas Cary of Newburyport, Massachusetts, 1762–1806, New England Historic Genealogical Society, Boston
GBC	George Blankern Cary
LBSP	Cary, Letterbook for the Simon Plantation, St. Kitts, Special and Area Studies Collections, George A. Smathers Libraries, University of Florida, Gainesville
LC	Lucius Cary
MC	Margaret Cary
MHS	Massachusetts Historical Society, Boston
NEHGS	New England Historic Genealogical Society, Boston
SC	Samuel Cary
SC Jr.	Samuel Cary, Jr.
SC Papers	Samuel Cary Papers, Massachusetts Historical Society, Boston
SGC	Sarah Gray Cary

Introduction

1. Peterson, *The Price of Redemption*, 3; Valeri, *Heavenly Merchandize*, 243, 234–35; Warren, *New England Bound*, 53; and Smith, *Slavery, Family, and Gentry Capitalism*, 21.

2. Sypher, "Hutcheson and the 'Classical' Theory of Slavery," 263; Moniz, *From Empire to Humanity*, 33; and Davis, *The Problem of Slavery*, 49.

3. Brown, *Moral Capital*, 152; Harris, *Executing Race*, 12; and Gikandi, *Slavery and the Culture of Taste*, 4.

4. Harvard University, *Quinquennial Catalogue,* 179.

5. Shipton, *Sibley's Harvard Graduates,* 401.

6. Margaret Graves Cary's diary, *CL,* 61–64. See also Kiger, "The Diary of Margaret Graves Cary."

7. Unless otherwise noted, the source for newspaper citations is the online database Early American Newspapers, Series 1, 1690–1876, Readex, 2004–, http://infoweb.news bank.com.

8. MC to GBC, January 23 and February 24, 1843, *CL,* 4, 7.

9. Paton, *Elizabeth Cary Agassiz,* 2; MC to GBC, January 23, 1843, *CL,* 5; Shipton, *Sibley's Harvard Graduates,* 32.

10. MC to GBC, January 23 and February 24, 1843, *CL,* 5, 7.

11. "Boston, MA: Church Records, 1630–1895," *The Records of the Churches of Boston,* CD-ROM, NEHGS. These records, in turn, clarify earlier, inaccurate sources about Sarah's birthplace.

12. Mather, *The Walk of the Upright, with Its Comforts,* 22; Joseph Badger painted Ellis Gray's portrait "about 1750"; four replicas were "painted about 1758" and acquired by the Massachusetts Historical Society, the American Antiquarian Society, and private owners. Park, *Joseph Badger,* 18–19.

13. October 2, 1762, transcriptions from DRTC.

14. Will of Samuel Cary, of Charles Town County of Middlesex Province of Massachusetts Bay, PROB 11/961/284, Public Record Office, National Archives, Kew, UK.

15. November 30, 1763, and October 10, 1764, DRTC.

16. MC to GBC, February 24, 1843, *CL,* 8–9; and MC to GBC, March 3, 1843, *CL,* 13; July 1770 and December 5, 1770, DRTC.

17. Kidder, *History of the Boston Massacre,* 29.

18. MC to GBC, March 3, 1843, *CL,* 13–14.

19. MC to GBC, March 9, 1843, *CL,* 15; November 5, 1772, DRTC.

20. Hirshler, *John Singleton Copley in America,* 123.

21. *DHC,* 311.

22. Imbarrato, *Women Writing Home.*

Chapter 1 · Seeking Fortune

1. Captain Howland left Boston on March 17, 1764, on the sloop *Hampton,* from the Port of Piscataqua, in New Hampshire; in the shipping lists, Jeremiah Smith is listed as the "Master's Name" for the *Seaflower,* a sloop that left on April 17. No captain is named on these lists, but as noted in the *New Hampshire Gazette,* Captain Kellie returned on this ship from St. Kitts on May 24, 1764. Captain Pike sailed for St. Kitts on May 18 on the *Swallow,* and Captain Branscomb left May 24 on the *Molly.* In addition, one ship in August, two in November, and one in December all left from Portsmouth, but the earlier departures are more in accordance with other records about Samuel's arrival. Massachusetts Naval Office Shipping Lists, 1686–1765, CO 5/848, 850, the National Archives, Kew; *New Hampshire Gazette*: Newspaper Abstracts, 1756–1769, Online database from records compiled by Sean Furniss, NEHGS.

2. MC to GBC, February 24, 1843, *CL,* 7.

3. Will of Charles Spooner of Harley Street Cavendish Square, Middlesex, PROB 11/1194/18, Public Record Office; and "Spooner of St. Christopher," in Oliver, *Caribbeana,* 1:3.

4. SC to William Manning, February 10, 1766, LBSP.

5. SC to William Manning, October 5, 1766; and SC to Joseph Sill, December 6, 1766, LBSP.

6. Samuel Baker, *A New and Exact Map of the Island of St. Christopher in America, According to an Actual and Accurate Survey Made in the Year 1753*, John Carter Brown Map Collection, C-6511-000, John Carter Brown Library, Brown University.

7. O'Shaughnessy, *An Empire Divided*, 60; Steele, *Grenada*, 63–64; Burnard, "Harvest Years?" 547–48; and Beckles, "Capitalism, Slavery and Caribbean Modernity," 778.

8. "Directions."

9. Morgan, *Slave Counterpoint*, 258–59.

10. Ward, *British West Indian Slavery*, 13; Williams, *Capitalism and Slavery*, 86; and Watts, *The West Indies*, 327.

11. Spence, "Ameliorating Empire," 48; and Ragatz, *The Fall of the Planter Class*, 248. See Tobin, *Cursory Remarks upon the Reverend Mr. Ramsay's Essay on the Treatment and Conversion of African Slaves in the Sugar Colonies* (1785).

12. Roberts, "Uncertain Business," 251; Higman, *A Concise History of the Caribbean*, 105.

13. Draper, *Price of Emancipation*, 38–39, 17; Brown, *Moral Capital*, 51; O'Shaughnessy, *An Empire Divided*, 4; and Zacek, "Class Struggle," 74.

14. Carretta, *Phillis Wheatley*, 100–101.

15. Amussen, *Caribbean Exchanges*, 41, 94; Burnard, "The Atlantic Slave Trade," 91–92; and O'Malley, *Final Passages*, 320.

16. Knight, *Working the Diaspora*, 49.

17. Dunn, *Sugar and Slaves*, 302, 224; and Smelser, "The Contentious Empires," 8.

18. Higman, *A Concise History of the Caribbean*, 99; Walsh, *Motives of Honor*, 21–22; and Morgan, *Slave Counterpoint*, 287.

19. Brown, *Moral Capital*, 153.

20. Carey, *British Abolitionism*, 108.

21. Gould, "The African Slave Trade," 202.

22. Beckles, "The Wilberforce Song," 114.

23. Ragatz, *The Fall of the Planter Class*, 3, vii; Burnard, *Planters, Merchants, and Slaves*, 268; and Burnard, "The American Revolution," n. p.

24. Newman, *A New World of Labor*, 232.

25. Campbell, *Candid and Impartial Considerations*, 172.

26. Ward, *British West Indian Slavery*, 208.

27. Burnard and Garrigus, *The Plantation Machine*, 4.

28. Smith, *Slavery, Family, and Gentry Capitalism*, 278.

29. SC to William Manning, July 26, 1768, LBSP.

30. Taylor, *American Colonies*, 307.

31. Shields, *American Poetry*, 853. Coincidentally, as Gilmore notes, Charles Spooner, Bourryau's uncle, was "married to Grainger's wife's sister Mary," Gilmore, *The Poetics of Empire*, 8–9, 12, 14.

32. SC to Charles Bowken, February 11, 1767, LBSP.

33. Krise, *Caribbeana*, 10; and Egan, "The 'Long'd-for Aera,'" 195.

34. Frohock, *Heroes of Empire*, 167; Shields, *Oracles of Empire*, 71; Ellis, "Incessant Labour," 52; Thomas, "Doctoring Ideology," 82; and Silva, "Georgic Fantasies,"128.

35. Shields, *Oracles of Empire*, 73; Frohock, *Heroes of Empire*, 176; Ellis, "Incessant Labour," 46; Thomas, "Doctoring Ideology," 87; and Mulford, "New Science," 87.

36. Grainger, *The Sugar-Cane*, 238, 244.

37. Frohock, *Heroes of Empire*, 176.

38. Grainger, *More Common West-India Diseases*, 69–70.

39. Isaac, *Landon Carter's Uneasy Kingdom*, 57, 72.

40. Grainger, *The Sugar-Cane*, 168.

41. Zacek, "Cultivating Virtue," 15.

42. Turnbull, *Letters to a Young Planter*, 37.

43. SC to Peter Symons, March 10, 1769, LBSP.

44. Haggerty, *"Merely for Money"?*, 15.

45. McCusker and Menard, *The Economy of British America*, 145.

46. SC to William Hammond, September 25, 1769, LBSP.

47. SC to William Manning, January 9, 1769, LBSP.

48. *London Gazette*, November 29, 1793.

49. SC to Richard Cary, March 30, 1769; and SC to Nathaniel Cary, June 16, 1769, LBSP.

50. Cary account book, SC Papers, MHS.

51. SC to Joseph Sill, July 25, 1769; and SC to Peter Symons, September 15, 1769, LBSP.

52. Will of John Bourryau of Island of Grenada, West Indies, PROB 11/955/239, Public Record Office; "Bourryau of St. Kitts," in Oliver, *Caribbeana*, 3:251–53.

53. SC to Joseph Sill, October 26, 1769; and SC to Charles Spooner, October 26, 1769, LBSP.

54. SC to Charles Spooner and Joseph Sill, January 5, 1770; and SC to Joseph Sill, January 5, 1770, LBSP.

55. SC to Samuel Sandbach, January 12, 1770, LBSP.

56. July 27, 1770, DRTC.

57. SC to Alex Gray [January 1770], LBSP.

58. Ibid.

59. Dunn, *Sugar and Slaves*, 252; Burnard, *Planters, Merchants, and Slaves*, 265–66; Sweet, *Bodies Politic*, 69; Vasconcellos, *Slavery, Childhood, and Abolition*, 65; and Burnard, "Slave Naming Patterns," 326.

60. Cugoano, *Thoughts and Sentiments*, 7.

61. Ibid., 151n2.

62. Quintanilla, "The World of Alexander Campbell," 237; "Alexander Campbell," Legacies of British Slave-ownership, online database, University College London, www.ucl.ac.uk/lbs/ (hereafter Legacies).

63. Cugoano, *Thoughts and Sentiments*, 16.

64. Wheeler, *The Complexion of Race*, 259.

65. Equiano, *Interesting Narrative*, 60–61, 251n122; and Falconbridge, *Narrative of Two Voyages*, 216–17.

66. Hartigan-O'Connor, *The Ties That Buy*, 157; and Smallwood, *Saltwater Slavery*, 161.

67. SC to Peter Robert Luard, February 18, 1770; SC to Joseph Sill, February 18, 1770, LBSP; Joseph Sill to SC, March 26, 1770, LBSP; and Joseph Sill to SC, March 28, 1770, SC Papers, MHS.

68. SC to Charles Spooner, May 17, 1770; William Arrendell to Captain John Kiddall, May 19, 1770; and SC to Joseph Sill, May 27, 1770, LBSP.

69. DRTC.

70. SC to William Smith, September 3, 1770, LBSP. Additional details about the estate appear in the will of Samuel Cary, the National Archives, Kew.

71. Charles Spooner and Joseph Sill to SC, November 12 and 28, 1770, SC Papers, MHS.

72. Joseph Sill to SC, March 5, 1771, SC Papers, MHS; SC to Joseph Sill, April 2 and 17, 1771; and SC to Charles Spooner, April 17, 1771, LBSP.

73. SC to Peter Robert Luard, April 17, 1771, LBSP.

74. Roberts, "Yankey dodle," 129.

75. Joseph Sill to SC, February 26, 1772, SC Papers, MHS.

76. Joseph Sill to SC, November 5, 1773, SC Papers, MHS.

77. "John Bourryau of Grenada," Legacies.

78. *London Gazette*, March 3, 1792, 153.

79. "John Bourryau of Grenada."

Chapter 2 · Building Prosperity

1. SGC to Henry Cary, March 9, 1819; and MC to GBC, March 9, 1843, *CL*, 230, 16.

2. February 8 and 15, 1774, DRTC; and Knowlton, *British Shipping Records.*

3. Jonathan Cary to [Davenport and Wentworth], May 1774, the Beinecke Lesser Antilles Collection, Hamilton College, Clinton, New York.

4. Edwards, *The History, Civil and Commercial*, 381–82, 386–87. Current atlas records show that Grenada is twenty-one miles long and twelve miles wide.

5. US Bureau of the Census, *A Century of Population Growth*, 11; and Newman and Holton, *Boston's Back Bay*, 15.

6. MC to GBC, March 9, 1843, *CL*, 17–18.

7. Ibid., 16–18.

8. MC to GBC, March 24, 1843, *CL*, 25.

9. MC to GBC, March 9, 1843, *CL*, 15, 17–18.

10. Moitt, *Women and Slavery in the French Antilles*, 39.

11. Ibid.

12. MC to GBC, March 24, 1843, *CL*, 25–26.

13. *DHC*, 321.

14. O'Shaughnessy, "Redcoats and Slaves," 108–9.

15. Watts, *The West Indies*, 279.

16. SC to William Smith, August 25, 1778, SC Papers, MHS; and Quintanilla, "The World of Alexander Campbell," 251. For additional perspective, J. R. Ward in "The Profitability of Sugar Planting," explains, "As early plantation records are so scarce, it may never be possible to establish conclusively what were the usual rates of profit before the middle of the eighteenth century" (205).

17. SC to William Smith, August 25, 1778; and SC to Joseph Sill, October 20, 1778, SC Papers, MHS.

18. SGC to Mary (Polly) Smith Gray, October 29, 1779, CF Papers III, MHS; "Boston, MA: Church Records, 1630–1895," NEHGS; and Abigail Adams to John Adams, October

20–22, 1777, Adams Family Papers: An Electronic Archive, MHS, www.masshist.org/dig italadams.

19. SGC to Mary (Polly) Smith Gray Smith Gray, October 29, 1779, CF Papers III, MHS.

20. Zaczek, *Censored Sentiments*, 13; and Dierks, *In My Power*, 56.

21. Silver, *Sketches of the New Church*, 61; and MC to GBC, March 9, 1843, *CL*, 19.

22. St. Andrews Regiment (Grenada Militia), British, 18 December 1778–5 January 1779, reel 6, vol. 3, Revolutionary War orderly books, MHS.

23. "Boston, MA: Inhabitants and Estates of the Town of Boston, 1630–1822 (Thwing Collection)," NEHGS; Boston, MA: Deaths, 1700–1799, online database, NEHGS; and Elizabeth Storer Smith to Isaac Smith Jr., April 12, 1780, Smith-Carter Family Papers, MHS.

24. SGC to Mary Smith Gray, May 25, 1780, CF Papers III, MHS.

25. John Thaxter to John Adams, September 19, 1780, *Founding Families: Digital Editions of the Papers of the Winthrops and the Adamses*, edited by C. James Taylor, MHS, www.masshist.org/publications/apde2/.

26. John Adams to Benjamin Franklin, September 29, 1780; Franklin to Adams, October 8, 1780; and Samuel Andrews to Adams, March 12, 1782, *Founding Families*, MHS.

27. Conway, *The British Isles*, 62–63; "Boston, MA: Inhabitants and Estates," NEHGS; "Last Wednesday departed this life, after a tedious illness, Ellis Gray, Esq," *Boston Independent Ledger*, July 16, 1781. Margaret Cary identifies consumption as the cause of death for both William and Ellis, MC to GBC, March 3, 1843, *CL*, 11.28. MC to GBC, March 24, 1843, *CL*, 27.

29. Ux is short for the Latin *uxor* meaning "wife"; January 26, 1785, DRTC.

30. SGC to Mary Gray Otis, March 29, 1785, CF Papers III, MHS.

31. SGC to Mary Gray Otis, May 20, 1786, CF Papers III, MHS.

32. SGC to Mary Gray Otis, May 24, 1787, *CL*, 70.

33. Roberts, "Yankey dodle," 288; and MC to GBC, March 9, 1843, *CL*, 18–19.

34. Roberts, "Yankey dodle," 288.

35. Hamilton, *Scotland, the Caribbean*, 42.

36. MC to GBC, March 9, 1843, *CL*, 20.

37. SC to Charles Spooner, May 1, 1780, SC Papers, MHS.

38. Charles Spooner to SC, October 2 and December 4, 1780; and SC to Charles Spooner, February 15 and April 13, 1781, SC Papers, MHS.

39. *CL*, 23.

40. Hayes, *A Colonial Woman's Bookshelf*, 33; Kelley, *Learning to Stand and Speak*, 166; Charles Spooner to SC, March 6, 1782; and "Cash paid on Account of Miss M. Cary," SC Papers, MHS.

41. MC to GBC, March 9, 1843, *CL*, 20.

42. SC Jr. to Sarah Tyler Gray, August 23, 1789, *CL*, 74.

43. MC to GBC, April 14, 1843, *CL*, 35.

44. *CL*, 24.

45. Haggerty, *'Merely for Money'?*, 57.

46. MC to GBC, April 4, 1843, *CL*, 28–30.

47. Ibid., 31–32.

48. Hewitt, *Correspondence and American Literature*, 11; Pearsall, *Atlantic Families*, 71; Hayes, *A Colonial Woman's Bookshelf*, 73; and Bannet, *Empire of Letters*, 46.

49. SGC to SC Jr., undated, 1790, *CL*, 76–77. "Smallcloaths" refers to close-fitting knee breeches.

50. Ibid., *CL*, 77–78.

51. MC to GBC, March 24, 1843, *CL*, 26.

52. SGC to SC Jr., 1790, *CL*, 77–78.

53. MC to GBC, March 3, 1843, *CL*, 11.

54. SGC to SC Jr., 1790, *CL*, 77–78.

55. Ibid., 79.

56. Ibid., 79–82.

57. SC Jr. to SGC, May 19, 1791, CF Papers III, MHS.

58. *CL*, 82.

59. SGC to SC Jr., 1790, *CL*, 82–83.

60. Ibid., 84; and Pope, *Works of Alexander Pope*, 2:462, lines 13–16.

61. SC Jr. to SGC, Wednesday, June 1791, CF Papers III, MHS.

62. The Sarah and Samuel Cary children would eventually include Samuel Cary (1773–1810); Margaret Graves Cary (1775–1868); Charles Spooner Cary (1778–1866); Lucius Cary (1782–1825); Sarah Cary (1783–1838); Henry Cary (1785–1857); Ann Montague Cary (1787–1882); Edward Cary (1789–1808); Harriet Cary (1790–1873); Thomas Greaves Cary (1791–1859); George Blankern Cary (1792–1846); Robert Howard Cary (1794–1867); and William Ferdinend Cary (1795–1881), Massachusetts: Vital Records, 1621–1850, Online database, NEHGS.

63. *CL*, 42–43.

64. *DHC*, 312–13.

Chapter 3 · *Relocating and Adjusting*

1. *CL*, 44–46; Perkins quoted in Hill, "Necrology of the New England Historic Genealogical Society," 323–24; *DHC*, 312–13; Pratt, *Seven Generations*, 61–62.

2. SC Jr. to Sarah Tyler Gray, May 31 and June 11, 1791, CF Papers III, MHS.

3. SGC to SC Jr., July 14, 1791, CF Papers III, MHS. Sarah is referring to Beawes and Mortimer, *Lex Mercatoria Rediviva*.

4. Pearsall, *Atlantic Families*, 47.

5. *CL*, 43.

6. SC Jr. to SGC, July 30, 1791, CF Papers III, MHS.

7. Dierks, *In My Power*, 101.

8. SC Jr. to SGC, July 30, 1791; and SGC to SC Jr., April 20, 1792, CF Papers III, MHS.

9. SC Jr. to SC, July 27, 1791, CF Papers III, MHS.

10. SC Jr. to David Barry, Sunday morning, 1791, CF Papers III, MHS.

11. Samuel refers here to a "Joe" or a "Johannes" in Portuguese currency, which is measured in gold; 36s sterling would then be a "half-Joe." And according to the United States Continental Congress et al., *Propositions Respecting the Coinage of Gold, Silver, and Copper* (1785), "The golden piece will be 1/5 more than a half joe, and 1/15 more than a double guinea. It will be readily estimated then by reference to either of them, but more readily and accurately as equal to 10 dollars" (10).

12. SC to David Barry, September 20, 1791, SC Papers, MHS.

13. *CL*, 44.

14. SGC to SC Jr., November 11, 1791, CF Papers III, MHS; MC to Edward Cary, No-

vember 1, 1853, *CL*, 39; Wightman, *Annals of the Boston Primary School Committee*, 63; and *CL*, 48.

15. SGC to SC Jr., November 11, 1791, CF Papers III, MHS.

16. Cott, *The Bonds of Womanhood*, 112–13n19.

17. SGC to SC Jr., December 16, 1791; April 20, 1792; and July 10, 1792, CF Papers III, MHS.

18. Cott, *The Bonds of Womanhood*, 104; and Kelley, "The Need of Their Genius," 251, 253.

19. *CL*, 53–54.

20. SC Jr. to SC, August 8, 1791; and SC Jr. to SGC August 8, 1791, CF Papers III, MHS.

21. SGC to SC Jr., October 2, 1791, CF Papers III, MHS.

22. Appleby, *Inheriting the Revolution*, 170.

23. *CL*, 48.

24. Boston, MA: Marriages, 1700–1809, online database, NEHGS.

25. *CL*, 47–48.

26. SGC to SC Jr., November 11, 1791; and March 4, 1792, CF Papers III, MHS.

27. SGC to SC Jr., April 20, 1792, CF Papers III, MHS.

28. SC Jr. to SC, St. George's, July 7, 1792, CF Papers III, MHS.

29. SC to SC Jr., July 13, 1792, SC Papers, MHS.

30. SC Jr. to SC, July 31, 1792, CF Papers III, MHS.

31. SGC to SC Jr., September 13 and November 25, 1792, CF Papers III, MHS.

32. SC Jr. to SC, November 19, 1792, CF Papers III, MHS.

33. Candlin and Pybus, *Enterprising Women*, 95.

34. SGC to SC Jr., May 24, 1794, CF Papers III, MHS.

35. SC Jr. to SGC, September 4, 1794, CF Papers III, MHS.

36. Mercy Otis Warren to SGC, June 24, 1793, Richards and Harris, *Mercy Otis Warren*, 239–40.

37. SGC to SC Jr., December 17, 1794, CF Papers III, MHS.

38. US Census Office, *Return of the Whole Number of Persons* (1801), 8.

39. *DHC*, 313.

40. United States, *Return of the Whole Number of Persons* (1791), 23; and US Census Office, *Return of the Whole Number of Persons* (1801), 8.

41. *DHC*, 313.

Chapter 4 · *Slave Revolts and Shifting Fortunes*

1. *CL*, 49.

2. O'Shaughnessy, *An Empire Divided*, 41; Edwards, *The History, Civil and Commercial*, 376.

3. Spence, *Radical Cause*, 8; and Geggus, "Slavery, War, and Revolution," 8–9.

4. Rediker, *The Slave Ship*, 319, 326.

5. Ibid., 311, 327; and Rawley, *London, Metropolis of the Slave Trade*, 130. Rediker also notes that the image of the *Brooks* was "first drawn and published by William Elford and the Plymouth chapter of the Society for Effecting the Abolition of the Slave Trade in November 1788" (308); see also Spooner, *Short Reasons against the Abolition of the Slave Trade*.

6. Duffy, "The French Revolution and British Attitudes," 83.

7. Cox, "Fedon's Rebellion," 14.

8. Grenada Planter, *A Brief Enquiry*, 16; and Turnbull, *Narrative*, 29.

9. Cox, "Fedon's Rebellion," 13.

10. "Reports that 'a General Insurrection of the French Free Coloured People broke out in this Island on the night of the 2d instant,'" CO 101/34/9, the National Archives, Kew.

11. Duffy, *Soldiers, Sugar, and Seapower*, 146; Grenada Planter, *A Brief Enquiry*, 101; Turnbull, *Narrative*, 102; and Hay, *A Narrative*, 76–77, 83–84. See also Craton, *Testing the Chains*, 188.

12. Wise, *A Review*, 100.

13. SC Jr. to Joseph Marryat, May 6, 1795, quoted in Montague, Montague, and Montague, "The Island of Grenada in 1795," 533–34.

14. SC Jr. to SC, May 12, 1795, quoted in ibid., 534–35.

15. Candlin, *The Last Caribbean Frontier*, 6, 185n16.

16. Craton, *Testing the Chains*, 183; Cox, "Fedon's Rebellion," 17; and Candlin, *The Last Caribbean Frontier*, 6.

17. Phillip, "Producers, Reproducers, and Rebels," n. p.; and Candlin and Pybus, *Enterprising Women*, 75.

18. SC Jr. to SC, May 12, 1795, quoted in Montague, Montague, and Montague, "The Island of Grenada in 1795," 535–36.

19. Turnbull, *Narrative*, 47–48.

20. Garraway, *A Short Account*, quoted in Montague, Montague, and Montague, "The Island of Grenada in 1795," 532.

21. MC, *CL*, 50.

22. SGC to SC Jr., July 14, 1795, CF Papers III, MHS.

23. *DHC*, 314n63.

24. SGC to SC Jr., July 14, 1795, CF Papers III, MHS.

25. SC Jr. to SC, August 12, 1795, quoted in Montague, Montague, and Montague, "The Island of Grenada in 1795," 536–37.

26. SGC to SC Jr., November 13, 1795, CF Papers III, MHS.

27. Ibid.

28. SC Jr. to SC, November 18, 1795, CF Papers III, MHS.

29. Cox, "Fedon's Rebellion,"15; Craton, *Testing the Chains*, 183; and Davis, *Inhuman Bondage*, 210–11.

30. *CL*, 51, 53.

31. MC to Edward M. Cary, November 1, 1853, *CL*, 40.

32. SGC to SC Jr., May 11, 1796, CF Papers III, MHS.

33. SC Jr. to SC, May 1, 1796, CF Papers III, MHS.

34. SC Jr. to SC, August 7, 1796, CF Papers III, MHS.

35. Ibid.

36. Candlin, *The Last Caribbean Frontier*, 19; Duffy, *Soldiers, Sugar, and Seapower*, 239; Craton, *Testing the Chains*, 210; Steele, *Grenada*, 143; and Candlin and Pybus, *Enterprising Women*, 29.

37. SC Jr. to SC, August 7, 1796, CF Papers III, MHS.

38. SC to SGC, November 11, 1796, *CL*, 123–24.

39. SC to SGC, December 26, 1796, *CL*, 126.

40. Gares, "Stephen Girard's West Indian Trade," 325.

41. SC to SGC, December 26, 1796, *CL*, 127.

42. SGC to SC Jr., February 4, 1797, CF Papers III, MHS.

43. SC to SGC, January 4, 1797, *CL*, 130.

44. Palmer, *Stoddert's War*, 74–75.

45. SC to SGC, January 5, 1797, CL, 128–29, 51. Additionally, marriage records for "Pompey Brooks" and "Pompy Brooks" show, "Pompey, negro, and Lydia Worrow, Indian, of Chelsea, Nov. 22, 1796, in Chelsea" (Medford marriages); "Pompy (of Medford, int.) and Lydia Worrow, Nov. 22, 1796. Blacks" (Chelsea marriages), Massachusetts: Vital Records, 1621–1850, NEHGS. Pompey's wife, Lydia, is also referred to as "Nancy," as in Samuel Cary's letter to Sarah Cary, February 4, 1797: "I have sent to town for two thousand feet of boards to board up the mule pen, which will make me a small chamber and a room to dine in. Nancy, as soon as I got to St. George's, came to me, and when I was coming up in a sloop, offered to break up housekeeping and come with me. She was keeping shop, and, Mr. Stephens, who is in St. George's, tells me, doing very well." CL, 133.

46. Campbell, *A Journey Over Land to India*, 129–30.

47. SC to SGC, January 21, 1797, *CL*, 131–32.

48. Ibid., 132.

49. SGC to SC Jr., February 4, 1797, CF Papers III, MHS.

50. *CL*, 51; *DHC*, 314.

51. SC to SGC, February 4, 1797, CF Papers III, MHS.

52. SC to SGC, March 15, 1797, *CL*, 135–36.

53. "A Plan of Mt. Pleasant Estate . . . surveyed July 1797," SC Papers, MHS. Regarding the abbreviation A.R.P., from the *Oxford English Dictionary*—"acre, n.": "2a. A measure of land area, originally as much as a yoke of oxen could plough in a day, later defined by English statute as an area 220 yards (40 poles) long by 22 yards (4 poles) broad (equal to 4,840 square yards, 4 roods, or approx. 4,047 square metres), or its equivalent of any shape." "acre, n." *OED Online*, accessed July 14, 2017, www.oed.com.

Chapter 5 · Recovery and Renewal

1. "Samuel Bennett, merchant, of Philadelphia was married on November 23, 1796, to Ruth Dobel, of Bristol." Dorland, "Second Troop," 279n8.

2. James N. Green, e-mail message to author, June 22, 2012.

3. LC to SGC, January 23, 1797, CF Papers III, MHS.

4. LC to SGC, February 25, March 10, and July 1, 1797, CF Papers III, MHS. The New Theatre was also known as the Chestnut Street Theatre.

5. Ibid.

6. LC to SGC, June 1, 1797, CF Papers III, MHS.

7. Rowson and Rust, *Charlotte Temple*, 26.

8. LC to SGC, July 1, 1797, CF Papers III, MHS; and Pope and Horace, *The First Epistle*, [23].

9. LC to SGC, July 1 and October 9, 1797; and January 4, 1798, CF Papers III, MHS.

10. SC to SC Jr., June 1, 1798, SC Papers, MHS.

11. SGC to SC, August 25, 1798, CF Papers III, MHS.

12. Gares, "Stephen Girard's West Indian Trade," 326.

13. SC Jr. to SGC February 3, 1799; and SGC to SC Jr., March 29, 1799, CF Papers III, MHS.

14. SC to SC Jr., January 12, 1799; and SC Jr. to SC, March 29, 1799, SC Papers, MHS.

15. SGC to SC, June 21, 1799, CF Papers III, MHS.

16. Gares, "Stephen Girard's West Indian Trade," 330.

17. LC to SGC, July 3 and July 14, 1799, CF Papers III, MHS.

18. LC to SGC, July 14, 1799, and August 4, 1799, CF Papers III, MHS.

19. LC to SGC, October 4 and December 3, 1799, CF Papers III, MHS.

20. Mercy Otis Warren to SGC, June 8 and August 18, 1799, Richards and Harris, *Mercy Otis Warren*, 245–47, 204.

21. Mercy Otis Warren to SGC, August 23, 1800, ibid., 249.

22. Mercy Otis Warren to SGC, February 7, 1802, ibid., 250.

23. Richards and Harris, *Mercy Otis Warren*, 257.

24. SGC to SC Jr., November 12, 1799, CF Papers III, MHS.

25. LC to SGC, May 8, 1800, CF Papers III, MHS.

26. Ibid. William Sandbach owned the Resource Estate.

27. SGC to SC Jr., June 17 and October 28, 1800, CF Papers III, MHS.

28. LC to SGC, July 4, 1800, CF Papers III, MHS.

29. LC to SGC, October 22, 1800, CF Papers III, MHS.

30. Palmer, *Stoddert's War*, 6.

31. SGC to SC, November 19, 1800, *CL*, 162.

32. SC Jr. to SGC, November 29, 1800, CF Papers III, MHS.

33. Sarah is paraphrasing Macduff from Shakespeare's *Macbeth*: "I cannot but remember such things were, / That were most precious to me" (4.3.225–26).

34. SGC to SC Jr., January 6, 1801, CF Papers III, MHS.

35. According to the Legacies profile for Edmund Thornton, William's father, "In 1785 Edmund Thornton was shown in Grenada in partnership with Thomas Campbell, and in 1786 again in Grenada in partnership with Jeremiah Williamson."

36. SC Jr. to SC, September 15, 1801, CF Papers III, MHS.

37. SGC to SC, October 1801, CF Papers III, MHS.

38. LC to SGC, December 8, 1801, CF Papers III, MHS.

39. LC to SC, February 14, 1802, CF Papers III, MHS.

40. SGC to SC Jr., February 20, 1802, CF Papers III, MHS.

41. More, *Strictures on the Modern System of Female Education*, 1:188–87; Swift, "A Letter to a Young Lady on Her Marriage," *Miscellanies in Prose and Verse*, vol. 2, (London: Motte, Benjamin, 1727), 319–37.

42. SGC to SC Jr., March 31, 1802, CF Papers III, MHS.

43. SGC to SC Jr., October 17, 1802, CF Papers III, MHS.

44. MC to Edward M. Cary, November 1, 1853, *CL*, 40.

45. LC to SGC, June 2, 1807, CF Papers III, MHS.

46. Scoville, *The Old Merchants of New York City*, 118, 122–23.

47. SGC to LC, September 2, 1807, CF Papers III, MHS.

48. SGC to LC, December 16, 1807, CF Papers III, MHS.

49. The *Essequebo & Demerary Royal Gazette*, transcriptions from Guyana Colonial Newspapers, www.vc.id.au/edg/transcripts.html.

50. CFDC, MHS.

51. See also Schurink, "Manuscript Commonplace Books, Literature, and Reading in Early Modern England"; Stabile, *Memory's Daughters*; Stallybrass, "Benjamin Franklin "; and Wilson, "Thomas Jefferson's Early Notebooks."

52. Bear and Stanton, introduction to Jefferson, *Jefferson's Memorandum Books*, 1:xvii, xxi.

53. CFDC, MHS.

54. Taylor, *The Black Carib Wars,* iv–v.

55. The verse is from King James Version. In the New Revised Standard Version, 1 Peter 4:8 reads, "Above all, maintain constant love for one another, for love covers a multitude of sins." Michael D. Coogan, ed., *The New Oxford Annotated Bible* (New York: Oxford University Press, 2010).

56. CFDC, MHS.

57. Pope, *Works of Alexander Pope*, 7:199.

58. Clark, "Culture Contact in the Palau Islands," 95.

59. Jefferson, *Notes on the State of Virginia, Writings*, 188–89.

60. Morley, Steele, and Addison *The Spectator*, 41–42.

61. Roberts, "Yankey dodle," 296.

62. According to newspaper notices, the ship was the *Union*: "DIED. . . . On his passage from Martinique, to Marblehead (on board sch. Union) Mr. Samuel Carey, mer. of Chelsea." *Columbian Centinel*, November 14, 1810. This information was repeated in the *Boston Gazette* on November 15, as well as in the *Repertory* and the *Newburyport Herald* on November 16, 1810.

63. SGC to LC, November 18, 1810, CF Papers III, MHS.

Chapter 6 · *Sustaining a Family*

1. The *Essequebo & Demerary Royal Gazette*, October 13, 1810; LC to Ann Cary, November 1810, *CL*, 178–79.

2. LC to SGC, undated, CF Papers III, MHS. This letter is most likely from 1812, as Lucius notes his pending "Voyage" and plans to visit Chelsea afterwards: "I am just about to begin my Voyage and that the Lapse of a few months will bring me into the midst of my dear Friends at the Retreat." Moreover, this letter comes before the next one in the Cary Family Papers, which is dated May 20, 1812, further suggesting that it was written in 1812. 3. LC to SGC, May 20, 1812, CF Papers III, MHS.

4. Adams, "Count Edward de Crillon," 53.

5. LC to Ann Cary, June 5, 1812, *CL*, 185–88.

6. *CL*, 52–53.

7. MC to Edward M. Cary, November 1, 1853, *CL*, 41.

8. LC to SGC, undated, 1812, *CL*, 190.

9. LC to SGC, February 1, 1814, CF Papers III, MHS; "coûte que coûte, phr," *OED Online*, accessed July 14, 2017, www.oed.com.

10. LC to SGC, January 10, 1815, CF Papers III, MHS.

11. LC to SGC, March 1, 1815, CF Papers III, MHS; and SGC to Henry Cary, March 23, 1815, *CL*, 207.

12. Taylor, *The Transportation Revolution*, 58.

13. Scoville, *The Old Merchants of New York City*, 122.

14. Ann Cary to Harriet Cary, July 16, 1818, *CL*, 261, 264.

15. LC to SGC, August 28 and October 15, 1818, CF Papers III, MHS.

16. SGC to LC, November 13, 1818, CF Papers III, MHS.

17. Henry Cary to SGC, May 19, 1819, *CL*, 282. This Gilbert Stuart painting titled

Mrs. Samuel Cary (1819) was part of an exhibition at Harvard's Fogg Museum in 1934. The painting's current location appears to be unknown.

18. LC to SGC, April 20, 1824, CF Papers III, MHS.

19. Cox, "British Caribbean," 294; and Ryden, *West Indian Slavery*, 185, 277.

20. MC to Edward M. Cary, November 1, 1853, *CL*, 41.

21. LC to SGC, July 13 and August 5, 12, and 29, 1825, CF Papers III, MHS.

22. Ann Cary to LC, September 28, 1825, *CL*, 311–12.

23. LC to Thomas Cary, October 8, 1825, *CL*, 310–11.

24. Henry Cary to Thomas Cary, September 28, 1826, with letter from Joseph Bette to Messrs. J. Marryat and Son, August 27, 1826, *CL*, 318–19. In that Joseph Marryat had died in 1824 and this letter is addressed to "J. Marryat and Son" in London, Bette's letter is directed to the firm in general and to Marryat's son, Joseph Marryat, a London merchant and a member of the firm Joseph Marryat and Sons. "Joseph Marryat," Legacies; "Monumental Inscriptions in England relating to the West Indians," in Oliver, *Caribbeana* 2:372, 380.

25. MC to Edward M. Cary, November 1, 1853, *CL*, 41–42.

Archival Sources

Adams Family Papers: An Electronic Archive. Massachusetts Historical Society, Boston. www.masshist.org/digitaladams.

Baker, Samuel. *A New and Exact Map of the Island of St. Christopher in America, According to an Actual and Accurate Survey Made in the Year 1753.* John Carter Brown Map Collection, C-6511-000. John Carter Brown Library, Brown University.

Beinecke Lesser Antilles Collection. Hamilton College, Clinton, New York.

Boston, MA: Births, 1700–1800. Online database. New England Historic Genealogical Society, Boston. https://www.americanancestors.org/DB27/i/0. Originally published as *A Report of the Record Commissioners of the City of Boston Containing Boston Births from A.D. 1700 to A.D. 1800* (Boston: Rockwell and Churchill, City Printers, 1894).

Boston, MA: Deaths, 1700–1799. Online database. New England Historic Genealogical Society, Boston. https://www.americanancestors.org/DB34/t/0. Originally published as Robert J. Dunkle and Ann S. Lainhart, *Boston Deaths, 1700–1799* (Boston: New England Historic Genealogical Society, 1999).

"Boston, MA: Inhabitants and Estates of the Town of Boston, 1630–1822 (Thwing Collection)." *Inhabitants and Estates of the Town of Boston, 1630–1800 and The Crooked and Narrow Streets of Boston, 1630–1822.* CD-ROM. Boston, Mass.: New England Historic Genealogical Society, 2001.

Boston, MA: Marriages, 1700–1809. Online database. New England Historic Genealogical Society, Boston. https://www.americanancestors.org/DB174/i/0. Originally published as *Report of the Record Commissioners of the City of Boston, Containing the Boston Marriages from 1700 to 1751,* vol. 28 (Boston: Municipal Printing office, 1898), and *Records Relating to the Early History of Boston, Containing Boston Marriages from 1752 to 1809,* vol. 30 (Boston: Municipal Printing Office, 1903).

"Boston, MA: Church Records, 1630–1895." *The Records of the Churches of Boston.* CD-ROM. Boston: New England Historic Genealogical Society, 2002.

Cary, Rev. Thomas. The Diaries of the Rev. Thomas Cary of Newburyport, Massachusetts, 1762–1806. Online database. New England Historic Genealogical Society, Boston. https://www.americanancestors.org/DB76/i/0. Original manuscripts: Diary of Rev. Thomas Cary, 1762–1776, 1778–1806 (mss 640), R. Stanton Avery Special Collections, NEHGS.

Cary, Samuel. Letterbook for the Simon Plantation, St. Kitts. Special and Area Studies Collections. George A. Smathers Libraries, University of Florida, Gainesville. http://ufdc.ufl.edu/UF00101464/00001.

Cary, Samuel. Samuel Cary Papers. Massachusetts Historical Society, Boston.

Cary Family Diaries and Commonplace Books, 1798–1817. Massachusetts Historical Society, Boston.

Cary Family Papers III. Massachusetts Historical Society, Boston.

Colonial Office Records. The National Archives, Kew, United Kingdom.

Founding Families: Digital Editions of the Papers of the Winthrops and the Adamses. Edited by C. James Taylor. Massachusetts Historical Society, Boston. www.masshist.org/publications/apde2/.

Legacies of British Slave-ownership. Online database. University College London, www.ucl.ac.uk/lbs/.

Massachusetts: Vital Records, 1621–1850. Online database. New England Historic Genealogical Society. https://www.americanancestors.org/DB190/i/0.

New Hampshire Gazette: Newspaper Abstracts, 1756–1769. Online database from records compiled by Sean Furniss. New England Historic Genealogical Society, Boston. https://www.americanancestors.org/DB1654/t/0.

Paterson, Daniel, and Pinel. *A New Plan of the Island of Grenada, from the Original French Survey of Monsieur Pinel Taken in 1763 by Order of Government, and Now Published with the Addition of English Names, Alterations of Property, and Other Improvements to the Present Year 1780 by Lieutt. Daniel Paterson.* C-6105-000. John Carter Brown Library, Brown University.

Public Record Office. The National Archives, Kew, United Kingdom.

Revolutionary War orderly books at the Massachusetts Historical Society. Microfilm P-394, 6 reels. Massachusetts Historical Society, Boston.

Smith-Carter Family Papers. Massachusetts Historical Society, Boston.

Books, Articles, and Papers

Adams, Henry. "Count Edward De Crillon." *American Historical Review* 1, no. 1 (1895): 51–69. www.jstor.org/stable/1834016.

Amussen, Susan Dwyer. *Caribbean Exchanges: Slavery and the Transformation of English Society, 1640–1700.* Chapel Hill: University of North Carolina Press, 2007.

Appleby, Joyce O. *Inheriting the Revolution: The First Generation of Americans.* Cambridge, MA: Belknap Press, 2000.

Bannet, Eve Tavor. *Empire of Letters: Letter Manuals and Transatlantic Correspondence, 1688–1820.* Cambridge: Cambridge University Press, 2005.

Beawes, Wyndham, and Thomas Mortimer. *Lex Mercatoria Rediviva: Or, the Merchant's Directory: Being a Complete Guide to All Men in Business* . . . London: Printed for J. Rivington and Sons, T. Longman, B. Law, S. Crowder, T. Cadell, G. Robinson, J. Sewel, and R. Baldwin, 1783.

Beckles, Hilary McDonald. "Capitalism, Slavery and Caribbean Modernity." *Callaloo* 20, no. 4 (1997): 777–89. www.jstor.org/stable/3299407.

———. "The Wilberforce Song: How Enslaved Caribbean Blacks Heard British Abolitionists." *Parliamentary History* 26, no. 4 (2007): 113–26. doi:10.1353/pah.2007.0029.

Brown, Christopher Leslie. *Moral Capital: Foundations of British Abolitionism*. Chapel Hill: University of North Carolina Press, 2006.

Burnard, Trevor G. "The American Revolution, the West Indies, and the Future of Plantation British America." *Common-Place: The Interactive Journal of Early American Life* 14, no. 3 (Spring 2014). www.common-place-archives.org/vol-14/no-03/burnard.

———. "The Atlantic Slave Trade." In *The Routledge History of Slavery*, edited by Gad J. Heuman and Trevor G. Burnard, 80–97. London: Routledge, 2011.

———. "Harvest Years? Reconfigurations of Empire in Jamaica, 1756–1807." *Journal of Imperial and Commonwealth History* 40, no. 4 (2012): 533–55. doi:10.1080/03086534.2 012.724234.

———. *Planters, Merchants, and Slaves: Plantation Societies in British America, 1650–1820*. Chicago: University of Chicago Press, 2015.

———. "Slave Naming Patterns: Onomastics and the Taxonomy of Race in Eighteenth-Century Jamaica." *Journal of Interdisciplinary History* 31, no. 3 (2001): 325–46. www .jstor.org/stable/207085.

Burnard, Trevor G., and John D. Garrigus. *The Plantation Machine: Atlantic Capitalism in French Saint-Domingue and British Jamaica*. Philadelphia: University of Pennsylvania Press, 2016.

Campbell, Donald. *A Journey over Land to India: Partly by a Route Never Gone Before by Any European*. London: Cullen, 1795.

Campbell, John. *Candid and Impartial Considerations on the Nature of the Sugar Trade: The Comparative Importance of the British and French Islands in the West-Indies: With the Value and Consequence of St. Lucia and Granada, Truly Stated: Illustrated with Copper-Plates*. London: R. Baldwin, 1763.

Candlin, Kit. *The Last Caribbean Frontier, 1795–1815*. Basingstoke: Palgrave Macmillan, 2012.

Candlin, Kit, and Cassandra Pybus. *Enterprising Women: Gender, Race, and Power in the Revolutionary Atlantic*. Athens: University of Georgia Press, 2015.

Carey, Brycchan. *British Abolitionism and the Rhetoric of Sensibility: Writing, Sentiment, and Slavery, 1760–1807*. New York: Palgrave Macmillan, 2005.

Carey, Brycchan, Markman Ellis, and Sara Salih, eds. *Discourses of Slavery and Abolition: Britain and Its Colonies, 1760–1838*. New York: Palgrave Macmillan, 2004.

Carretta, Vincent. *Equiano, the African: Biography of a Self-Made Man*. Athens: University of Georgia Press, 2005.

———. *Phillis Wheatley: Biography of a Genius in Bondage*. Athens: University of Georgia Press, 2011.

Chamberlain, Mellen. *A Documentary History of Chelsea: Including the Boston Precincts of Winnisimmet, Rumney Marsh, and Pullen Point, 1624–1824*. 2 vols. Boston: Massachusetts Historical Society, 1908. https://archive.org/details/documentaryhisto04 cham.

Clark, Geoffrey. "Culture Contact in the Palau Islands, 1783." *Journal of Pacific History* 42, no. 1 (2007): 89–97. www.jstor.org/stable/40346573.

Conway, Stephen A. *The British Isles and the War for American Independence*. New York: Oxford University Press, 2000.

Cott, Nancy F. *The Bonds of Womanhood: "Women's Sphere" in New England, 1780–1835*. New Haven, CT: Yale University Press, 1977.

Cox, Edward L. "The British Caribbean in the Age of Revolution." In *Empire and Nation: The American Revolution in the Atlantic World,* edited by Eliga H. Gould and Peter S. Onuf, 274–94. Baltimore: Johns Hopkins University Press, 2005.

——. "Fedon's Rebellion 1795–96: Causes and Consequences." *Journal of Negro History* 67, no. 1 (1982): 7–19. www.jstor.org/stable/2717757.

Craton, Michael. *Testing the Chains: Resistance to Slavery in the British West Indies.* Ithaca, NY: Cornell University Press, 1982.

Cugoano, Quobna Ottobah. *Thoughts and Sentiments on the Evil of Slavery and Other Writings.* Edited with notes and introduction by Vincent Carretta. New York: Penguin, 1999.

Curtin, Philip D. *The Rise and Fall of the Plantation Complex: Essays in Atlantic History.* Cambridge: Cambridge University Press, 1990.

Curtis, Caroline Gardiner Gray, ed. *The Cary Letters: Edited at the Request of the Family.* Cambridge, MA: Riverside Press, 1891.

Davis, David Brion. *Inhuman Bondage: The Rise and Fall of Slavery in the New World.* New York: Oxford University Press, 2006.

——. *The Problem of Slavery in the Age of Revolution, 1770–1823.* Ithaca, NY: Cornell University Press, 1975.

Dierks, Konstantin. *In My Power: Letter Writing and Communications in Early America.* Philadelphia: University of Pennsylvania Press, 2009.

Dorland, W. A. Newman. "The Second Troop Philadelphia City Cavalry." *Pennsylvania Magazine of History and Biography* 45, no. 3 (1921): 257–91. https://archive.org/details /pennsylvaniamagav45hist.

Draper, Nicholas. *The Price of Emancipation: Slave-ownership, Compensation and British Society at the End of Slavery.* Cambridge: Cambridge University Press, 2010.

Duffy, Michael. "The French Revolution and British Attitudes to the West Indian Colonies." In *A Turbulent Time: The French Revolution and the Greater Caribbean,* edited by David Barry Gaspar and David Patrick Geggus, 78–89. Bloomington: Indiana University Press, 1997.

——. *Soldiers, Sugar, and Seapower: The British Expeditions to the West Indies and the War against Revolutionary France.* Oxford: Clarendon Press, 1987.

Dunn, Richard S. *Sugar and Slaves: The Rise of the Planter Class in the English West Indies, 1624–1713.* Chapel Hill: University of North Carolina Press, 1972.

Edwards, Bryan. *The History, Civil and Commercial, of the British West Indies: With a Continuation to the Present Time.* 1793. Reprint, London: Printed by T. Miller for G. and W. B. Whitaker, 1819.

Egan, Jim. "The 'Long'd-for Aera' of an 'Other Race': Climate, Identity, and James Grainger's 'The Sugar-Cane.'" *Early American Literature* 38, no. 2 (2003): 189–212. www.jstor.org/stable/25057314.

Ellis, Markman. "'Incessant Labour': Georgic Poetry and the Problem of Slavery." In *Discourses of Slavery and Abolition: Britain and Its Colonies, 1760–1838,* edited by Brycchan Carey, Markman Ellis, and Sara Salih, 45–62. New York: Palgrave Macmillan, 2004.

Equiano, Olaudah. *The Interesting Narrative and Other Writings.* Edited by Vincent Carretta. New York: Penguin, 2003.

Falconbridge, Anna M., Christopher Fyfe, Isaac DuBois, and Alexander Falconbridge. *Narrative of Two Voyages to the River Sierra Leone During the Years 1791–1792–1793.*

The Journal of Isaac Dubois/with an Account of the Slave Trade on the Coast of Africa [by] Alexander Falconbridge. Liverpool: Liverpool University Press, 2000.

Falconer, William, and Peter Markoe. *The Shipwreck: A Sentimental and Descriptive Poem, in Three Cantos*. Philadelphia: Prichard and Hall, 1788. Originally published as *The Shipwreck: A Poem, in Three Cantos, by a Sailor* (London, 1762).

Foster, Thomas A. *Women in Early America*. New York: New York University Press, 2015.

Frohock, Richard. *Heroes of Empire: The British Imperial Protagonist in America, 1596–1764*. Newark: University of Delaware Press, 2004.

Gares, Albert J. "Stephen Girard's West Indian Trade 1789–1812." *Pennsylvania Magazine of History and Biography* 72, no. 4 (1948): 311–42. www.jstor.org/stable/20088028.

Garraway, D. G. *A Short Account of the Insurrection of 1795–96*. St. George's, Grenada: Printed by Chas. Wells and Son at the "Chronicle" Office, 1877.

Gaspar, David Barry, and David Patrick Geggus, eds. *A Turbulent Time: The French Revolution and the Greater Caribbean*. Bloomington: Indiana University Press, 1997.

Geggus, David Patrick. "Slavery, War, and Revolution in the Greater Caribbean, 1789–1815." In *A Turbulent Time: The French Revolution and the Greater Caribbean*, edited by David Barry Gaspar and David Patrick Geggus, 1–49. Bloomington: Indiana University Press, 1997.

Gikandi, Simon. *Slavery and the Culture of Taste*. Princeton, NJ: Princeton University Press, 2011.

Gilmore, John. *The Poetics of Empire: A Study of James Grainger's "The Sugar Cane" (1764)*. London: Athlone Press, 2000.

Gould, Philip. "The African Slave Trade and Abolitionism: Rereading Antislavery Literature, 1776–1800." In *Periodical Literature in Eighteenth-Century America*, edited by Mark Kamrath and Sharon M. Harris, 201–19. Knoxville: University of Tennessee Press, 2005.

Grainger, James. *An Essay on the More Common West-India Diseases: And the Remedies Which That Country Itself Produces: to Which Are Added, Some Hints on the Management, &c. of Negroes*. London: Printed for T. Becket and P. A. De Hondt, 1764. http://nrs.harvard.edu/urn-3:HMS.COUNT:1162196.

———. *The Sugar-Cane: A Poem, In Four Books*. 1764. In *Caribbeana: An Anthology of English Literature of the West Indies, 1657–1777*, edited by Thomas W. Krise, 166–260. Chicago: University of Chicago Press, 1999.

Grenada Planter. *A Brief Enquiry into the Causes Of, and Conduct Pursued By, the Colonial Government, for Quelling the Insurrection in Grenada: From Its Commencement on the Night of the 2d of March, to the Arrival of General Nichols, on the 14th of April 1795. In a Letter from a Grenada Planter to a Merchant in London*. London: Printed for R. Faulder, New Bond-Street, 1796.

Haggerty, Sheryllynne. *"Merely for Money"?: Business Culture in the British Atlantic, 1750–1815*. Liverpool: Liverpool University Press, 2012.

Hamilton, Douglas. *Scotland, the Caribbean, and the Atlantic World, 1750–1820*. Manchester: Manchester University Press, 2005.

Harris, Sharon M. *Executing Race: Early Women's Narratives of Race, Class, and the Law*. Columbus: Ohio State University Press, 2005.

Hartigan-O'Connor, Ellen. *The Ties That Buy: Women and Commerce in Revolutionary America*. Philadelphia: University of Pennsylvania Press, 2009.

Harvard University. *Quinquennial Catalogue of the Officers and Graduates, 1636–1930.* Cambridge, MA: The University, 1930. http://nrs.harvard.edu/urn-3:HUL.ARCH:1133986.

Hay, John. *A Narrative of the Insurrection in the Island of Grenada, Which Took Place in 1795.* London: Printed for J. Ridgeway, 1823.

Hayes, Kevin J. *A Colonial Woman's Bookshelf.* Knoxville: University of Tennessee Press, 1996.

Hewitt, Elizabeth. *Correspondence and American Literature, 1770–1865.* Cambridge: Cambridge University Press, 2004.

Higman, B. W. *A Concise History of the Caribbean.* New York: Cambridge University Press, 2011.

Hill, Hamilton Andrews. "Necrology of the New England Historic Genealogical Society." *New England Historical and Genealogical Register* 45 (1891): 320–26. https://archive.org/details/newenglandhistor45wate.

Imbarrato, Susan Clair, ed. *Women Writing Home, 1700–1920: Female Correspondence across the British Empire.* Vol. 6, *USA.* General editor Klaus Stierstorfer. London: Pickering and Chatto, 2006.

Isaac, Rhys. *Landon Carter's Uneasy Kingdom: Revolution and Rebellion on a Virginia Plantation.* New York: Oxford University Press, 2004.

Jefferson, Thomas. *Jefferson's Memorandum Books: Accounts, with Legal Records and Miscellany, 1767–1826.* 2 vols. Edited by James A. Bear and Lucia C. Stanton. Princeton, NJ: Princeton University Press, 1997.

Jefferson, Thomas, and Merrill D. Peterson. *Writings.* New York: Library of America, 1984.

Keate, George. *An Account of the Pelew Islands: Situated in the Western Part of the Pacific Ocean. Composed from the Journals and Communications of Captain Henry Wilson, and Some of His Officers, Who, in August 1783, Were There Shipwrecked, in the Antelope, a Packet Belonging to the Honourable East India Company.* London: Printed for G. Nicol, Bookseller To His Majesty, Pall-Mall, 1788.

Kelley, Mary. *Learning to Stand and Speak: Women, Education, and Public Life in America's Republic.* Chapel Hill: University of North Carolina Press, 2006.

———. "'The Need of Their Genius': A Woman's Revolution in Early America." In *Women in Early America,* edited by Thomas A. Foster, 246–69. New York: New York University Press, 2015.

Kidder, Frederic. *History of the Boston Massacre, March 5, 1770: Consisting of the Narrative of the Town, the Trial of the Soldiers: and a Historical Introduction, Containing Unpublished Documents of John Adams, and Explanatory Notes.* Albany, NY: J. Munsell, 1870. https://www.loc.gov/law/help/rare-books/pdf/john_adams_1870_history.pdf.

Kiger, Joshua Allan. "The Diary of Margaret Graves Cary: Family and Gender in the Merchant Class of 18th Century Charlestown." Master's thesis, Miami University, 2014.

Knight, Frederick C. *Working the Diaspora: The Impact of African Labor on the Anglo-American World, 1650–1850.* New York: New York University Press, 2010.

Knowlton, John, comp. *British Shipping Records, Portsmouth, New Hampshire: Index 7, Jul. 31, 1770–Sept. 7, 1775.* Portsmouth, NH: Portsmouth Athenaeum, 2014.

Krise, Thomas W. *Caribbeana: An Anthology of English Literature of the West Indies, 1657–1777.* Chicago: University of Chicago Press, 1999.

Martin, Samuel. *An Essay upon Plantership: Humbly Inscribed to . . . George Thomas, Esq; . . . the Fourth Edition, with Many Additions from Experiments Made Since the Last Edition. by Samuel Martin, Senior, Esq.* London: Antigua, 1765.

Mather, Samuel. *The Walk of the Upright, with Its Comforts: A Funeral Discourse after the Decease of the Reverend Mr. William Welsted [sic], Who Died April 29th. and Mr. Ellis Gray, Who Died on January 7th Proceeding It. Colleague Pastors of a Church in Boston. Preached to Their People in the New Brick Meeting-House, on May 6. 1753.* Boston: Printed for Michael Dennis, at the corner of Scarlet's Wharf, 1753.

McCusker, John J., and Russell R. Menard. *The Economy of British America, 1607–1789.* Chapel Hill: University of North Carolina Press, 1985.

Moitt, Bernard. *Women and Slavery in the French Antilles, 1635–1848.* Bloomington: Indiana University Press, 2001.

Moniz, Amanda B. *From Empire to Humanity: The American Revolution and the Origins of Humanitarianism.* New York: Oxford University Press, 2016.

Montague, Joel, Mariam Montague, and Shahnaz Montague. "The Island of Grenada in 1795." *Americas* 40, no. 4 (1984): 531–37. www.jstor.org/stable/980860.

More, Hannah. *Strictures on the Modern System of Female Education: With a View of the Principles and Conduct Prevalent among Women of Rank and Fortune.* 2 vols. London: Printed by A. Strahan, for T. Cadell Jun. and W. Davies, 1799. https://archive.org/details/stricturesonmod03moregoog.

Morgan, Philip D. *Slave Counterpoint: Black Culture in the Eighteenth-Century Chesapeake and Lowcountry.* Chapel Hill: University of North Carolina Press, 1998.

Morley, Henry, Richard Steele, and Joseph Addison. *The Spectator: A New Ed., Reproducing the Original Text, Both as First Issued and as Corr., by Its Authors.* London: G. Routledge, 1883.

Mulford, Carla. "New Science and the Question of Identity in Eighteenth-Century British America." In *Finding Colonial Americas: Essays Honoring J. A. Leo Lemay,* edited by Carla Mulford and David S. Shields, 79–103. Newark: University of Delaware Press, 2001.

Naval Office Shipping Lists for Massachusetts, 1686–1765. East Ardsley, UK: Micro Methods, 1968.

Naval Office Shipping Lists for New Hampshire, 1723–1769. East Ardsley, UK: Micro Methods, 1966.

Newman, Simon P. *A New World of Labor: The Development of Plantation Slavery in the British Atlantic.* Philadelphia: University of Pennsylvania Press, 2013.

Newman, William A., and Wilfred E. Holton. *Boston's Back Bay: The Story of America's Greatest Nineteenth-Century Landfill Project.* Boston: Northeastern University Press, 2006.

Oliver, Vere Langford, ed. *Caribbeana: Being Miscellaneous Papers Relating to the History, Genealogy, Topography, and Antiquities of the British West Indies.* 6 vols. London: Mitchell, Hughes and Clarke, 1910–1919.

O'Malley, Gregory E. *Final Passages: The Intercolonial Slave Trade of British America, 1619– 1807.* Chapel Hill: University of North Carolina Press, 2014.

O'Shaughnessy, Andrew Jackson. *An Empire Divided: The American Revolution and the British Caribbean.* Philadelphia: University of Pennsylvania Press, 2000.

———. "Redcoats and Slaves in the British Caribbean." In *The Lesser Antilles in the Age of European Expansion,* edited by Robert L. Paquette and Stanley L. Engerman, 105–27. Gainesville: University Press of Florida, 1996.

Palmer, Michael A. *Stoddert's War: Naval Operations During the Quasi-War with France, 1798–1801.* Columbia: University of South Carolina Press, 1987.

Pares, Richard. *A West-India Fortune.* 1950. Hamden, CT: Archon Books, 1968.

Park, Lawrence. *Joseph Badger (1708–1765): And a Descriptive List of Some of His Works.* Boston: University Press, 1918.

Paton, Lucy Allen. *Elizabeth Cary Agassiz: A Biography.* Boston: Houghton Mifflin, 1919.

Pearsall, Sarah M. S. *Atlantic Families: Lives and Letters in the Later Eighteenth Century.* Oxford: Oxford University Press, 2008.

Peterson, Mark A. *The Price of Redemption: The Spiritual Economy of Puritan New England.* Stanford, CA: Stanford University Press, 1997.

Phillip, Nicole. "Producers, Reproducers and Rebels: Grenadian Slave Women, 1783–1838." Paper presented at the Grenada Country Conference, January 2002, University of the West Indies. www.open.uwi.edu/sites/default/files/bnccde/grenada/conference/papers/phillip.html.

Pope, Alexander. *The Works of Alexander Pope: Including Several Hundred Unpublished Letters, and Other New Materials.* Collected in part by John W. Croker, with introduction and notes by Whitwell Elwin and William J. Courthope. 10 vols. London: Murray, 1871–1879. https://catalog.hathitrust.org/api/volumes/oclc/213508869.html.

Pope, Alexander, and Horace. *The First Epistle of the Second Book of Horace, Imitated.* London: Printed for T. Cooper, 1737. http://name.umdl.umich.edu/004809259.0001.000.

Pratt, Walter Merriam. *Seven Generations: A Story of Prattville and Chelsea.* Norwood, MA: Privately printed, 1930.

Quintanilla, Mark. "The World of Alexander Campbell: An Eighteenth-Century Grenadian Planter." *Albion: A Quarterly Journal Concerned with British Studies* 35, no. 2 (2003): 229–56. www.jstor.org/stable/4054136.

Ragatz, Lowell Joseph. *The Fall of the Planter Class in the British Caribbean, 1763–1833: A Study in Social and Economic History.* New York: Octagon Books, 1928.

Ramsay, James. *An Essay on the Treatment and Conversion of African Slaves in the British Sugar Colonies.* [London], 1784. Reprint, Cambridge: Cambridge University Press, 2012.

Rawley, James A. *London, Metropolis of the Slave Trade.* Columbia: University of Missouri Press, 2003.

Rediker, Marcus. *The Slave Ship: A Human History.* New York: Viking, 2007.

Richards, Jeffrey H., and Sharon M. Harris. *Mercy Otis Warren: Selected Letters.* Athens: University of Georgia Press, 2009.

Robbins, Chandler. *A History of the Second Church, or Old North, in Boston: To Which Is Added a History of the New Brick Church.* Boston: Published by a committee of the Society, 1852.

Roberts, James W. "'Yankey dodle will do verry well here': New England Traders in the Caribbean, 1713 to circa 1812." PhD diss., Johns Hopkins University, 2011. ProQuest: 3492579.

Roberts, Justin. "Uncertain Business: A Case Study of Barbadian Plantation Management, 1770–93." *Slavery and Abolition* 32, no. 2 (2011): 247–68. doi:10.1080/0144039X.2010.547679.

Rowe, Nicholas. *The True End of Education, in, The Poetical Preceptor; Or, a Collection of Select Pieces of Poetry; Extracted from the Works of the Most Eminent English Poets . . . the Fourth Edition; Corrected, Etc.* London: S. Crowder, 1790.

Rowson, Susanna, and Marion Rust. *Charlotte Temple: Authoritative Text, Contexts, Criticism.* New York: Norton, 2011. Originally published in 1791 as *Charlotte, A Tale of Truth.*

Ryden, David Beck. *West Indian Slavery and British Abolition, 1783–1807.* Cambridge: Cambridge University Press, 2009.

Schurink, Fred. "Manuscript Commonplace Books, Literature, and Reading in Early Modern England." *Huntington Library Quarterly* 73, no. 3 (2010): 453–69. doi:10.1525/hlq.2010.73.3.453.

Scoville, Joseph Alfred. *The Old Merchants of New York City.* Vol. 4, by Walter Barrett, clerk [pseud.]. New York: Carleton, 1870. Reprint, New York: Greenwood Press, 1968.

Shields, David S. *American Poetry: The Seventeenth and Eighteenth Centuries.* New York: Library of America, 2007.

——. *Oracles of Empire: Poetry, Politics and Commerce in British America, 1690– 1750.* Chicago: University of Chicago Press, 1990.

Shipton, Clifford K. *Sibley's Harvard Graduates.* Vol. 9, *Biographical Sketches of Those Who Attended Harvard College in the Classes 1731–1735 with Bibliographical and Other Notes.* Boston: Massachusetts Historical Society, 1956.

Silva, Cristobal. "Georgic Fantasies: James Grainger and the Poetry of Colonial Dislocation." *ELH* 83, no. 1 (2016): 127–56. doi:10.1353/elh.2016.0000.

Silver, Ednah C. *Sketches of the New Church in America on a Background of Civic and Social Life: Drawn from Faded Manuscript, Printed Record, and Living Reminiscence.* Boston: Massachusetts New Church Union, 1920.

Smallwood, Stephanie E. *Saltwater Slavery: A Middle Passage from Africa to American Diaspora.* Cambridge, MA: Harvard University Press, 2008.

Smelser, Marshall. "The Contentious Empires." In *The American Revolution and the West Indies*, edited by Charles Toth, 5–12. Port Washington, NY: Kennikat Press, 1975.

Smith, S. D. *Slavery, Family, and Gentry Capitalism in the British Atlantic: The World of the Lascelles, 1648–1834.* Cambridge: Cambridge University Press, 2010.

Spence, Caroline Quarrier. "Ameliorating Empire: Slavery and Protection in the British Colonies, 1783–1865." PhD diss., Harvard University, 2014. http://nrs.harvard.edu/urn-3:HUL.InstRepos:13070043.

Spence, William. *The Radical Cause of the Present Distresses of the West-India Planters Pointed Out, and the Inefficiency of the Measures Which Have Been Hitherto Proposed for Relieving Them, Demonstrated . . .* London: Hansard and Sons, for T. Cadell and W. Davies, in the Strand, 1807.

Spooner, Charles. *Short Reasons against the Abolition of the Slave Trade.* [London?], 1789.

Stabile, Susan M. *Memory's Daughters: The Material Culture of Remembrance in Eighteenth- Century America.* Ithaca, NY: Cornell University Press, 2004.

Stallybrass, Peter. "Benjamin Franklin: Printed Corrections and Erasable Writing." *Proceedings of the American Philosophical Society* 150, no. 4 (2006): 553–67. www.jstor.org/stable/4599024.

Steele, Beverley A. *Grenada: A History of Its People.* Oxford: Macmillan Caribbean, 2003.

Sweet, John Wood. *Bodies Politic: Negotiating Race in the American North, 1730–1830.* Baltimore: Johns Hopkins University Press, 2003.

Sypher, Wylie. "Hutcheson and the 'Classical' Theory of Slavery." *Journal of Negro History* 24, no. 3 (1939): 263–80. www.jstor.org/stable/2714380.

Taylor, Alan. *American Colonies.* New York: Viking, 2011.

Taylor, Christopher. *The Black Carib Wars: Freedom, Survival, and the Making of the Garifuna.* Oxford: Signal Books, 2012.

Taylor, George Rogers. *The Transportation Revolution, 1815–1860.* Vol. 4 of *The Economic History of the United States,* edited by Henry David, Harold U. Faulkner, Louis M. Hacker, Curtis P. Nettels, and Fred A. Shannon. New York: Rinehart, 1951.

Thomas, Steven W. "Doctoring Ideology: James Grainger's 'The Sugar Cane' and the Bodies of Empire." *Early American Studies* 4, no. 1 (2006): 78–111. www.jstor.org/stable/23546535.

Tobin, James. *Cursory Remarks upon the Reverend Mr. Ramsay's Essay on the Treatment and Conversion of African Slaves in the British Sugar Colonies.* London: Printed for G. and T. Wilkie, 1785.

Turnbull, Gordon. *Letters to a Young Planter; Or, Observations on the Management of a Sugar- Plantation: To Which Is Added, the Planter's Kalendar.* London: Printed by Stuart and Stevenson for J. Strachan, 1785.

——. *A Narrative of the Revolt and Insurrection of the French Inhabitants in the Island of Grenada.* Edinburgh: Printed for A. Constable, 1795.

United States. *Return of the Whole Number of Persons within the Several Districts of the United States: According to "An Act Providing for the Enumeration of the Inhabitants of the United States," Passed March the First, One Thousand Seven Hundred and Ninety-One.* Philadelphia, PA: Printed by Childs and Swaine, 1791.

US Bureau of the Census. *A Century of Population Growth: From the First Census of the United States to the Twelfth: 1700–1900.* Washington, DC: Government Printing Office, 1909.

——. *Heads of Families at the First Census of the United States Taken in the Year 1790: Massachusetts.* Washington, DC: Government Printing Office, 1908.

US Census Office. *Return of the Whole Number of Persons Within the Several Districts of the United States: According to "an Act Providing for the Second Census or Enumeration of the Inhabitants of the United States."* Washington: Printed by order of the House of Representatives, 1801.

US Continental Congress, Robert Morris, Thomas Jefferson, and Continental Congress Broadside Collection. *Propositions Respecting the Coinage of Gold, Silver, and Copper.* New York, 1785. www.loc.gov/item/90898209.

Valeri, Mark. *Heavenly Merchandize: How Religion Shaped Commerce in Puritan America.* Princeton, NJ: Princeton University Press, 2010.

Vasconcellos, Colleen A. *Slavery, Childhood, and Abolition in Jamaica, 1788–1838.* Athens: University of Georgia Press, 2015.

Walsh, Lorena S. *Motives of Honor, Pleasure, and Profit: Plantation Management in the Colonial Chesapeake, 1607–1763.* Chapel Hill: University of North Carolina Press, 2010.

Ward, J. R. *British West Indian Slavery, 1750–1834: The Process of Amelioration.* Oxford: Clarendon Press, 1988.

——. "The Profitability of Sugar Planting in the British West Indies, 1650–1834." *Economic History Review* 31, no. 2 (1978): 197–213. www.jstor.org/stable/2594924.

Warren, Wendy. *New England Bound: Slavery and Colonization in Early America*. New York: Liveright, 2016.

Watts, David. *The West Indies: Patterns of Development, Culture, and Environmental Change Since 1492*. Cambridge: Cambridge University Press, 1987.

Wemms, William, and John Hodgson. *The Trial of William Wemms, James Hartegan, William M'cauley, Hugh White, Matthew Killroy, William Warren, John Carrol, and Hugh Montgomery: Soldiers in His Majesty's 29th Regiment of Foot, for the Murder of Crispus Attucks, Samuel Gray, Samuel Maverick, James Caldwell, and Patrick Carr, on Monday Evening, the 5th of March, 1770, at the Superior Court of Judicature, Court of Assize and General Goal Delivery, Held at Boston. the 27th Day of November, 1770, by Adjournment*. Boston: Printed by J. Fleeming, 1770.

Wheeler, Roxann. *The Complexion of Race: Categories of Difference in Eighteenth-Century British Culture*. Philadelphia: University of Pennsylvania Press, 2000.

Wightman, Joseph M. *Annals of the Boston Primary School Committee: From Its First Establishment in 1818, to Its Dissolution in 1855*. Boston: G. C. Rand and Avery, 1860.

Williams, Eric E. *Capitalism and Slavery*. 1949. Reprinted with a new introduction by Colin Palmer. Chapel Hill: University of North Carolina Press, 1994.

Wilson, Douglas L. "Thomas Jefferson's Early Notebooks." *William and Mary Quarterly* 42, no. 4 (1985): 434–52. www.jstor.org/stable/1919028.

Wise, Thomas Turner. *A Review of the Events, Which Have Happened in Grenada, from the Commencement of the Insurrection to the 1st of May; by a Sincere Wellwisher to the Colony*. Grenada: Printed for the author in Saint George, 1795.

Wood, Gordon S. *Empire of Liberty: A History of the Early Republic, 1789–1815*. Oxford: Oxford University Press, 2009.

Wyman, Thomas Bellows. *The Genealogies and Estates of Charlestown in the County of Middlesex and Commonwealth of Massachusetts, 1629–1818*. Edited by Henry H. Edes. Boston: D. Clapp and Son, 1879.

Young, Edward. *The Complaint: Or, Night-Thoughts on Life, Death, and Immortality: To Which Is Added, a Paraphrase on Part of the Book of Job*. London: Printed for A. Millar; and R. and J. Dodsley, 1765. https://archive.org/details/complaintonlife00youngoog.

Zabin, Serena R. *Dangerous Economies: Status and Commerce in Imperial New York*. Philadelphia: University of Pennsylvania Press, 2009.

Zacek, Natalie. "Class Struggle in a West Indian Plantation Society." In *Class Matters: Early North America and the Atlantic World*, edited by Simon Middleton and Billy G. Smith, 62–75. Philadelphia: University of Pennsylvania Press, 2008.

——. "Cultivating Virtue: Samuel Martin and the Paternal Ideal in the Eighteenth-Century English West Indies." *Wadabagei: A Journal of the Caribbean and Its Diasporas* 10, no. 3 (Fall 2007): 8–31.

Zaczek, Barbara Maria. *Censored Sentiments: Letters and Censorship in Epistolary Novels and Conduct Material*. Newark: University of Delaware Press, 1997.